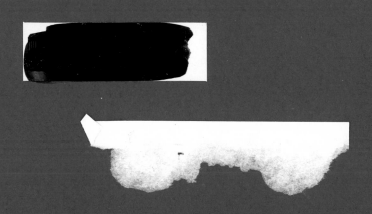

WITHDRAWN

The Romance of the Shoe

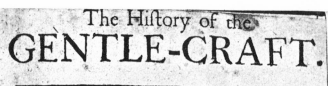

The History of the
GENTLE-CRAFT.

A *Gentle Craft* that hath the Art,
To steal soon into a LADIES Heart;
Here you may see, what Youth and Love can do,
The Crown doth stoop to th' Maker of a Shooe.

ST. CRISPIN FITTING A SHOE ON PRINCESS URSULA.

See p. 54.

From a copy of *The History of Gentle Craft*, preserved in Cordwainers' Hall, London.
Title page, with date, missing. It is evidently, however, the edition of 1676.

Photo Mr. Geo. Avenell.

THE ROMANCE OF
THE SHOE

BEING

The History of Shoemaking

IN ALL AGES, AND ESPECIALLY IN ENGLAND AND SCOTLAND.

BY

THOMAS WRIGHT

*(Author of " The Romance of the Lace Pillow," " The Life of
William Cowper," " The Life of John Payne," etc.)*

———

WITH 146 ILLUSTRATIONS.

———

LONDON :

C. J. FARNCOMBE & SONS, Ltd., 30 IMPERIAL BUILDINGS,
LUDGATE CIRCUS, E.C.4.

———

1922

Detroit: Reissued by Singing Tree Press, Book Tower, 1968

THIS WORK

IS

DEDICATED

TO

MR. JAMES MANFIELD J.P.

Library of Congress Catalog Card Number 68–26624

CONTENTS.

CHAPTER I

EGYPT, ASSYRIA, GREECE.

CHAPTER II

ROME, BRITAIN, AND SAXON AND NORMAN ENGLAND.

CHAPTER II.—*Continued.*

CHAPTER III

THE PLANTAGENETS, LANCASTER AND YORK.

CHAPTER IV

THE TUDORS.

CHAPTER V

THE STUARTS. SHOEMAKERS' TOKENS AND SIGNS.

CHAPTER VI

THE FIRST THREE GEORGES. THE HARDY TRIAL. LATE TOKENS.

CHAPTER VI.—*Continued.*

CHAPTER VII

THE OLD STITCHMEN.

CHAPTER VIII

SHOEMAKERS' HOLIDAYS, SONGS, CHAP-BOOKS AND PROVERBS.

CHAPTER IX

MACHINERY. THE FOOTWEAR PRESS.

Chapter IX.—*Continued.*

CHAPTER X

ANECDOTES. SHOEMAKER WIT AND HUMOUR.
THE SHOE IN FICTION AND POETRY.

LIST OF PLATES.

PREFACE

BORN in a shoe town, and interested most of my life in the personality of the shoemaker, it is not surprising that I should take pleasure in the history of the industry. What is really surprising is that no work of the kind has ever before been written. Tiny books on the subject have appeared; different phases of it have been dealt with in magazine articles; and Baudouin, Lacroix, Devlin, W. E. Winks and Mr. S. S. Campion have in various ways laid the industry under obligations; but this is the first attempt to offer a comprehensive view of the subject. Dealing with so vast a period as six thousand years or more, I have been obliged to write compendiously. On every page, however, I have endeavoured to bring into prominence the personality and the psychology of the shoemaker; and the more I have studied this good fellow the more I have felt drawn to him.

I have endeavoured to be accurate, and I can only say that if any reader should draw my attention to inaccuracies or serious omissions, he may count on my gratitude.

While writing this book I placed myself in correspondence with, and called on, a number of manufacturers, heads of Technical Schools, and operatives, taking particular care to see as many as possible of the old stitchmen. On all sides I was received with the greatest courtesy and kindness, and I wish to thank very warmly all who have so generously helped me. To make a complete list of their names would occupy many pages, for I must have interviewed or written to hundreds of persons; but I wish to thank particularly Mr. James Manfield, J.P., to whom this work is dedicated, for loan of books and other assistance; the Lord Mayor of Norwich (Mr. H. N. Holmes); Mr. George Avenell, for taking so many photographs for me; Mr. Frank Plucknett, for reading my proofs and many other services; Mr. Roland Gorbold, for loan of photographs and other kindnesses; Mr. P. G. Trendell, of the Victoria and Albert Museum; Mr. Bernard Kettle and Mr. Frank Lambert, of the Guildhall Library and Museum, London; Mr. C. H. W. Mander, Cordwainers' Hall, London; Mr. A. Adcock, Northampton; Mr. C.C.Campion, Northampton; Mr. Reginald Brown, Public Library, Northampton; Mr. J. F. Blakeborough; Mr. F. Bostock, Northampton; Major C. A. Markham, Northampton; the Principals of the Technical Schools at Bristol, Leeds, Norwich, Leicester and Northampton, who are referred to by name in Chapter IX.; the Editors of the leading Trade Journals (and in particular, Mr. T. A. Roberts, of *The Footwear Organiser*, whose kind help has been incessant); and the Editors of the *Northampton Herald*, *Northampton Mercury*, *Northampton Independent*, *The Wellingborough News*, *The Kettering Leader* and *The Kettering Guardian*.

I am also indebted in various ways to Mr. Alfred Ager, Northampton; Mr. J. Allsopp, South Wigston; Mr. G. H. Anderson, Kings Lynn; Messrs. A. and W. Arnold, Northampton; Mr. W. Ashton, Wigan; Mr. E. Avery, Maidstone; Mr. W. J. Barnes, Northampton; Mr. H. G. Barker, Northampton; Messrs. W. Barratt & Co., Northampton; Mr. Henry Bostock, Stafford; Mr. H. J. Bostock, Stafford; Mr. J. S. Billingham, Marefair, Northampton; Mr. W. E. Billingham, Bridge Street, Northampton; Mr. C. S. Carter, Louth; Mr. H. Clark, Batley; Messrs. Cridland & Rose, Bristol; The Cordwainers' Company, London; The Authorities, Cordwainers' Hall, London; Sir James Crockett; Dr. A. D. Denning, Stafford; Messrs. Derham Brothers, Bristol; Mrs. A. B. Douglas (daughter of John Askham), Wellingborough; Messrs. Dowie & Marshall, London; Mr. W. C. Edwards, Mark Lane, London; Mr. Allan A. Falconer, Duns; Mr. Roland Farey, Northampton; Mr. H. W. Glover, Leicester; Mr. W. Griffin, Long Buckby; Mr. S. H. Hamer, Halifax; Miss W. Haward, Girton College, Cambridge; Mr. A. H. Howell, Paisley; Mr. H. L. Longuet Higgins,

Turvey; Mr. W. R. Leech, Lowestoft; Mr. T. W. A. Lingard, London; Messrs. William, Ernest and Joseph Mann, Northampton; Mr. T. Matthews, Northampton; Mr. D. McNaught, Kilmaurs; Mr. Alex. T. Morrison, Aberdeen; Mr. Martin, Whitworth Street, Northampton; Mr. A. Norris, Bexhill-on-Sea; Norvic Shoe Company, Norwich; Messrs. Padmore & Barnes, Northampton; The Patten Makers' Company, London; Mr. Spencer Percival, Kettering; Mr. Alfred Peters, Padiham; Dr. T. Pinches, London; Sir Henry Randall, Northampton; Mr. F. C. Robinson, Leicester; Mr. George Rye, Norwich; Mr. George Searle, Heavitree; Mr. Francis Sexton, Northampton; Messrs. Charles Smith, Northampton; Mr. H. Shelton, Weston Underwood; Mr. William Stephens, Great Houghton; Mr. W. Steward, Bedford; Mr. H. F. Swann, Northampton; Mr. J. H. Talbot, Olney; Mr. A. E. Tebbutt, Northampton; Mr. G. C. Turner, Leicester; Mr. C. M. W. Turner, London; Mr. Henry Twiss, Limerick; Rev. G. Temple, Grendon Rectory; Mr. Arthur Wakerley, Leicester; Mr. Arthur Ward (Ward & Gent), Northampton; Mr. John Warren, Northampton; Mr. A. W. Waters, Leamington; Mr. W. G. Watson, Stafford; Mr. D. Woodroffe, Northampton; Mr. Martin Wright, Leicester; Mr. John W. Wilson, Manchester; Rev. J. Johnstone Walker (Boughton Rectory); Mr. W. D. Price, Rhyl; Mr. J. C. Willison, Manchester; Mr. H. Cowley, Olney; and M. George Ross, Lessines, Belgium.

THOMAS WRIGHT.

Cowper School,

Olney, Bucks.

September 16*th*, 1922.

THE ROMANCE OF THE SHOE

CHAPTER I.

EGYPT, ASSYRIA, GREECE

1. SHOEMAKING has time out of mind been regarded rather as an art than as a trade. Many of the sandals of ancient Egypt were surprisingly beautiful, and Apollo, god of the arts, was the tutelary deity of the shoemakers of Greece and Rome. Recognising the link between god and craft, the Emperor Augustus placed at the entrance of *Sandaliarium vicus* (sandal street), where the shoemakers congregated, a statue of " the god with loosely-floating hair "—held back, no doubt, by a brainband[1]—**Apollo Sandaliarius.** In its hand was probably a lyre, and at its sandalled feet a reticulated omphalos[2] and a crow—the bird which the jealous god sent to spy upon his mistress Coronis. Anciently almost every shoemaker indulged in a crow which he taught to talk, and there is a hoary jest of one who kept his bird in a cage in order to see whether it would

[1] He was usually represented either with a brainband or bays.
[2] A stone in a net. Round the omphalos was a serpent.

B

live three hundred years. At the birth of Apollo hill and valley burst into singing, and joyousness was a characteristic of his cult. The coins of Rhodes reveal him as the sun flooding with his brilliance all creation; those of Cos represent a youth dancing and beating a tambourine in his honour.

In art there are only revolutionaries or plagiarists. The shoemaker is a revolutionary. As already remarked, he regards his handiwork, and justifiably, as one of the arts, for if it is useful, it is also in many of its manifestations, bewitchingly beautiful. But he declines to be a copyist, and he is never satisfied with it or with himself. He wants something better and still better; consequently, he is continually advancing. In these days of steam power, machine displaces machine, and the shoeman is ever ready to change when need or entreaty requires. In the days of the antique world the worker of Zephyrion refused to ape his brother of Sicyon. Five thousand years pass, and "Derham Bros." of Bristol write to me proudly: "This firm is not only one of the oldest in the city, but also one of the most progressive." It is the same spirit. The alert manufacturer of to-day shakes hands over the centuries with his ochre-coloured brother of Egypt, and with him who contrived buttoned footgear for King Jamshyd.

Other characteristics of the shoemaker are his youthful buoyancy of spirit, his abandon, and his

passion for liberty. His thoughts are clad in gay
colours. His cheerfulness and mirth give a vital
warmth to his home. He laughs even in his sleep.
He is addicted to sport, whippets and pigeons
being particularly to his taste. At Leicester his
recreation on St. Monday was rabbit coursing on
the Pastures.[1] The Northamptonian has a taste
for the obscurity of the woods at night, where
the bark of the fox mingles with the hoot of the
owl. Possibly it is the poetry of these solemn
recesses that attracts him ; but whatever it is he
returns with it in a sack, glining at you out of the
corners of his eyes as he passes. He loves
excitement and grasps the fact that to live is itself
a great adventure.

He is devoted to music and song. Whenever
you come upon him in literature he is "singing
merrily." In passing his house you often hear the
chirp of the fiddle. In *The Cobler of Canterburie*[2]
(1590) he sits on his three-legged stool "in the
shop where he sung like a nightingale." Dekker's
merry cobbler of Ware[3] "did," while he worked,
"continually sing; so that his shop seemed a
verrie birdcage." Rounds were his delight. It
was a ditty trilled at a bench that led St. Crispin
to take to the lapstone[4] and the crescent-shaped
knife.[5]

[1] Now Abbey Park. [2] See Chapter 4.
[3] Thomas Dekker (1570—1641).
[4] A stone laid in the lap and used as an anvil by a shoemaker in
hammering his leather. Now, a flat iron without the handle is used.
[5] Now, a clicking knife is used.

In every English struggle for liberty the shoe-maker has taken part. He doffed his apron and exchanged his hammer for a culliver in answer to the menace of the Armada; he flung aside his last in order to hustle Darcie, the minion of Queen Elizabeth, when that insolent upstart sought to encroach upon the rights of London. He sent Bradlaugh to Parliament. A deputation of stitchmen once waited on Sir Robert Peel in order to lay before him the wants of the trade societies. " How is it," asked Peel, " that you people are foremost in every movement ? " and then, with a twinkle in his eye, " If there is a conspiracy or political movement, I always find one of you in it." It is to the credit of the craft, however, that in whatever degree their actions at any particular date have been censured, these actions have ultimately been warmly acclaimed. What yesterday was sedition to-day is patriotism. Any coward can go with the times. It takes a hero to go against them, and all the stitchmen were heroes. The shoemaker loves a spectacle. If there are sights to be seen he is abundantly in evidence. " But wherefore," asks Flavius in *Julius Cæsar*, " art thou not in thy shop to-day ? why dost thou lead these men about the streets ? " " Truly, sir," is the arch reply, " to wear out their shoes to get myself more work."

2. The old Stitchmen were the most ardent of Radicals, except in so far as their own personal habits and methods were concerned, and in these they were the most conservative of Conservatives. They were out to reform everybody except themselves. They were quite sure that the repeal of the laws of primogeniture and entail would turn England into Eden ; but they were as haughty towards cobblers and other low-down shoemen[1] as any lord in Parliament could possibly be to a mere tradesman. If the good man believed in the verbal inspiration of Saints Hardy and Bradlaugh, on the other hand no amount of arguing could induce him to admit fresh air into his stuffy workshop. If by chance he got a mouthful of it, he looked serious, and began to compose an inscription for his grave-rail in St. Giles's churchyard. Fresh air was all very well in its place—and that place was out of doors.

Still, with all their weaknesses, the old stitchmen, as Mr. Henry Bostock[2] remarked to me, were " a fine, dignified, patriarchal race. They were intellectual giants—a class by themselves." But although shoemakers have characteristics in common, each prides himself on his difference from others—grasping the fact that a man's personality is his most precious possession, his " jewel of self."

The operatives of to-day may be divided into

[1] It was the same in France. "The shoemakers, proud like other aristocracies, never fraternised with the cobblers."—*La Croix*, p. 177.
[2] Of the Lotus Company, Stafford. May 12th, 1920.

two broad classes, first, the men whose failings are so obvious that comment is unnecessary; secondly, the reflective men. The man of the second class, whether religionist or free thinker, is brisk in thought and a respecter of learning. He loves a book. A phrase, or even a single word, fires his fancy, quickens his senses, and gives a pleasing commotion to his soul. He makes maps of his thoughts. He takes pride in his allotment. But whatever his bias he goes his own way. He is King and High Priest to himself. The men of both classes are argumentative and combative.

The manufacturers may also be grouped. The first, the small and fast diminishing class, consists of those who might with advantage to themselves give more thought to the condition of their factories and the welfare of their employees. The second, the large and constantly increasing class, consists of those ideal captains of industry who carry all before them owing to their sunny disposition and alacrity of mind. They are advocates of light, ventilation and recreation. If they are strict, they are also genial and generous. Their keen and alert business methods and shrewd common sense enable them to cope with the most difficult problems. To walk through their factories is to feel their beneficent influence. With masters like these, friction between employer and employed is reduced to a minimum, and the two great bodies, *The Incorporated Federated Associations of*

Boot and Shoe Manufacturers of Great Britain and the *National Union of Boot and Shoe Operatives*, have through their secretaries, time after time, smoothed away difficulties and brought about just and satisfactory compromises.

The shoemaker's turn for conviviality often landed him in the Dark House,[1] and it also made possible Cruikshank's terrible " Saint Crispin's Day."[2] That picture, however, is misleading. It needs a companion — the merry but thoughtful worker who has developed into the dexterous operative, the village sage, the fluent preacher, the racy politician, the resourceful manufacturer and merchant prince.

The trade has two principal ends in view— *Utility*, for the shoe must be strong and serviceable ; and *Presentability*, for it must satisfy the eye, especially when it is intended for the ladies. Under both heads there has always been a little friction with the public, who, however, are themselves chiefly to blame. Again and again, it is true, admiration has been expressed for the beautiful lines of a child's foot, and humanity is troubled because, as years progress, this perfect object is often, through pressure of ill-shaped footgear, cruelly distorted. If the foot, which sustains the whole weight of the body, goes wrong,

---

[1] The village " Round House," though it was often hexagonal. It had no windows.

[2] Cruikshank's *Comic Almanack*, October, 1836.

naturally the superstructure must suffer. Yet how thoughtlessly it has been abused! The foot of the adult ought to be as comely and as free from deformity as that of the child, and would be if only the public, putting aside bias and ignoring fashion, would ask for the ideal shoe, that is to say, one which corresponds with the shape that nature has given to that marvel of beauty, the human foot—a shoe in particular that does not force the big toe out of its natural position. The child's shoe at the present day is nearly always everything that could be wished.

3. When the world was young, the foot of the magnificent sun-gilded savage was flawless. His legs were strong and stout as the bole of a palm. His feet, fleshy and fanlike, grasped rather than trod the earth. His toes were almost as prehensile as his fingers.[1] On such solid trunks a gold-brown Eve, as Gauguin paints her, looked shyly out of the corners of her eyes when a sinister blue and vermilion demon up among the foliage attacked her with his oily blandishments. On such solid trunks a gold-brown Adam listened, open-mouthed and aghast, to their amazing conversation. Eventually (whatever we may think of the narrative) came trouble, to be followed, however, by the magnificent declaration, "I am God All-sufficient,"[2]

[1] The Hindoo to-day often picks up small articles with his toes. Gunnar, the legendary Swedish hero, played his harp with his feet.
[2] Gen. xvii. 1 (Geneva Bible).

which has ever since been the comfort of harried humanity.

4. And then the world took to foot-gear—the most ancient sort of which we have record being the Egyptian **Tab-teb**, which consisted of plaited papyrus strip or hide secured by thongs. But with the ladies the sandal was something very much more than a protection for the feet. Immemorially, they grasped that in walking, as the eyes are usually directed downwards, the first object that one sees when approaching any-body is the foot; consequently they craved orna-ment and colour. The shoemaker, delighted to indulge so charming a caprice, readily complied; with the result that the sandal, with its pigments that rivalled the plumage of the ibis and the parrot, its touches of Nubian gold, and all the other luxuries of effect, became as indispensable a weapon in the armoury of the Egyptian girl as its successor—the ravishing little " Norvic " shoe—is to her even more bewitching English sister. She used it as she used her unguents and the pearl-white lotus blossom that set off her Ptolemy-black plaited hair; and it gave her confidence as she walked delicately through the streets of Memphis or Naukratis. When she—say Tutu [Pl. 2]—died, closing a life which had been an idyll in order to enter upon a second and even more idyllic life, she left her sandals behind; for we notice that in the other world where, seated on a chair of ebony, she

is playing draughts with her husband (Ani) in a
sequestered green and yellow arbour,[1] she is barefooted.   What a pleasant, quiet bower of delights
the Egyptians made heaven, and what an uninviting noise-manufactory we moderns have made
of it, filling it with the din of perpetual bell ringing
and trumpet blowing!   The Hebrew prophet, like
the Egyptian painter, looked forward to something
infinitely better than that.   Does not Isaiah say
(in Cranmer's version), " My people " (delicious
phrase !) " shall dwell in the ynnes of peace " ?[2]

We get very near to pretty Tutu when we view
through glass in a Museum her

> " Tiny slippers of gold and green
>   Tied with a mouldering, golden cord."[3]

But the Egyptian girls, who were fond of sport,
often exchanged the fragile " slipper " for the sub-
stantial sandal of gazelle[4] skin tanned pink, and
we hear of one of them, who was an impassioned
lyrist, inviting her lover to come to the marsh
tangles birding with her.   Before setting out she
kohled her eyes and attached her ear ornaments—
both of which operations, as every sportsman
knows, are very necessary if you would bring home
any sort of a bag.   And he went — with his

[1] *Book of the Dead*.   Papyrus of Ani.
[2] Inns of peace.   Isa. xxxii. 18.
[3] Sir Edwin Arnold, *Potiphar's Wife*."
[4] The gazelle skin sandals of Tutu, wife of Ani, are in her toilet box
which is preserved in the British Museum, No. 24,708, 4th Egyptian
Room.

hunting-cat and his throw-stick—also simply in
order to hunt the wild birds—so he said.

5. Queen **Hat-shep-set** (B.C. 1600) used to
put "oil of ani" (whatever that was) on her
feet, and as, according to her own account, her
skin was "made of gold," it must have peeped
very provokingly from between the thongs of
her dainty sandals, which sparkled with gems
graven by cunning jewel-smiths and turned up at
the toe. With her head adorned with a gold band
and the *uraeus*,[1] and in her dress of diaphanous
white linen, she hypnotised all comers. She was
delightful when pleased, while, for instance, the
soles of her feet were being tickled, by a slave,
with a peacock's feather, but if she happened to
be moody, then it was "Look out!" She was
frugal of words, though she was a woman. Her
palace was a perfumery. Her dungeon was not a
perfumery. She fostered the sandal trade, and
on the walls of Thebes, one of her cities, are
delineated sandal makers plying their craft and
using hammers, awls and crescent knives not
unlike those of the old English stitchmen, and
hard by are the comb, wedge, mallet and grease-
horn in which the awl was dipped [Pl. 1].

I spoke of the diaphanous character of the
queen's robe. The dresses of all the Egyptian
ladies were so cobwebby that the outlines of their
slender bodies could be seen through them.

---

[1] A snake ornament.

When fully dressed they had, so to speak, nothing on except their shoes, unless you count for dress that which Petronius prettily calls "woven air." As to the men, while the favoured aristocrat indulged in a long and often inconveniently curved sandal, the down-trodden peasant, who was unable to go to the expense of making himself miserable, had to put up with a really comfortable shoe that approximated to the shape of his foot.

6. It was a tab-teb that **Moses** removed before the burning bush. When a Hebrew died his brother was expected to marry the widow. If he refused, she would in the presence of the elders pull off his shoe and bitterly reproach him.[1] To escape the odium, however, a man might "sell his shoe," that is pass on the responsibility to the next of kin. It was in this way that Ruth, fresh from the cornfields—and herself fresh as morning dew—became the mate of Boaz.

One pair of early Egyptian sandals in the British Museum is of white leather with tooled ornamentation, another is rosetted, and the toes of a third are gilded and tasselled. Such were the "slippers" worn by beautiful and trinketed princesses who resided in cedar palaces hidden away in the recesses of cool palm groves; by the ladies of Zion whom **Isaiah** describes as walking with "stretched forth necks and wanton eyes," and

---

[1] See Deut. xxv. 10.   In Deut. xxxiii. 25 we read of military shoes shod with iron and brass.

making a continual tinkling with their feet ; and by the Tyrian frailties of that old song of which the same prophet (xxiii. 16) gives so mournful a snatch, and which may be paraphrased :

> " Hie, harlot, through the city hie !
> Thy haunting beauty fled ;
> And on thy soft, sweet lute rely
> And siren song for bread."

I do not think these wanton, if charmingly shod, worshippers of Astarte loved the prophet. As they passed him in the street, they no doubt muttered contemptuously, "The spiritual man is mad ! "[1]

Looking back on these ancient fashions—especially those of Egypt—we experience the subtle charm felt when setting foot on a foreign shore. I salute the artisan who placed his genius and his gay ideas at the service of Anquet, Tutu and the other seductive ladies of that architectural and vermilion-loving land ; and if I had lived in those days I would have drunk his health from a gold cup with a spirited figure of a he-goat for a handle. We can all do without food [for a little while] but without colour we should die.

7. The Egyptians represented their pschent-covered,[2] or hawk-headed **Gods** as sometimes with and sometimes without shoes (" His feet were shod with sardonyx "), but the priests who,

[1] Hosea ix. 7.

[2] The pschent was the united crown of the two kingdoms—Upper and Lower Egypt. It was a linen mitre within a gold crown.

in vests of gossipion,[1] performed their acts of worship before the impassivity of these weird deities, were barefooted. " Ten hundred shaven priests did bow to Ammon's altar day and night." The attendants of the podgy and ob- scene hippopotamus-goddess Taurt; the cory- bants who crashed cymbals and danced franti- cally before Cybele; the sages who at Sunium looked into Minerva's sea-green eyes; the wantons who rattled the sistrum and burnt perfume before Isis[2]; all followed the same custom, as did those who dealt in ceremonial magic, whether white or black[3]; but the priest of Apollo Ismenius (and this is significant) was shod. Bare, too, usually were the feet of the Cumæan sibyl in her dismal cavern when, in her delirium, with quivering frame and hair erect, she became the mouthpiece of a god, and curdled with her shrieks the blood of the trembling suppliant, though sometimes on such occasions only one foot was unshod, and is so shown on painted vases; but necromancers wore palm-leaved sandals with wooden soles.

The mourner also went unsandalled, but **Ezekiel,** when told that the desire of his eyes was to be taken from him, obeyed the divine

[1] A soft, white material.

[2] The worship of Isis left the initiated person " in a mystic ecstasy in which he saw things unspeakable." The gifts bestowed on her temple by persons in this state of mind were often of prodigious value. A Spanish woman, for example, gave a silver statue with eight emeralds set in the sandals.

[3] White magic was concerned with the evocation of angels, black with that of devils.

injunction and put shoes on his feet. " At even,"
runs the pathetic passage, " my wife died, and I
did in the morning as I was commanded."

But if the mourner went unsandalled, so also
very often did the reveller—the Egyptian dancing
girl, for instance, who, in a robe transparent as
water, and with a lotus blossom slipped between
her extended fingers, postured, to the music of the
dulcimer, so superbly that onlookers fainted with
delight ; and the Greek peasantry, who performed
their rhythmic dances to the provocation of pipe
and cymbal.

8. Egyptian shoe companies are heard
of at an early date, and the curriers and
tanners also grouped themselves. In Cleopatra's
reign four members of a Curriers' Corporation
sold a building plot to one Nechouthes for
" 601 pieces of copper." The vendors were a
black, Pamothes, and his " yellow " workmen.
Doubtless these old curriers prospered.[1] As they
say in *The Arabian Nights*, " God the most High
blesseth trade." I like to think of Nechouthes as
a genius who turned out leather which was so good
that not only his rivals but also his successors
spoke its praises, and I can hear him saying to us
from his grave :

---

[1] Then, as now, there were three distinct classes—tanners, curriers and
shoemakers. In an Egyptian picture may be seen the tanner at work
drawing a spotted skin from an urn containing alum, and the currier
preparing the skin, extending it and spreading it out in rolls ready to be
delivered to the shoemaker.

"So live, that when you're dead and leave this world's
    confusing hive,
The folk will say, ' He is not dead ; he's very much
    alive.' "

The red, yellow and blue shoes worn by the
swarthy Ethiopians of Meroe, who were twelve
feet high,[1] must have been both handsome and
enormous.

9. Among the rock carvings of the **Hittites**
are representations of boots similar to those
still worn in Mesopotamia [Pl. 3]. As to the
latter, the upper is cut from yellow leather
and lined with red, and sometimes the leg,
which has a huge tassel in front, is turned down
a little or even half way.[2] The fashion, after
lasting 4,000 years, is still the rage. But this is
a gentleman's boot. Ladies, and especially English
ladies, are less easy to please. When a shoe—to
say nothing of a hat—has been the mode even for
only one thousand years they, unreasonably, begin
to clamour for a change.

Skin and leather were used from an early date
in **Babylonia.** In the tongue of the Sumerians
skin was called " su " and leather " e," its hiero-
glyph being the representation of a tank excavated
in the ground ; in that of the Akkadians, a later
race, the " e " becomes " ea," but both forms
stand for the place where the steeping was done.

---

[1] Herodotus. See also Isaiah xlv. 14.
[2] *Footwear Organiser*, April, 1920. Article by Mr. Roland Gorbold.

Plate 1

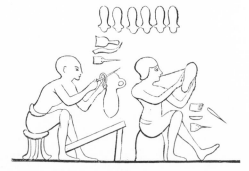

EGYPTIAN SANDAL MAKERS. Time of Hal-shep-set, B.C. 1600. See p. 11.

THE LION HUNT. Showing the foot-gear of Assyrian Slaves. See p. 17.

British Museum. *Footwear Organiser,* March, 1921.

Plate 2

ASHUR-NASIR-PAL,
King of Assyria about B.C. 885—860.   See p. 17.

ANI AND HIS WIFE TUTU,
who is carrying a sistrum in her right hand.   See pp. 9 and 10.

The Sumerians used the words *mulu*,[1] an indoor shoe, and *su-esir*, an out-of-door shoe. The Akkadian for shoe was *senu*, and that for the thong, *mesenu*. To draw on the shoe was symbolical of taking a long journey. Hence in one text containing incantations, the wish is expressed that some sorceress " may place her shoes on her feet for ever "—that is, go away and never return. And she has certainly gone, and Babylon itself has gone, and to the wail of the witch has succeeded the boom of the bittern.

The foot covering of the **Assyrians** consisted of a sole of wood or leather to which a back part was attached, covering the heel, and leaving the toes and the instep exposed [Pl. 3.] In such sandals King Ashur-nasir-pal (B.C. 885—860) is seen on one bas-relief, carrying his bow and pouring out a libation, and on another grasping the staff of sovereignty [Pl. 2]. In similar sandals King Ashur-ban-ipal (B.C. 668—627) with plaited beard fingered the baked books in his cuneiform library; or, seated in his garden, quaffed with his queen purple wine, while the bul-bul sang among his roses, and the bleeding head of his enemy Te-umman dangled among the leaves of an overhanging tree. The Assyrian slave wore boots with tops resembling a modern gaiter but laced in front [Pl. 1].

10. Ancient Lydia did an enormous trade in

[1] Cf. the Italian *mula* and the English *mule*, a slipper.

C

dainty and aromatic footgear for women. It
was with a Lydian slipper that Omphale beat
the wretched Hercules when he became "a
woman's property," and spun among maids. Unhappily, slippers can be removed far too easily,
and there have been examples in all ages of
ladies who have been over handy with them.

Sappho, the poetess (fl. B.C. 610), whose
intense soul yearned after beauty both of dress
and phrase, used to encase her feet in " broidered
shoes of various delightful colours wrought by
Lydian art," and she was evidently thinking of
her own charming footgear, peeping from beneath
her saffron robe, when, overwhelmed by a storm
of the senses and carried beyond herself, she sang
to the patkis[1] her lost song of " The golden
sandals of dawn," and almost drove mankind
frenzied.

Apparently the " slippers " of **Rhodope,** the
original of Cinderella, were also Lydian. Incontestably they were not of glass.[2] While yet a
child she entered the household of a Thracian
named Iadmon, her fellow servant being the
fabulist Æsop who—a foil to her loveliness—was
ugly as an ægipan. From Thrace she drifted to
Egypt. She scented her hair with musk and
stained her feet with henna.

---

[1] A sort of harp.

[2] It is said that a Frenchman created this delusion by writing the word
verre (glass) in mistake for *vair* (fur), the two words being pronounced
alike.

"Her jests were theme of lute and lyre,
A proverb was her lip."

Charaxus, the brother of Sappho, lavished upon
her the whole of his fortune. Whether she smiled
or whether she pouted, he was her abject slave.
In one of Sappho's poems is a burning appeal to
the gods to free Charaxus from his philtred bond-
age. Rhodope is next heard of (and she was still
a mere girl) at Naukratis, confounding men's
senses and bartering her smiles for emeralds. She
was pious, however, in her fashion, for she sent
costly offerings to the neighbouring temple of
Aphrodite.[1] One day, while she was bathing, an
eagle swooped down and flew off with one of her
sandals, which he carried to the palace at
Memphis. The king, astonished at its smallness,
ordered a search to be made for the owner, who
was discovered to be, not a demure maid with a
mop and a pail, but a very self-possessed young
thing in captivating attire, seated on a carpeted
dais, with an incense pot burning odoriferous
gums and the other appurtenances of her calling.
They at once conducted her to the king, who had
been awaiting her with a pleased impatience.
Charmed with her person and wit, he very
discreetly asked no awkward questions; and as
she was willing, or unwilling (it did not in the least
matter which), he without further ado made her

---

[1] Heliodorus: *Theagenes and Chariclea*, Bk. 2. Another lady,
Aglaonike, gave to the temple of Kypris (Venus), her "little scented
shoes." *Anthologiæ Græcæ Erotica*, ed. by W. H. Paton, p. 124.

his queen. Some of the other ladies of Naukratis, who had their own views as to who should have been chosen (and they were the originals of Cinderella's step-sisters), were inclined at first to show displeasure. But it is not a bit of good for every girl to want to marry a king. There never were enough kings to go round, and they seem to get scarcer every year. Though in a foreign land, Rhodope remembered with affection her native country, and she sent to the temple of Delphi a present of ten iron "obelisks," each large enough to roast an ox; and with the rest of her wealth she erected the Third Pyramid.

Boots and shoes of elegant make were worn in Persia in the days of Darius and Xerxes (B.C. 521 —472); and on some of the bas-reliefs of Persepolis are represented buttoned shoes with openings leaving part of the instep exposed [Pl. 3].

11. Of the Athenian leather-folk in the days of Socrates[1] and later, we get many glimpses in the plays of Aristophanes[2] and other Greek classics. The tanners, shoemakers and cobblers were separate communities, and in Athens there was great sub-division of labour. One man cut out the leather, another closed; one made men's shoes, another women's. We know pretty well, too, how the shoemaker spent his day, for instance,

---

[1] Socrates, B.C. 469—399.
[2] Aristophanes, B.C. 444—380.

about 414 B.C. **Cerdo,**[1] say, turns out of bed at cock-crow, shuffles on his clothes, and hurries, bird-cage in hand, into his workshop. As the morning advances, customers drop in. A lady wants *embades* (house-slippers) ; a hunting man, *kothornoi* (buskins) ; and a short girl, in a crimson chlamys,[2] cork soles.

An acquaintance, Metro, after introducing a lady painted with alkanet[3] and her daughter, says to them : "A craftsman more kindly disposed to your sex you could not find. In his art he is unerring; his shoes compare with the handiwork of Athena, and are an enchantment to the senses." " Thank you, Metro," says Cerdo, " I always try to give satisfaction." " Dremylas " (calling to a raw apprentice), " chairs ! Hang it, stupid ! asleep again ! Pistas " (calling to another lad), " hit him till he wakes up ! Your pardon, ladies, but nobody ever did have such apprentices ; what can I do for you ? "

" This silly chit has been playing at ' Hunt the Slipper ' with her friends and in the scuffle the latchet has got torn off, and I want some shoes."

" Oh, the latchet can soon be righted ! Will you have parrot-coloured shoes ? or have you any other preference ? "

---

[1] The common name for shoemakers in Greece and Rome.

[2] Cloak.

[3] *Alkanna tinctoria.* Not to be confounded with our *anchusa.* The Athenians used it as our ladies are said to use rouge.

The lady makes her purchase; he thanks her, and bows her out.

A dapper and essenced exquisite,[1] now swinging a twisted cane and now fiddling with the flowers in his ears, asks for the very latest "Alcibiades."[2] A huntsman, who is used to being well shod (*euknemis*),[3] demands strong buskins. A flute player wants what no English shoemaker could supply—a pair of musical shoes (*kroupeza*), and Cerdo obliges him with a thick-soled article which has under the toes a deep fissure with a metal arrangement which, under the pressure of a skilful foot, plays a tune [Pl. 4]. A couple of Arcadians, bent on seeing the violet-crowned city, its palaces and temples, next look in. Has he any moon shoes?[4] Noticing that Cerdo looks surprised, one of them says loftily, "We are *proselenoi*,[5] and wear this reminder of our antiquity."

Soon after they are gone there comes from his house the sound of singing. It is his wife, who is roasting for his dinner "three choenixes of kidney beans," mixing wheat with them. He falls soberly to his simple meal and then gets angry with her for something (or nothing). She answers back. Quoting Susarion, he says impatiently, "As for

---

[1] This scene is built upon one of the *Mimes* of Herodas, about B.C. 265.

[2] Alcibiades, B.C. 452—404. Shoes named after him.

[3] The Mounts Factory Co., Northampton, have made this word the basis of their trade mark: "The ' Euknemida ' Derby."

[4] Shoes decorated with moons.

[5] *i.e.*, Older than the moon.

woman, there is no living with her—or without her." She whimpers, he kisses her, and promises a seat at the theatre. Next morning they set off like two lovers, he carrying his entrance money (a three-obol piece) in his mouth for fear of losing it on the way; and amid shouting, pushing and laughter they take their places with the multitude in the vast semi-circle. The play is Aristophanes' *Knights*, and Cerdo's feelings on witnessing it are mingled. On the one hand it hurts him to see a leader of the people—Cleon—ridiculed so mercilessly; on the other, he is secretly pleased, for is not Cleon a tanner! and shoemakers and tanners have time out of mind been at variance.

But if he is sometimes uncomfortable at seeing the demagogue so roughly handled, he sits aghast and with open mouth to hear how unceremoniously the gods are treated by this daring playwright. Zeus[1] is kicked, Poseidon[2] flouted, and even his very own Apollo insulted. In short, the world has gone crazy, and the honest man can scarcely believe his eyes and ears.

The play over, he decides to waste an hour at the " Thinking Shop " of Socrates. As he passes through the streets he reads, as he has so often read before (for he loves an aphorism), the sentences, " Know thyself," " Look to the end of life," &c., on the mutilated Hermæ.[3] Just as he

---

[1] Jupiter.   [2] Neptune.
[3] Stone pillars surmounted by the head of Hermes (Mercury). They were mysteriously mutilated B.C. 415.

enters the "Thinking Shop," Iphicrates the general, who had been a shoemaker,[1] is leaving. As afterwards transpired, the subject discussed had been that of courage, and Iphicrates used to say that he owed everything to the heartening words of Socrates. Inside, Cerdo elbows a fellow-craftsman, the leather cutter Simon, who takes down the conversation,[2] which is of so noble a character that those who hear it go away "almost inspired"; and Cerdo is no exception for, lifted above himself, he returns to his wife in a glow of excitement. "Ah," says he, "people say there is no such place as Kardia[3] [Heart-town], but I have been to it."

12. Empedocles, the sublime philosopher and poet, who, lavish alike in attire and in diction, is perhaps the most gorgeous figure in literature, wore shoes of richly wrought brass. He moved like a diademed god, to him incense was unceasingly offered, and he closed (we are told) his spectacular career[4] by plunging head-long into the crater of Etna, which threw out, along with burning lava, all that was left of him— his shoes of richly wrought brass. **Diogenes** the

[1] Once, when some puppy taunted him with his calling, he replied: "I shall be the highest of my race; you are the lowest of yours!" On another occasion, when asked, "Who are you?" he replied, "One who leads others." "The worst words," he used to say, "that a general can utter are, I should not have expected it." See Chapter 2 and also Cornelius Nepos and Plutarch.

[2] See Diogenes Laertius.

[3] See Aristophanes' *The Birds*, lines 1464—1480.

[4] B.C. 412.

Cynic,[1] folded in his tub, wore sandals of palm
leaves, which were as clumsy as his wit was
exquisite. As became a philosopher he was spare
in body, but not so spare as the Coan Philetas,[2]
who wore shoes with leaden soles "for fear the
wind should blow him away."

But far more inconvenient than the footgear of
either Diogenes or Philetas was that of **Xenophon**
and his Ten Thousand during that terrible march[3]
to the Euxine. Their smart military buskins
having worn out, they improvised shoes made from
raw hides which, as the frost caused the clasps to
perforate the flesh and the hides to adhere to the
skin, had to be removed at night. Owing, however, to Xenophon's irresistible gaiety which
extracted mirth out of the most formidable
occurrences,[4] these difficulties were overcome.
And ours can be overcome, and so can everybody's. We too can emerge, as did Xenophon
and his host, into the country of the merry
Mosynicians—into Jolly Land.

13. In the 3rd century B.C. the city most
famous for the elegance of its shoes was **Sicyon,**
near Corinth, the native place of Apelles, the
influence of whose exquisite art affected the
footwear made there. Its staple was women's
shoes, and when the customs of Greece spread

[1] Diogenes died B.C. 323.
[2] Born at Cos, died about B.C. 290.
[3] B.C. 401.
[4] See Xenophon's *Anabasis*.

over sea and Rome emulated Sicyon, the sybaritic Italian took in particular to the imported novelty. The sturdier folk, however, would scarcely look at it. " You wouldn't catch me in Sicyonians," said Cicero. " Still, I grant you they are comfortable."

It was from a saying of Apelles that originated one of the most ancient of the shoemaker proverbs. Many painters when signing their works add the word *pinxit*,[1] but Apelles signed his, "Apelles epoiei" (Apelles faciebat),[2] to signify that the work was merely in hand—that he was open at any time to improve it; a lovely idea, for man himself can be best defined as an unfinished animal, his mind being always growing. It was also his custom to expose his pictures in a public place, and to hide behind them with a view to benefiting by the criticisms of passers by. A cobbler having detected a fault in the shoes of a figure of Venus (for whom the lovely Campaspe had stood as model), Apelles corrected it. Next day the cobbler began to take exception to the leg, when Apelles darted from behind the picture and, almost scaring the critic out of his life, said, " Let the cobbler stick to his last ! " This saying, after being bandied about, ultimately took the Latin form, *Ne supra crepidam sutor*. Very appropriately the motto (date 1560) is to be seen over the gateway of a Northamptonshire mansion—

---

[1] Painted it.

[2] Apelles was painting it ; *i.e.*, he had it in hand.

Dingley Hall. Another ancient saying, " Now
you've put your foot into it," to-day implies misfortune, but the Greeks used it differently, for one
of Pindar's heroes, Agesias, slipped " his lucky
foot into his sandal." In Plato's *Theaetetus* there
is a reference to putting the shoe on the wrong
foot, showing that even at that early date there
were " lefts and rights."

14. In all ages there have been persons who
were unhappy unless they were provided with
Noisy boots, and the fops of Alexandria had
this weakness. When Simichidas (in Theocritus)
took part in the festival of Demeter he wore
half boots which made the stones under foot
ring as he walked ; the macaronis of London
added a new joy to life by wearing heel-tips which
clinked ; and in the 19th century a condition of
some of the West Indian orders received at
Northampton was that the boots " must squeak."

The Egyptians, who were the inventors of
Name shoes, had a spiteful habit of painting on
the sole of their sandals the figure of an enemy,
whom they could thus every day insult by treading
him under foot ; and a sandal of this sort, on the
sole of which appeared the figure of a Jew, was
taken from the mummy case of a certain
Harsontioft [Pl. 4]. The custom is also alluded
to in *The Arabian Nights.*[1] The Egyptian insult,
however, was the Greek compliment and proof of

---

[1] Payne's Translation, III., p. 251.

affection, whence the charming custom for the lover or husband to carve on the soles of his sandals the name of his sweetheart or wife— Phryne, Leda, or whatever it might be—in order that wherever he trod he might leave a witness of his devotion to her.[1] The images of most of the **Greek gods** were provided with a luxurious kind of white footgear called phaecasia. Hermes[2] affected golden *pedila*,[3] which were usually winged [Pl. 4]. Nor should the beautiful idea be lost sight of that he is also given a winged helmet, signifying that if he was swift of foot he was also swift in thought. Artemis[4] hunted the deer in *kothornoi*, and it was while she was at her toilette and preparing for the chase, and while

> " Hard by her upon the ground
>   Sat her virgins in a round,
>   Bathing their
>   Golden hair,"[5]

that Eros[6] discharged at her and them his troublesome arrows. In B.C. 356 her temple at Ephesus was burnt down by the shoemaker Herostratus. But even Zeus[7] had his troubles, and ultimately succumbed to them (or so the Cretans who showed

---

[1] Sometimes a portrait was also engraved.

[2] Mercury.

[3] The *pedila* were without soles, but had straps which united under the foot, soles being unnecessary for a being who moved through space without touching the ground. The *talaria* of the Roman Mercury were similar.

[4] Diana.

[5] Robert Greene's Works (Collins's ed.), II., p. 302.

[6] Cupid.   [7] Jupiter.

his tomb used to say), an event that must have been a severe blow to the *phaecasia* trade. But the deadliest blow of all came on that desolate night when a wailing was heard and a voice from the sea proclaimed that Pan was dead—that the reign of the gods was over. The shoe trade survived it, however. It survives everything. It sought and found new markets.

15. If Athens and Sicyon were alive to the provocative power of pretty footgear, so also was Maccabean Jewry. The " lady **Judith,**" before setting out on her perilous expedition, drew " sandals upon her feet . . . to allure all men that should see her." If the libidinous eyes of " huge Holofernes " had not, as old Robert Burton puts it, been ravished with " Judith's pantofles," he might not have perished so ingloriously, and the lady might not have lived to tell any sort of tale.

The love of gay footgear was not, however, confined to pretty women. When Alexander the Great invaded India (B.C. 326),[1] he received submission from a king who wore not only clothing of gold and purple, but also sandals of gold set with precious stones. It pleases us better, however, to read of the simpler taste of the legendary **Rama.**[2] Exiled for 14 years by his father, the king of Ayodhya, Rama had made his

---

[1] Quintus Curtius. Bk. 9.
[2] See the *Ramayana*, one of the epics of India.

way, accompanied and cheered by his faithful
wife Sita, into a forest, leaving his brother Bharet
to take his honours.   Bharet, however, a noble-
hearted prince, begged Rama's sandals in order
that he might place them on the throne, saying:
" The sight of them will nerve my heart to duty,
until you return to take again your rightful seat."
So on Rama's throne they were placed, and there
they remained until, in due course, he and Sita,
whose devotion had saved him, returned to royal
Ayodhya.   " I am tired," says Payne, " of hearing
how death came and levelled the pride of this man
and that man, but I love to read,

> " ' How heroes and goddesses, other for other,
>   Tamed death ;
>   How Isis, Neith, Sita, won husband and brother
>   New breath.' "[1]

[1] *Ibn et Tefrid.*

CHAPTER II.

ROME, BRITAIN AND SAXON AND NORMAN ENGLAND

16. The popular shoe of ancient **Etruria** was the *pero*, made of unwrought leather; but important men, the augur, for instance, who carried a *lituus* (a curved wand), wore top boots similar to those now used by fishermen [Pl. 5]. In almost all ages, the more important the man the bigger his boots, and the augur, what with his boots and his wand, is letting us know that he is somebody. The English hunting squire, by means of his " Tebbutts,"[1] conveys to us the same information. It has been said that it is the mind that makes the man. This is a mistake ; it is the boot. The word *lituus* also means a trumpet, and it is evident that the Etrurian *lituus* was a combination of trumpet and wand. The trumpet has no equal among instruments of music. It is quite wonderful how many persons you can disturb with it at one and the same time. Every man should be taught to blow his own trumpet, with one exception—the shoe

[1] See Chapter 7, § 97, " Long Boot Closing."

manufacturer, who, to judge by his advertisements in the trade journals, does not need teaching. The Etrurians also made a hinged or jointed clog of wood and bronze.

17. The Romans had two principal kinds of footgear, the **Solea**[1] and the **Calceus.** The former, which covered only the sole of the foot, was worn in the house; the latter, which covered the whole of it, out of doors; and both were fastened with a *lorum* or thong. *Calcei*, which turned up at the toe, were called *calcei repandi.* The ladies of Pompeii inclined to white,[2] red, or gilded *soleae.* Of the love-lorn Erycinas[3] and Cydippes of the period, Ovid, as translated by Marlowe, says :

> " Jewels and gold their virgin tresses crown,
> And stately robes to their gilt feet hung down."

A painting at Herculaneum represents a girl in yellow shoes with yellow shoe-ties dancing and playing cymbals ; and in similar footgear, no doubt, the daughter of Herodias " tumbled," as the Anglo-Saxon version has it, before King Herod. A woman might wear *soleae* in the streets, but a man who went out in them would expose himself to banter. Julius Cæsar, on occasion,

---

[1] The *crepida*, the *crepidula* and the *gallica* were varieties of the *solea.* The crepida made a noise in walking ; hence the name.

[2] Shoes of snow-white leather steeped in alum. Ovid : *Ars Amatoria*, III., 271.

[3] Erycina, a surname of Aphrodite (Venus). A favourite name for girls in Rome.

Plate 3

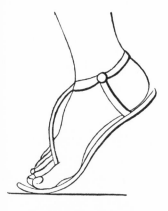

EGYPTIAN SANDAL.

See p. 9.   See also plate 2.

From *Ye Gentle Craft*, by S. S. CAMPION.

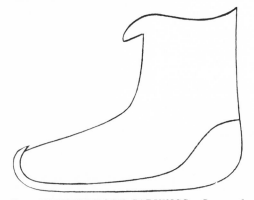

From HITTITE ROCK CARVINGS. See p. 16.

Footwear Organiser, April, 1920.

ASSYRIAN SANDAL.

See p. 17.   See also plate 2.

From HITTITE ROCK CARVINGS. See p. 16.

Footwear Organiser, April, 1920.

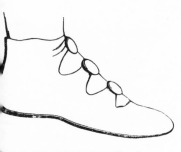

HOE OF PERSEPOLIS. See p. 20.

From *Ye Gentle Craft*, by S. S. CAMPION.

MODERN MESOPOTAMIAN YELLOW AND
CRIMSON BOOT.   See p. 16.

Photo Mr. Rowland Gorbold.

Plate 4

KROUPEZA. MUSICAL SHOE.
See p. 22.

TREADING ONE'S ENEMY
UNDER FOOT. (Egyptian.)

See p. 27.

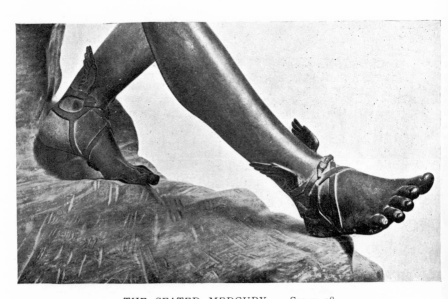

THE SEATED MERCURY. See p. 28.

From The Museo Nazionale, Naples. *Footwear Organiser*, March, 1921.

indulged in golden soles, while the shoes of Heliogabalus were sewn with jewels. Senators affected black buskins, ornamented with the letter " C " in gold,[1] and those of curule rank strutted in scarlet *mullei*.[2] The variety of *calceus* worn by soldiers was the *caliga*, a spiked shoe [Pl. 5], whence the name Caligula,[3] bestowed by the soldiery on Caius Cæsar, who as a child had roughed it in the camp.[4] The *lorum* or thong was useful in other ways. With it you could chastise your slave or your wife, according to fancy, though in the latter case there was the disadvantage that she might, unkindly, when you were off your guard, hit you back, giving you a nasty knock with her slipper.

18. The quality, when they dined out, went in their *calcei* which, in the vestibule, were exchanged for *soleae*. Let us follow **Calenus,** the lover of Cynthia, say. The time has come for the guests to take their places—barefooted —on the " ivory couches, elevated couches of ivory," spread with gilded coverlets. A slave brings snow water for Cynthia's hands and feet, but Calenus pushes him aside and

---

[1] Horace, *Sat.* i. 6, 26. The " C " was a reference to the hundred patricians first established by Romulus.

[2] Named after the red mullet, a fish.

[3] Emperor, A.D. 37—41.

[4] Officers wore the *campagus*. We also read of the *carbatina*, which reached the knee, the calf pieces being kept in position by straps passing through eyelet holes; the *cothurnus*, worn by tragedians; the *soccus*, worn by comedians; and the *baxea*, made of fibre.

D

removes her *soleae* with his own fingers, and while touching her pretty toes he has no eyes for the ebony and gold which on all sides surround him, or even for the flame-coloured gods in blue nimbuses, who look down from the painted walls. He had eyes, however, for her face and her hair which, being sprinkled with gold dust, made her look as though she also were on fire. Calenus is fortunate if, having drawn off Cynthia's shoes, he is able to continue in her favour. For the sex (it seems) is fickle, and a richer man, who formerly perhaps had stood for sale, with chalked feet, on the market place, might step in and carry off the prize.

Among the Roman shoe proverbs is one attributed to Paulus Aemilius (B.C. 230—160), a senator who, after living many years with his wife Paphyria, decided, to the surprise of his friends, to divorce her. " Is she not good-looking ? Has she not borne you five children ? Is she not faithful ? " they enquired. " This is a presentable shoe," he replied, putting out his foot, " but it is only the wearer that can tell where it pinches." Divorce is not so easy to-day, but Paphyria still at times ruffles Paulus. Many remedies have been suggested, but open bribery perhaps is the best—buying her, for example, a pair of high-legged boots at Stead and Simpson's.

19. It was through the shoemakers' quarter that **Augustus** rode in triumph after the defeat of Antony, B.C. 29, on his way to the temple of Jupiter Capitolinus. In front went the musicians, followed by the led oxen intended for sacrifice, carriages full of spoils, and cap-tives in chains. Lastly, in a gilded chariot, with his face covered with vermilion, rode Augustus himself, laurelled, and imperially robed. The thunderous applause of the multitude mingled with the blare of trumpets. As the magnificent show passed through *Sandaliarium Vicus* there stepped from the crowd a shoemaker carrying a crow in a cage. A great hush suc-ceeded, and in the midst of it the bird, to the amusement of Augustus and his train, squawked out, "*Ave, Cæsar, victor imperator!*" ("Hail, Cæsar, conqueror and emperor!") Augustus then and there promised to purchase it for 20,000 crowns.

Another shoemaker, uncertain whether Antony or Augustus would be victor, had taught his crow to salute both, and next day he took it to the palace, after having well lessoned it to say, "*Ave, CÆSAR, victor imperator!*" but the obstinate bird, instead of doing as he was told, squawked out, "*Ave, ANTONIUS, victor imperator!*" ("Hail, Antony, conqueror and emperor!") The court listened aghast, but Augustus, instead of showing displeasure, praised the man's skill, and granted him a share of the 20,000 crowns.

A third shoemaker, hearing of the good fortune

of his comrades, tried hard to teach his crow the magical words, but in vain ; and the disappointed teacher cried out in his vexation, "*Opera et impensa periit!*" ("This is all I get for my trouble!") At last, however, the dull bird got by heart the requisite speech, and the shoemaker hurried with him to the palace. But Augustus, when greeted, replied impatiently, "I am tired of talking crows ; take it away!" He had scarcely spoken when the bird squawked out, "*Opera et impensa periit!*" and Augustus was so amused that he not only made the purchase, but gave the shoemaker an even larger sum than he had paid for the other crows.

At Rome it was considered an ill omen if one's shoes were nibbled by mice. "What should you think," a credulous person once asked Cato, "if you found that mice had nibbled your shoes?" "Nothing extraordinary in that," replied Cato. "Now it would have been really wonderful if my shoes had nibbled the mice." Another early jest about shoes is that of a young man who dreamed that he had struck his foot against a sharp nail. "Ah," was the comment, "what a pity you took off your shoes before going to bed."

20. To the period of Augustus also belonged **Alfenus,** the young shoemaker of Cremona, who —a Latin Dick Whittington—forsook his lapstone and trudged off to Rome, where he rose to legal and consular dignity. Among his friends were the poets Virgil, whom he helped to recover

Plate 5

LOMBARDIC.

ROMAN.　See p. 32.

CALIGA.　See p. 33.

GREEK　MONODERMON.

Footwear Organiser, August, 1919.

AUGUR with LITUUS.　(Etruscan.)

See p. 31.

Plate 6

ROMAN SANDAL. Guildhall Museum, London.

Photo Mr. Geo. Avenell.

ROMAN SHOE OF PIERCED LEATHER.

Found on the National Safe Deposit Company's Site, Queen Victoria Street, London.

Guildhall Museum. *Photo Mr. Geo. Avenell.*

an estate that was nearly lost, Horace and Catullus, and the two former paid well merited tributes to him. Probably Alfenus, who knew a good shoe when he saw one, often twitted Virgil about his footgear. But if Virgil's shoes were unfashionable (and they were always too large for his feet), they comported with his untidy hair and ill-shaven chin. " But then, what does that matter !" as Horace, himself a modish man, used to say, "a Virgil is a Virgil," and so he is, even though his feet are not made for his boots, and though his chin resembles a worn-out broom. With Catullus, unhappily, Alfenus had some difference, whence the reproachful lines commencing, "*Alfene immemor atque unanimis false sodalibus*" (" Alfenus, false to your faithful friends"). Let us hope that the quarrel was composed, and that the shoemaker-lawyer shared many an after flagon with the lover of Lesbia.

In the reign of Tiberius a shoemaker who lived near the temple of Castor and Pollux had an only daughter, and both his apprentices, **Antonius and Pixta,** fell in love with her. The girl chose Antonius, who made a pet of a crow which he taught to utter the names of the Cæsars, Tiberius and his associates, Germanicus and Drusus. Every morning it used to fly to the top of the tribunal of judgment, from which, turning towards the Forum, it saluted the Cæsars, and then uttered piercing cries, as if pleased with its performance

The people of Rome acquired a deep affection for the bird, and Antonius became proud of it. But one day, while it was flapping its wings preparatively to the customary speech, an arrow pierced the air and the poor bird fell dead. That Pixta had done the deed was beyond doubt, and the people were so exasperated that they rushed upon him and trampled him to death ; while to the crow was accorded a public funeral.

In the same reign our Lord was crucified. When on the way to Calvary, says the legend, He was insulted by a shoemaker named Ahasuerus. " I shall rest," said our Lord, " but you shall not die. You shall perpetually wander." And in a contrite spirit he has ever since wandered over the earth. A chap book of the year 1769 tells how he landed at Hull, in England, where somebody drew his picture, " in which he looked neither old nor young," but just as he did when he began his many centuried journey.[1]

21. Among the most infamous creatures of Rome was the murderous, voluptuous, wonderfully bedizened **Messalina,** wife of the emperor Claudius.[2] In her yellow wig (her own hair was black), and with her face smeared with red paint, she was no doubt very seductive. Her hand was as soft as the skin of a serpent, but then she was

---

[1] On this legend were founded Godwin's *St. Leon*, Sue's *Wandering Jew*, and Croly's *Salathiel*.

[2] Emperor, A.D. 41—54. Messalina was killed A.D. 48.

a serpent; and the story of her fantastic moods
and her deviltries, as recorded in the lurid pages of
Suetonius and Tacitus, is well-nigh past belief.
Among the courtiers of Claudius with whom she
dallied was a certain Lucius,[1] who was prepared
to rise in the world by any grovelling device.
Observing that Claudius was "infinitely addicted"
to Messalina, an idea germinated, and he begged
of her, as the greatest favour she could do him, to
allow him to pull off her sandals. Having removed
one of them, he carried it away, and kept it
constantly between his robe and his tunic, kissing
it passionately from time to time[2] whenever he
thought the yellow wig was looking. There were
many pretty and wholesome girls just then in
Rome, but nobody would do except a fusty
empress. He had his reward. And so we say of
a man who has risen to eminence by fulsome
flattery, " He has kissed Messalina's slipper."

A far more evil character, however, than Lucius
was the shameless, hunch-backed and bibulous
Vatinius, the cobbler of Beneventum—the man
with the nose (the biggest nose in history), who
climbed to power under Nero by taking up the
infamous occupation of an informer. Despite his
nose—which became him as the terrible beak
becomes the murderous bird of prey—and despite
his knavery, he was certainly a man of humour.

---

[1] Father of the Emperor Vitellius.
[2] Suetonius' *Life of Vitellius*, Ch. 2.

Nero,[1] who as emperor was *princeps senatus*, had for the senate nevertheless an intense detestation ; and Vatinius once startled and delighted him by saying, " I hate you, Cæsar, because you are a senator." Thus the rascal had courage as well as wit, for jesting with Nero was like entering the cage of a lithe and ferocious tiger. Vatinius— and by his " coarse buffoonery the Muses were every day disgraced "—was a mighty drinker, and as he knew of no pot big enough, or convenient enough, for his extravagant needs, he invented one with four spouts, which looked something like noses. Great sot, big pot ! From whichever point of the compass you approached it, there was a chance for a drink. Apparently, it was more like a vat than a pot—Vatinius and his vat ! People, speaking under their breath, used to say : " The noses of Vatinius's pot are long, but not so long as his own sinister nose "—thus glancing at the fiendish skill with which he ferreted out the unfortunates who had incurred the Emperor's odium. He became incredibly wealthy, and on one occasion gave for the entertainment of Nero a grand show of gladiators. His end is not known, but it is possible that he died comfortably in his bed after a long last draught from his beloved pot ; and it is possible, too, that somebody who was attached to him closed with a sigh his vinous eyes, and wept when his crooked body was placed on

[1] Emperor, A.D. 54—68.

the pyre. But perhaps his end was more tragic. To the wrong-doer—the man leprosied with crime —the ancient Roman was in the habit of saying: "*Dii laneos habent pedes*" ["The feet of the (avenging) deities are shod with wool"]; and those deities may have taken him unawares. Anyhow, his pot is his monument.

In A.D. 64 the greater part of Rome was destroyed by fire, the incendiary having been Nero himself; and no section of the community suffered more than the shoemakers, whose quarter was entirely ruined. It might be supposed that from a creature like Nero nothing good could possibly come. Roses, however, spring from sty-sweepings, and Nero, tyrant, matricide and incendiary, was author of the deathless saying, "The artist's home is everywhere." Certainly he made the artists of shoe-land scatter.

22. By the time of Martial[1] the craft had drifted into the **Argiletum.** As in Egypt, so in Rome and its provinces there were many artisan companies—the **Shoemakers' Guild** being one of them—whose principal objects were to promote cheerfulness of intercourse and to provide for burials. The members paid an entrance fee, and met in a guild house, which had its *lararium* (where the tutelary god and the lares—symbolised by a couple of serpents— were invoked, libations poured out, and odor-

[1] Martial died A.D. 104.

iferous gums burnt) and its panel with list of members. If the guild dwindled seriously, the affairs were wound up, and a declaration was made, with the attestation of witnesses, that it had ceased to exist. In one instance the addition was made by a wag (who no doubt laughed consumedly at his little jest) that persons who had recently died were not to consider that they had any claim on the society.

23. A poor lad—**Calvus**, say—comes up from the country to Rome in the hope of making his fortune, and apprentices himself to an uncle who is in the trade. He revels in Rome with its temples and its palaces. He despises his dull old village. " For joy, for crowds, for Rome is Calvus made ! " The shop (*sutrina*) is in one of the best streets. In order to attract custom the outside is covered with green, red and white squares, and the inside, which is distinguished, light and airy, is pillared and festooned. It is the " Manfield and Sons " of the time. Peeping within you would see the master busy at his last (*sutoris modulus*), while hopping about, now on his shoulder, now among the tools, is the inevitable crow. He can suit you with any colour or design, and if you have the misfortune to tread your shoes at the heel (*calcei talum obterere*) he will make them like new for seven *oboli* (ninepence).

Customers bustle in and wait impatiently to be

measured. One is insulting, and when he is gone,
Calvus, who could scarcely keep his temper,
mutters to himself, " The monkey is a monkey,
though he wears golden sandals."

The next customer is a vain girl, redolent of
cinnamon, and dressed to the edge of her finances,
who wants " tight loops " to her sandals. He
maladroitly suggests that a loop corresponding
with the size of her foot would be more comfortable, at which she flushes, and sharply bids him
produce what she requires. He manages, however, to slip in a compliment about the neatness of
her ankle, and that clears the air. She is succeeded by the elegant Apuleius, who from his
earliest years has devoted himself " to the
cultivation of literature alone, to the contempt
of all other pursuits," and who is in turn
accommodated.

When Calvus reaches early manhood, a little
black-eyed slip, daughter of a neighbouring bookseller, flutters his heart. Her name is Cytherid.
They exchange glances, but that is as far as he
dare venture. Still he has somehow to relieve his
feelings, so he takes a piece of red chalk and
scrawls on a neighbouring wall the words :

"CYTHERID PULCHRA " (Pretty Cytherid),

and as that has no effect, next day he writes
imploringly :

"VALE MEA CYTHERID FAC ME AMES"
(Darling Cytherid, do take some little notice of me.)[1]

and the next day, going by, he sees under it the delightful sentence, also in red chalk :

" CYTHERID AMAT CALVUM "
(Cytherid loves Calvus.)

One step leads to another.   In the warmth of his passion he tells her that she is as beautiful as Venus Physica, who has violet eyelids. The wedding takes place, and a little later the old uncle dies and Calvus succeeds to the business. He has his trials, but he has also a maxim to meet every case, his favourite being : " The strongest man is he who loses not his self-control, even though he be foully wronged."[2]

His baby is ill. He calls in the physician and, still not satisfied, he goes trembling to the temple of Apollo, where he is comforted by the sight of paintings representing cures.   He makes his gift. The baby recovers.   He works hard, and when his shop closes he shares a herring[3] and an onion with his wife. This high living sometimes upsets him and makes him think he needs a change, so on occasion he and she will indulge in a day in the country, with a cut sod for a couch and a cut sod for a table, and after the meal he will lie on his back inhaling the breath of the wild thyme.

---

[1] A free rendering.   The walls of Pompeii have many such graffiti.
[2] Menander.   [3] Halec, any small fish.

Plate 7

ST. HUGH and ST. WINIFRED.   See p. 48.

CARRYING OFF ST. HUGH'S BONES.   See p. 51.

Both plates are from the copy of *The History of the Gentle Craft*, preserved in Cordwainers' Hall, London.   Title page, with date, missing.   Edition of 1676.

Photo Mr. Geo. Avenell.

Plate 8

On left, Emperor Maximinus decrees persecution of the Christians. On right, Crispin and Crispianus bidding adieu to their mother at Durovernum. See p. 54.

From the copy of *The History of the Gentle Craft* (1676), preserved in Cordwainers' Hall, London.

Photo Mr. Geo. Avenell.

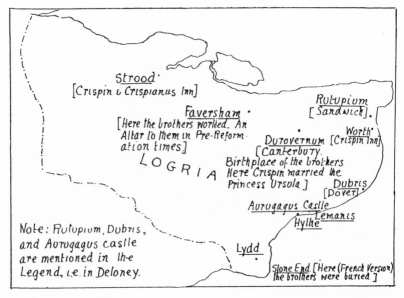

KENT—to show places associated with the St. Crispin Legend. See p. 54.

Sometimes, it is true, he is inclined to be envious of the wealthy fops who peacock it as they pass, just as was the shoemaker[1] in Lucian. Still, as a rule he is cheerful, and rightly, for really nothing can happen important enough to cause anybody to lose his peace of mind, and he has need of this stoical temper, for a little later death removes his precious Cytherid, and he casts on the pyre—stifling as best he can his sorrow—the shoes which he had last made for her, and which had given her so much pleasure. Eventually he himself dies, and his corpse is burnt by the Guild. It is true he never made his fortune, but he got as safely to " Hic jacet " as if he had been a Lucius or a Vatinius.

24. Not a few cobblers, however, did amass wealth, and **Martial** tells of one who, from stretching old skins with his teeth, became a landowner at Praeneste. Here he went the pace. With his head garlanded with roses, and his arm round a compliant girl, he drank to the sound of the lyre rich Falernian out of priceless cups which in his Bacchanalian frenzy he dashed to a thousand pieces as soon as he had used them. " Ah me ! " sighed Martial, " why did my old dad send me to an expensive school ? Why did I become a maker of poetry which nobody wants to buy ? " A similar

---

[1] Micyllus, who learnt wisdom from a cock. The cock, after praising the cobbler's occupation, pointed out that the rich man often meddles with affairs of state and comes to a violent end. " Well," comments Micyllus, " it is better to break one's back mending shoes, than to drink hemlock out of a gold cup."

sigh escaped long after from the lips of Nashe, who in his *Pierce Pennilesse* (1592) complained that there were so many mentally inferior to him who "had wealth at command," adding, "I called to mind a cobbler that was worth five hundred pounds." Think of that! Evidently leather is the trade! But it is no use sighing; we can't all live in Shoe Lane.

Some of the craft were "stump-foot men" (in all ages the trade has included a large number of **Cripples**) to whom other occupations were closed. Hard by the shoe shops in the Argiletum were the **Booksellers' Stalls**, thus, even in these early times, leather and literature hung together. But if the shoemakers, owing to their love of reading, needed the booksellers, on the other hand the booksellers could not have carried on without the help of the shoemakers and leather-sellers, for their books were scrolls—sheets of parchment rolled round a slip of wood and tied with thongs; consequently, the shoemaker could mend either a boot or a book.

It is pleasant to see the Roman shoemaker dropping into the shop of the Sosias, which had pillars on each side covered with the titles of books, which, of course, were hand written, laying down his four *denarii*, and bringing triumphantly away a copy of Tibullus. Back at his stall he opens it at random, and the first lines that meet his eye are the memorable:

"Nil opus invidia est ; procul absit gloria vulgi
Qui sapit, in tacito gaudeat ipse sinu."

("No envy I desire ; I lack the mob's applause, yet feel
no smart ;
The wise is he who silent locks his joy within his inmost
heart.")

As he reads them he feels that those two lines—to say nothing of the other swift and splendid poetry —are alone well worth his four *denarii*. Further perusal reveals to him that the work includes the burning elegies of Sulpicia. He reads again : Soul mixes with soul. He hugs his prize.

Not only men but gods also must have frequented the Roman boot shops, for both Neptune and Pluto figure in *calcei*, and even Venus, who when it became a question of attire was economical to a fault, invested in a pair of sandals made in the Argiletum. It was a Roman artificer who shod the polt-foot of the god-smith Vulcan. About A.D. 70 Vespasian erected in the shoe-makers' quarter the great Temple of Peace, which became a Museum and Library, but under Commodus (A.D. 191) the shoemakers again suffered fearfully by fire—the whole of their quarter, together with Vespasian's beautiful temple, being destroyed.

25. When the world turned Christian, it produced several shoemaker saints, among them being Anianus, who was converted by St. Mark while fixing a new thong to that apostle's shoe, and who died in A.D. 86, Bishop of Alexandria; and Alexander, who was appointed to the see of Comana, and suffered martyrdom about A.D. 270. Far more distinguished than these, however, are **Hugh of Wales,** Crispin and Crispianus. While it is evident that some of the events in their lives have historicity, it is equally clear that others were invented by Thomas Deloney,[1] but to endeavour to separate fact from fiction would be a mere waste of time.

Sir Hugh—the Simple Simon among saints— was son of a king of Powis (Welshpool), and while still a youth he fell in love with an icicle, Winifred, daughter of the king of Tegina (Flint-shire) [Pl. 7]. It was not only into Flintshire, however, that he had wandered, but also into the fair realm of illusion, for in the warmth of his fancy he invested her with a hundred virtues which she did not possess. The more he tried to quench his passion the more it flamed. Winifred, how-ever was bent upon "a religious life," and in order to avoid him, and to humour her bias, she retired to a lone house beside "a springing well." He followed her, however, and found her reading in an arbour, "and so intent was she on her devotions that he approached very near before she saw him, when immediately, a crimson blush spreading over her face, she arose and would have gone." To his piteous appeals she replies, " If your love be such

[1] See Chapter 4.

Plate 9

St. Crispijn en St. Crispinianus.

From Plate in Northampton Public Library.

MARRIAGE OF ST. CRISPIN AND PRINCESS URSULA.

See p. 55.

From a 17th Century Chap-book.

Plate 10

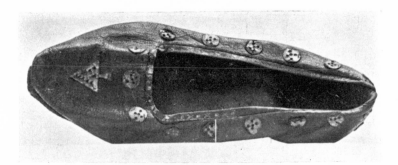

Shoe of reddish-brown leather, decorated with gilding.   Coptic.

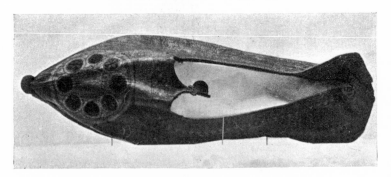

Shoe of reddish-brown leather, decorated with gilding and embroidery.   From a tomb at Akhmin.   Coptic, 5th Century.

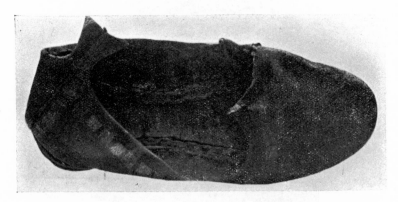

Maroon coloured leather. Upper cut in one piece and stitched to a stoutish sole. On the front are two concentric circles enclosing a flower. The back of the shoe extends upwards to facilitate pulling on.   Coptic, 5th Century.

THREE SHOES FOUND AT AKHMIN, EGYPT.   See p. 58.

Victoria and Albert Museum, South Kensington [370—1887].

Photo Mr. Geo. Avenell.

as that of brothers to sisters "—and there was more
in the same pious style—" I may then yield you
some redress, but if you aim at marriage, all
you can say is in vain, for I have vowed a chaste
and single life."

At that Sir Hugh turned mournfully away, and
then, instead of solacing himself with one of the
many other princesses with which these islands
were just then choke-full, he set off, in order to
lighten his heart and to see what Time, the
mother of wonders, would do, on a Continental
tour. At Venice some " lovely ladies of a certain
class welcomed him with a honied song " (which,
by the by, was not written[1] until 1300 years after
they were all dead) beginning :

" Welcome to Venice, gentle, courteous knight ;
    Cast off all care and entertain content.
If any here be gracious in thy sight,
    Do but request, and she shall soon consent.
Love's wings are swift, then be not thou so slow."

Whereupon Sir Hugh chimes in with :

" Oh, that fair Winifred would once say so ; "

and to each seductive stanza he makes the same
piteous response. He, in his simplicity, wonders
how it is that these simpering ladies are so very
kind, whereas their sister in Tegina is so painfully
cold. On learning the startling truth he avoids
them and after visiting Sicily returns to Britain.
On landing at Harwich he fell in with a merry

[1] It is by Deloney.

E

journeyman cordwainer, whose housemate he became, and from whom he learnt shoemaking. Then, like a ninny, he resolved to make one more attempt upon the Princess Winifred's frozen heart, and, "after the manner of fond lovers," he sang in praise of her a pleasant song which began :

" The pride of Britain is my heart's delight,"

and which in every line reflected his pensive melancholy. It was the era of the persecutions under Diocletian, and St. Hugh was among the first to be imprisoned for his faith. The shoe-makers, however, supplied his needs, and in requital of their kindness he called them " Gentle-men of the Gentle Craft," a name that has ever since clung to the fraternity ; and while in jail he made a " sugared song " about them in which he extols their courtesy and chivalry.

Winifred was also taken, and they mount the same scaffold. She is bled to death, and he is condemned to drink poison in which her blood had been mingled. Before emptying the cup he said, addressing the shoemakers who stood round: " My friends, I leave you—I have nothing else to leave— my bones." St. Winifred was buried by the well which took her name, and St. Hugh was strung up on a gibbet, where he became the food of ravens. Late one evening, however, while the owls hooted and the bats chippered, the journeymen coming to the gibbet and finding the bones picked clean, straightway stole them [Pl. 7], if they could be said to steal what already belonged to them; and in order " to turn them into profit and avoid suspicion," they decided to convert them into tools. One of the men, who had a gift for rhyme, then chimed in :

> " My friends, I pray you listen to me,
> And mark what St. Hugh's bones shall be."

Then follows a list of the tools : hand and thumb leathers, awls, stirrup, stropping-stick, &c.

> " And lastly, to clap St. Hugh's bones in
> An apron that's made of a jolly sheep's skin."[1]

From that time shoemakers' tools have been known as St. Hugh's bones, and bones (of the deer, however) are still used for rubbing the welt and the bottoms of the soles, being preferred to the wooden rubbing or " hollen " sticks because they do not heat.

26. From the depressing story of St. Hugh and his Winifred we come to the rollicking narrative of the sensible and very human **Saints Crispin and Crispianus.** Concerning them there are two quite different traditions. According to the first or *French version*, which is ludicrous rather than rollicking, Crispin and Crispianus, who were of noble birth, were born in Rome, whence at the time of the Diocletian persecution they escaped to Noviodunum (Soissons), where they made shoes,

---

[1] See Rowley's play, *A Shoemaker a Gentleman*, 1638. Deloney gives a different version.

not for profit but for the poor, whose conversion they accomplished. Thereupon Maximinus (Diocletian's associate in the empire) sent against the young men his creature, Rictius Varus. Led before Maximinus they were bidden to recant, and on their refusal they were handed over to Varus, who hung millstones round their necks and cast them into the Aisne. This, however, was a mere amusement for them, for they bobbed out of the water and made for the opposite shore like a pair of moorhens. Varus then plunged them into boiling lead, in which they sported like two healthy children at the sea-side, and in their abandon they splashed some of the metal into Varus's eye. In his exasperation, Varus then filled a cauldron with pitch, fat and oil, and into this mixture, when it was on the boil, the brothers were incontinently plunged [Pl. 17]; but in it they were so happy that they began to sing, and finally an angel (for what reason is not clear) came and lifted them out. Lastly, on November 8th, 288 A.D., they were beheaded on a plain near Soissons, which has since acquired the name of St. Crépin-en-Chaye. Why, after being beheaded, they did not like other decapitated saints pop their heads on their shoulders again and walk away smiling, I do not know. At this point the affecting story splits into two versions. According to one, the corpses were sent to England, and during a storm were cast on shore at a spot near Lidde in Kent, where a heap of stones was raised to their memory. Whatever grains of truth there may be in this story, it is certain that a corner of that coast now bears the name Stone End. According to the other version, their bodies were placed in three different churches[1]—two complete bodies in each church—in order that the sick could touch them and be miraculously cured. Some persons find it hard to believe that each saint had three bodies, and I admit that it is a wonderful story; but it would have been still more wonderful if each had had six or a dozen bodies. Over the spot at Soissons where the brothers were buried was erected a basilica, called St. Crispin the Great.

Later, arose on the site of their prison, an abbey called, to distinguish it from the basilica that contained the relics, St. Crispin the Little; and about 1350 was erected, also in their honour, in the plain of St. Crepin-en-Chaye, a third monastic church. But scarcely a vestige of any of these edifices now remains, the ruins of the latest having been demolished by German shells in the War of 1914—1918.

The *English Version*, a much breezier and far more convincing narrative, makes Crispin and his brother the sons of the queen of Logia (Kent). In order to escape persecution under Maximinus,

---

[1] In Rome, Toulouse and Soissons. We also hear of relics at Fulda, in Germany.

the youths, having donned "homlie garments,"
left their mother and their native town, Durovernum (Canterbury) [Pl. 8], to go where God might
lead them. At night they entered Faversham,
and as they approached a house "near the Crosse
Well" in Preston Street, there came from it a
pleasant song[1], each verse of which ended with
the Druidical " Hey derry down "—" Let us dance
round the oak "—a tree which has naturally been
very dear to the trade.

They knocked gently at the door. " Who's
there ? " said a voice, which turned out to be that
of a journeyman shoemaker. " What would you
have at this time of the night? Some saucy
knave or other, I warrant you." Then seeing two
comely youths who spoke submissively, he called
down his master, Robards, who, after looking
" wishtly " upon them, took them in, and it was
soon settled that they should be bound to him for
seven years. The excellence of their work procured for Robards the appointment of shoemaker
to Maximinus. One day Crispin was sent to
Canterbury with shoes for the Emperor's daughter,
Ursula, who straightway falls in love with him,
" and amorous glances " and " kind words " follow.
Pretending displeasure, however, she orders him
to take her measure " and to bring her a pair of
shoes more suitable to her humour ; " and then
she blushes like anything. He brings the shoes,

[1] The song is by Deloney.

"strokes" them on [Frontispiece]; her eyes sparkle, and she gives him an "angel" (which, as angels were not coined till a thousand years later, was rather clever of her). She asks him what pretty wench is mistress of his heart. He assures her that it is disengaged. After telling him that she will find him a wife, she enquires what sort would be most acceptable, and he replies: " I would have one fair, rich and wise. First, to delight mine eye ; secondly, to supply my want ; and thirdly, to govern my house."

" Her beauty I will refer to the judgment of your eyes," said the princess, " but you shall have a bagge full of rare virtues with her."

" Truly, madam," quoth Crispin, "such coins go not current among tanners, and I know if I should carry it to the market it would buy no sole leather."

She then—for the hermetic moment had come —declares her love for him, and " he was stricken into an ecstasie of joy," whereupon she gave him "a sweet kisse," and after he had "opened his estate and high birth to her," they arranged to meet again under " a great oak " in her father's park. Thither at the appointed time Crispin came, attended by a blind friar who, putting on spectacles, said, " You see what use is. Though I be blind and cannot see a letter, yet I cannot say mass without my book and these " [Pl. 9]. However, spectacles or no spectacles, the lovers do not care; so, Crispin got his wife, with an enchanted world thrown in, and the friar his fee.

In the meantime Crispianus who had become a soldier in the Roman army, had advanced against the Persian shoemaker-general Iphicrates[1] [another wonder, seeing that Iphicrates had been dead 600 years], and there was ding-dong fighting, as there always is when leather meets leather. The Persians being defeated, " sour war was ended with most sweet feasting." I said that at the time Crispianus fought with him, Iphicrates had been dead 600 years. Crispianus, however, was elated with his victory all the same; and to defeat an enemy who had been dead 600 years, to say nothing of giving him a good dinner afterwards, was a feat of which anybody might have been proud.

Maximinus honours Crispianus, and on hearing of the high birth of the brothers becomes reconciled to the marriage of Crispin and Ursula. Not only so, but he kissed their baby, saying as he held it in his arms, " A shoemaker's son is a prince born." The secret marriage was " confirmed openly on the 25th of October with feasting," and that day has ever since been the shoemakers' holiday.

The brothers were buried at Faversham, and their tomb is said to have been discovered in the

[1] The real Iphicrates was, as we have seen (p. 24), an Athenian, not a Persian.

ruins of the Benedictine Abbey there. After their deaths they were calendared, an altar was erected to their honour in the church and their house in Preston Street became a place of pilgrimage. Above the portal of the Shoemakers' Arbour (1679) at Shrewsbury, are the remains of two stone figures, which no doubt represent the two saints.[1]

If St. Crispin was the patron of the shoemakers as a body, the cripples among them paid honour to **St. Giles,** who flourished at Arles, in France, at the end of the 7th century. Wherever shoemakers, in mediæval times, congregated, a church dedicated to this saint was pretty certain to be erected. Thus we have in London St. Giles, Cripplegate (a significant word), a little way from the shoeland of St. Martin's, and St. Giles in the Fields, near the shoemakers' Dudley Street[2]; and there are churches to the saint in Northampton, Norwich and Edinburgh. Shoemakers were often called " Hopping Gileses."

27. The footwear of the **Ancient Britons** was the raw cow-hide shoe [Pl. 12], which resembled the latter-day pampootie of Scotland, and the cuaran of Ireland. With the advent of the Romans a great advance was made, and ankle

---

[1] Crispin became a common surname. The George Hotel at Colnbrook, Bucks, claims to have been founded in 1066 by a Milo Crispin. The third edition of the Geneva Bible (1568) was printed by John Crispin. Nos. 2 and 4 (corner shops) Roseberry Avenue, London, are the place of business of W. T. Crispin & Co., Boot Repairers.

[2] Monmouth Street.

boots of fine purple leather with hexagonal ornaments were sometimes worn.[1]

The shoes of the **Saxons** ['shoe' and 'thong'[2]
are Saxon words] were of a simple character, and
some had a series of openings across the instep.
Black half-boots turned over at the top and open
from instep to toe ; half-boots with double rows of
studs from toe to top and round the ankle ; and
shoes of gold stuff with lattice-pattern embroidery
were worn at court.

28. Our knowledge of the footwear of Coptic
Egypt in the 5th, 6th and 7th centuries is derived
largely from the finds at **Akhmin** preserved in
the V. and A. and other Museums [Pls. 10 and 11].
Some of the sandals are of maroon coloured
leather, embroidered and gilded. Around one
pair runs a border of rectangles united by a circle
enclosing a square on the instep. The sole of
another lovely specimen consists of a papyrus
middle between two layers of leather, the surface
of the upper layer being superbly decorated with
golden discs.[3] The lady of this period indeed was
as aesthetic in her tastes as her earlier sister. She

---

[1] A pair of this kind was found in a stone sarcophagus at Southfleet,
Kent, in 1902 [Pl. 12]. In the London Museum (Stafford House) are
sandals found in Moorgate Street, the uppers of which have many pieces
stamped out of them, giving them the appearance of net work, but they
are laced like a modern shoe and tied at the instep.

[2] 'Latchet' is Norman.

[3] Some of the shoes in the German collections are depicted in Herr
Frauberger's *Antike und Fruhmittelalterliche Fussbekleidungen aus
Achmin-Panopolis* (Antique and Early Century Footgear from Achmin-
Panopolis).

loved colour, ornament and perfume. " A scent of lotus about her hung." Such splendid footgear indeed even splendid words can but inadequately describe.

29. The **Tanners** of those days lived in the oak forests where they plied their trade, and among their haunts was Cannock Chase, now a heath, which formerly covered half Staffordshire. The local place names—Oakley, Acton and Swin- fen—would alone remind of this Titan forest and the droves of swine that fed on the acorns, or were preyed upon by the wolf and the scarcely less ferocious lynx.[1] The tanners used not only oak bark but also sweet gale, a plant which still grows at Gailey near Cannock. Their wives and children had many terrifying experiences, especially in January[2]—the pairing season, when the wolves were "full wood" (exceeding fierce) and the males, with eyes on fire, fought to the death while the forest re-echoed with their unearthly howls. When with their lank, repulsive shapes they made for the homestead, the inmates, with their live stock, were like defenders of a beleagured city. The cries of the terrified cattle mingled with the screams of little children. Even the moon, in Rabelais' vivid phrase, was not safe from their ferocity.

The story of **St. Bertelin** gives a lurid picture of life in these frightful recesses. As a youth he

---

[1] Cf. Loxley, near Uttoxeter, and see Duignan's *Staffordshire Place Names*, p. 18.

[2] Anglo-Saxon : Wolf-moneth.

became infatuated with a pretty Irish girl, whom he brought to England. He built himself a hut among the tanners of Cannock Chase, and while there his mistress gave birth to a child. One day on returning home he found a huddle of torn clothes, bones and blood. Both his mistress and his child had been devoured by wolves! With the horror of the appalling scene fierce upon him, and in a state of immedicable woe, he forsook his home and made his way to what is now Bastwick (Bertellswych, Bertelin's village).[1] But unable to endure himself in these horrid solitudes, so near the scene of the terrible tragedy, he tramped away to Croyland Abbey, where he " contemned the puddle and vanities of the world," became an " ermite," and in cilice and surcingle spent his time in " bithinking " (meditation).[2]

According to Villon the wolf was not an altogether useless animal :

> " An if the beasts in trap be ta'en,
>   The skins to fur his winter gown
>   As a right tanner I ordain." [3]

Shoes also were made from the skin, and a wolf's head " set to stew in tavern wine " was a common dish.

30. One day as **Robert the Devil**, Duke of Normandy, was looking out of a window at his castle, which was situated on a lofty and fantastic

---

[1] Near Stafford, which had a St. Bertelin's Church.

[2] He died at Ilam, Derbyshire, about A.D. 700.

[3] *Greater Testament*, chap. iii., Payne's Translation, p. 70.

rock near Falaise, he saw, drawing water from the stream below, a comely girl who turned out to be Arlette the daughter of a tanner. After a while she had a son, of whom he rather believed himself to be the father; and this son, " William the Tanner," as the men of Alençon called him, became the Conqueror of England. The **Normans,** it seems, had more enterprise than knowledge. Having heard of the opulence of Rome they, after due military preparation, made for Italy. On arriving at Luna (Luni) they took it for Rome and plundered it. Finding their mistake they again set out, but on their way they met a weazened old man in iron shoes. Said he, " I have come from Rome, but it is so far off that I have already worn out one pair like these," whereupon the Normans lost heart and returned dejectedly home.[1] To this legend two English stories bear resemblance—those of the Wrekin and " The Devil's Spadeful." According to the former, a Welsh giant who had a spite against the inhabitants of Shrewsbury, determined to block up the Severn with a load of earth, and drown the town. But losing his way, he found himself at Wellington, where he met a cobbler carrying a sack of boots and shoes. " Would you oblige by telling me how far it is to Shrewsbury, sir ? " enquired the giant, for he was very polite. The cobbler, thrown off his guard, was about to tell,

---

[1] See Michelet : *History of France*, chap. i.

but suddenly recovering himself he enquired cautiously, " What is your business there ? " " To fill up the Severn with this load." Then the cobbler, who thought it would never do to lose all his customers by drowning, said, " Well, it's a long journey, and I've worn out on the way all the boots and shoes in this sack." On hearing this the giant in despair dropped his load, and this formed the Wrekin. In the latter legend, the bad person is the devil, who carries " a spadeful of earth," and the doomed town Bewdley. On finding his errand hopeless, the devil drops the earth, with the result of the mound called " The Devil's Spadeful."[1]

The Normans delighted in very ornate shoes, some of which, as shown by a painting in distemper in the crypt of Canterbury Cathedral, had coloured bands decorated with dots round the top and down the instep, the toe being slightly twisted outward [Plates 12 and 13]. Robert Curthose wore short boots, hence his other nickname, *Curta ocrea*, and Rufus, the Ram's Horn Shoe,[2] the toes of which were twisted and filled with wadding.

31. The cordovanners or cordwainers, as shoemakers were then called, took their name from **Cordova,** whence came their leather, but the true Cordovan goat [the *musmon* or *mouflon*][3] had by

---

[1] Near the Stamford Road, about a mile from Bewdley.
[2] Invented by Robert Cornado (Robert the Horned).
[3] *Ovis musimon.*

1670 died out of Spain. Thomas Blount in his
Glossographia[1] says quaintly: " In the islands of
Corsica and Sardinia there is a beast called *musole*
not found elsewhere in Europe, horned like a Ram
and skinned like a Stag, his skin carried to
Cordova and there dressed makes our true
Cordovan leather." Naturally the goat and
leather are to the fore in **Don Quixote.** We
learn that the wench who girded on the knight's
sword[2] was a cobbler's daughter of Toledo, that
Sancho Panza started life as a goat-herd,[3] that
the Pleiads were in Spain called " The Seven
Goats,"[4] and that the Shoe Jig[5] was a popular
dance.

What Cordova was to the West, **Nishapoor**[6]
was to the East; and its stamped leathers, which
had a fragrance and quality that preserved them
from injury by insects, were used not only for
footwear, but also for binding the old Persian
books, " the sweet-scented manuscripts " of Omar
Khayyam and Attar.[7]

At an early date the English cordwainers began
to form themselves into **Companies,** one of the
first being that of Oxford, whose members obtained
their charter from Henry I. at the price of an
annual fine of one ounce of gold; and a part of

[1] " Or a Dictionarie interpreting Hard Words," 1670.
[2] Bohn s Ed., I., p. 43.   [3] Ibid., II., p. 389.
[4] Ibid., II., p. 304.   [5] Ibid., II., p. 463.
[6] Capital of Khorassim, Persia.
[7] Omar Khayyam died A.D. 1123, Attar, A.D. 1230.

the city was called " Parmuntria " (the quarter of
the leather-sellers). A distinction was always made
between confraternities and corporations.   The
confraternity regulated social intercourse, the corporation business matters. The one was associated
with the Church, the other with the Guildhall, and
each had its separate rules.   In Paris, owing to
repeated quarrels, the different classes, *cordonniers*
(shoemakers), *basaniers* (workers in basein) [1], and
savetiers (cobblers), were obliged not only to worship separately, but to hold their festivals on
different days.

[1] Sheep skin.

Plate 11

Frauberger. Plate 4, No. 15. Shoe and latchet, brown with red spots on the sole. See p. 58.

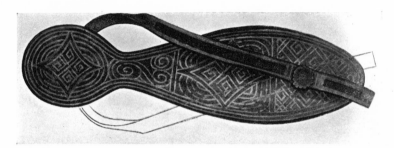

Frauberger. Plate 4, No. 16. Of red-brown leather dressed with alum with most beautiful decorations of red and gold. It evidently belonged to an illustrious person. The sole does not show the slightest sign of having been used. In possession of Count Gregor Stroganoff, of Rome. See p. 58.

Frauberger. Plate 4, No. 17. Sole consists of two layers of leather with papyrus between them. The surface of the upper leather is entirely gilded and decorated. Thongs, black and gold. 2nd Century. This lovely specimen is described as being in the South Kensington Museum, London, where it was photographed in 1888. See p. 58.

All the above are from *Antike und Frühmittelalterliche Fussbekleidungen aus Achmin-Panopolis* (Antique and Early Century Footgear from Akhmin-Panopolis), by Henrich Frauberger. Copy in Victoria and Albert Museum, South Kensington. Press mark, 24 (173) G. 3.

Photo Mr. Geo. Avenell.

Plate 12

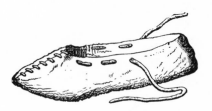

ANCIENT BRITISH SHOE MADE OF RAW COW-HIDE.
See p. 57.
From a Specimen in the Royal Irish Academy.

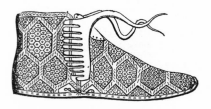

ANKLE BOOT.

Found in a Roman burial place at
Southfleet, Kent, in 1802.

See p. 58.

SAXON SHOE.
See p. 58.

PLAIN NORMAN SHOE.
See p. 62.

ORNAMENTAL NORMAN SHOE.

See p. 62, and see also plate 13.

CHAPTER III.

THE PLANTAGENETS, LANCASTER AND YORK

32. By the time of **Henry II.** the tanners had left the forests, owing to the enactment forbidding them to dwell outside a borough. The tanners themselves grumbled, but their wives felt very much safer encinctured by the blue town moat with its quacking ducks than in the forest clearing with its howling wolves. Long after the days of the frail Arlette, Falaise continued to make leather. Once when Henry II. and Hugo, Bishop of Lincoln, were conferring after a quarrel, Henry who had hurt a finger which he had bound with a strip of leather, called for needle and thread in order to tighten the bandage. The Bishop watched him through a few stitches and then, with the utmost composure, said to him, " *Quam similis es modo cognatis tuis de Falesia* " (" How much you now remind me of your cousins at Falaise ! ") Henry, overwhelmed at first by the astonishing impertinence, clenched his hands in anger ; then, the comic side appealing to him, he gripped his chair in order to restrain himself, and finally rolled on to the ground in convulsions of laughter.

F

After the murder of Becket relics of him drifted to the hospital of St. Nicholas, near Canterbury, and among them the upper leather of his shoe which, when visitors approached, was held out to be kissed. The shoes of Henry II. (ob. 1189), as shown on his tomb at Fontevraud, are green with bands of gold, the spurs being fastened with strips of red leather.

33. It was an event in the reign of Richard I. that gave birth to the Romance entitled, *The famous Hystory off George a Greene Pinder off the Towne off Wakefeild*, the chapters that concern us being those relative to the custom called **"Trayl-staff,"** which prevailed in "merry Bradstad" [Bradford]. The shoemakers, it seems, had " by long tradition observed a custom that no man of whatever degree soever" should "walk through the town with his staff upon his shoulders" unless he would "have a bout or two with some or other of the gentle craft." Among those attacked were the King, who was disguised, and his train. When asked the reason for this violence, the shoemakers answered "that it was a privilege they had which had been observed time out of mind." " Well," followed the King, " we are peaceable men, and rather than break your custom, we will drag our staves after us ; " and so they did. While this scene was being enacted, up came Robin Hood, the Pinder, and others, also in disguise, all of whom refused to trail. A combat ensues, but the shoemakers, as soon as they recognise their opponents, voluntarily submit. The King reveals himself, and the shoemakers, pardoned "for their rude and uncivil insolences," call for pipe and tabor and perform "a country morrice dance," which is so well ordered that they are bidden to ask any favour, in reason. They requested, and obtained, "that the law of Trayl-staff, which they held only by tradition, might be confirmed for ever."[1] The succeeding king, John, purchased at Northampton in 1213 a pair of boots for which he paid the extravagant sum of twelve pence, and ordered some women's boots, of which one pair was to be "embroidered with circles."

34. In the 13th century records of **Norwich** are many references to the parmenters[2] and cordwainers, and one of the old churches bears the significant name of St. Peter de Parmentergate. In spite, however, of the extent of the trade, the workers occupied a humble position in the social scale, and in 1463 there was trouble because a shoemaker was chosen for the common council, the question being whether his occupation disqualified him from taking the oath. In these records is laid down in quaint language what a cordwainer might or might not do. The tanners, who were not to sell "leddur" that was not "sufficiauntli tanned," were allowed to use only the hides of

---

[1] On this story was founded Robert Greene's Comedy, *George a Greene*, &c.   [2] See p. 64.

neat stock. All other skins had to go to the wittawer.[1]

On **Corpus Christi** Day the streets of the larger towns were lavishly decorated, and a procession was formed in which the pyx was carried under cloth of gold. At Winchester, in 1435, "the shomakers wh two lyghtes" were assigned the fourth place. After a choral service at church, there was a mystery or miracle play. At Norwich, on one occasion, the tanners, cordwainers and curriers represented "Moises and Aron with the children of Israel, and Pharo with his knyghts."[2]

At Chester, before the plays commenced, horsemen went round and proclaimed *The Banes*,[3]—the programme. On one occasion the tanners represented "The Fall of Lucifer," and the Corvysors (shoemakers) "Christ's entry into Jerusalem." In these plays, the scenes of which were fantastic and bold both in colour and idea, the devils, who were clad in wolves' and rams' skins, caused roars of laughter by their extravagant buffoonery.[4]

The first charter of the Chester cordwainers, who by the by had to provide for the use of the town every Shrove Tuesday a "balle of leather called a footballe of the value of 3s. 4d.," is dated

---

[1] Or white-tawyer, alum dresser.

[2] In the public library at Shrewsbury is an interesting MS. on the pageant in that town.

[3] Cf. "Banns of Marriage."

[4] See Rabelais, Bk. IV., chap. xii., &c. The Chester, York, Coventry and other Miracle Plays have been printed.

May 24th, 1371. At the close of the miracle
plays in Paris a figure representing the Almighty
stepped forward and made a speech which may be
rendered :

> " Listen, Crispin, my good friend ;
> Crispianus, too, attend,
> That on you may blessings pour,
> (None deserves a blessing more)
> You a church shall have. A new
> Pope some day will give it you,"—

a prophecy which seems to refer to the recognition
by Innocent II. in 1142 of the church of St. Crispin
the Great at Soissons.

The reign of Henry III. was marked by the
coming of the bare-footed friars. One of them
who found a pair of shoes, put them on in contravention of his vow. He dreamt that night that
robbers leapt on him with the cry, " Kill, kill! "
" I am a friar," he shrieked." " You lie! " was
the retort, " for you are shod." The friar raised
his feet in disproof, but the shoes were there. He
had forgotten to remove them before getting into
bed, and in a fit of repentance he flung them out
of the window, after which he never had an un-
quiet night. It is just as well for everybody before
getting into bed to notice particularly whether his
boots are off.

In 1261 **Jacques Pantaleon**, son of a shoemaker of Troyes, became Pope as Urban IV., and
two churches in the city are associated with his

name : St. Urban, which he erected on the site of his father's shop, and St. Pantaleon, which contains statuary by François Gentil (16th century), representing the arrest of St. Crispin and his brother [Pl. 23].

The shoes of the magnificently arrayed effigy of Henry III., in Westminster Abbey, are crossed by intersecting bands of gold, which form a covering of diamond shaped spaces, each containing the figure of a lion.   For shoe of Edward the First's reign see plate 18.

35.   At what date the **London Cordwainers** grouped themselves is unknown, but their first ordinance (in which the workers are described as *alutarii*[1]), was made in 1272. Their arms are a golden chevron and three goats' heads on an azure shield, with the motto, *corio et arte* (leather and skill) [Pl. 14], and for long the company included the tanners, the curriers and the leather dressers. The shoemakers, who clustered round the Royal Exchange, drifted later to St. Martin-le-Grand's at the other end of Cheapside where, like their brothers of ancient Rome, they were close to the bookshops (of Paternoster Row). The ordinance of 1272 was renewed in 1340, when " twelve good and lawful men were elected for the regulation of the misterie,"[2] and the first charter of incorpora-

---

[1] Makers up of leather dressed with alum.   Latin *aluta*.

[2] That is, "the trade," from *ministerium*, service.   The old spelling, as given above, is preferable to the modern spelling " mystery," which causes confusion with a word having quite a different meaning.

tion was granted in 1439 by Henry VI. In 1824 the powers of the company were curtailed, and the active control of the trade, which had been exercised for over six centuries, fell into disuse. Among the present duties and trusts which it fulfils is the administration of various charities, and the maintenance of the Technical College at Bethnal Green, which is superintended by Mr. F. Y. Golding.

The Cordwainers' Hall[1]—the fifth on the same site—built by Adam in 1788, had over the central window a medallion of a girl[2] spinning with a distaff, a reference to the adjoining Distaff Lane,[3] and to the thread used by the cordwainers ; and in the present hall (built in 1910) are preserved its two principal fire-places and some other of its features.

The Wardens of the Company in old times had plenty to do ; and one of them, Gregory de Rameseye, was in 1345 particularly vigilant. On March 12th, for example, he found in the possession of " John Joy," some " shoes of cordwain mixed with basen[4] ; " and later he hauled before the Lord Mayor for a similar offence a

---

[1] For account of the Cordwainers' Company and the Technical College see *The Footwear Organiser*, October, 1919.

[2] Perhaps Clotho, one of the Fates, spinning the thread of life.

[3] Distaff Lane extended from Friday Street to Old Change. The present Distaff Lane at right angles to it was formerly called Little Distaff Lane. See Ogilby and Morgan's *Map of London*, 1677.

[4] Dressed sheepskin.

certain William Cokk.   In each case the delinquent
was fined 40d.[1]

The trade of **Patten-making**[2] was formerly
carried on in St. Margaret Patten's Lane (now
Rood Lane), Fenchurch Street; the workers are
mentioned in 1379, and they (with the Galoche-
makers) were incorporated by Charles II. in 1670.
[For arms see Pl. 31, for pattens see Pls. 19 and
21.]

In 1754 the City Companies connected with
the shoe were: No. 6, the Skinners, whose hall was
in Dowgate Hill; No. 15, the Leather Sellers,
whose wardens were empowered to inspect sheep,
lamb and calf leather throughout the kingdom, and
whose hall was in Bishopsgate: No. 27, the Cordwainers; and No. 76, the Patten-makers, who had
no hall.   One of the duties of the various companies was to provide—in turn, apparently—
Whifflers,—"terrible, monstrous wilde men," to
clear the way for the Lord Mayor when on great
occasions he and his train moved through the
narrow streets with their gabled, mullioned and
drip-stoned houses.   Their dress was green, cow-
bells jangled at their girdles, they carried clubs
and, while making hideous noises, cast squibs
and other fireworks in order to scatter the crowds

---

[1] *Calendar of Letter Books of the City of London*, Bk. F., p. 124.

[2] The word patten is derived from the French *patte*, a foot, notwithstanding Gay *(Trivia*, 1715), who wrote:
   " The patten now supports each frugal dame,
      Which from the blue-eyed Patty takes the name."

of people who stood about gaping with wonder. If you had a hole burnt in your hat, or sticking-plaster on your nose, people assumed that you had been to the Lord Mayor's Show, and had been enjoying yourself. On these and other spectacular occasions there rode at the head of each company the "bedell,"[1] a gorgeous person in sounding scarlet, "accompanied by his minstrels in their golden chains, all on horses richly caparisoned, making great melodie."

36. All shoemakers (to say nothing of other folk) should honour the memory of **Sir John Shorne**,[2] Rector (1290 to 1314) of North Marston, Bucks, who in a time of drought produced, by striking his staff on the ground at a spot near his church, the spring that is still known as Sir John Shorne's well. By so doing he served only his own village, but his next act was to lay the whole world under indebtedness, seeing that he conjured the devil into a boot apparently of his own making. His story naturally found its way into church decoration, and he figured on the rood screens at Gately, Cawston and Suffield in Norfolk, and Sudbury in Suffolk [Pls. 14, 15]. In the Gately statue the devil is submitting very meekly with only his horns and head visible, though evidently he would like to be gone, but a tight fist holds him

---

[1] In Purvey's translation of Gen. xli. 43, where Joseph is described as being honoured, it is a "bidele" who cries, "Bow the knee."

[2] Clergymen were then called "Sir."

and there is really no chance. When Sir John died, however, and consequently lost grip, the devil, very meanly taking advantage of the situation, made off, and he has been at large ever since. I feel it my duty, however, to tell him not to be too confide it. There are good shoemakers in England still—fine public-spirited men—and he may once more be entrapped. In particular, if he really values his liberty, it would be well for him to keep away from Messrs. Lilley and Skinner, Messrs. Freeman, Hardy and Willis, the Lotus people, and other leading firms, for these are companies, and do not pass away like individuals. Like Tennyson's brook they go on for ever. Taken a second time, he would never get loose again. A sumptuous shrine with an image of Sir John thickly coated with silver,[1] was erected in his church, and apparently too it was provided with an arrangement that caused the devil to appear and disappear. In any case, multitudes flocked to see it and to drink of the spring, bringing rich offerings and taking away pilgrims' signs—figures of the saint stamped on thin sheet lead, with pins at the back for fastening to one's hat [Pls. 14, 15]; and the offerings increased rather than diminished, till the Reformation,[2] for all England knew that

---

[1] It was overlooked by a "watching window" belonging to an upper chamber which had, and still has, a fireplace.

[2] Some persons left legacies for the shrine. Joane Ingram, for instance, who died in 1519, bequeathed to "Master John Shorny's light" a pound of wax.

Sir John Shorne,
A gentleman born,
Conjured the devil into a boot.

To burn a candle before the shrine was an act of piety. Those who were over pious burnt two—one, as the profane said, for the saint, and the other for the devil,[1] and Sir John's fame seems to have eclipsed even that of Becket, for in the time of Bishop Hall[2] "Sir Shorne" had become a generic name for the Roman clergy, and both the Elizabethan gambling game and that well-known toy, "Jack in the box," evidently originated from Jack Shorne's "juggling image," and confusion in the toy-maker's mind.

37. In 1316 the shoemakers had another pope of their very own—**John XXII.**—who began life in a shoemaker's shop at Cahors. After the death of his predecessor, the conclave being unable to agree, he suggested that as a short way out of the difficulty they should allow him to select a pope. Falling into the trap, they agreed, and he chose himself. Despite his austerity and the simplicity of his tastes, he had for money an appetite that has rarely been exceeded. To kiss his slipper was a luxury that few could afford. In those days divorce was easy, and a man might get rid of his

[1] In Montaigne we read of a woman burning one candle to St. Michael and the other to the dragon.

[2] See *The Honour of the Maried Clergie*.

wife " for a mantle of miniver,"[1] but John XXII. wanted, of course, more than that, and he was as ready to permit marriages as to dissolve them, provided you did not approach him empty-handed. A rich citizen of Paris who wished to marry was troubled because he and the lady had stood god-parents to the same child. Would it be right for persons so nearly related to become man and wife? In order to ease his conscience, the ninny applied to the pope, who was of opinion that the difficulty could be got over. The necessary consideration was forthcoming, the scrupulous gentleman obtained his bride, and all Europe rocked with laughter, including John himself, who shook his meagre sides till they ached, and his " Ha, ha, ha ! what a comical world this is ! " comes echoing all down the ages.

But if John understood the weaknesses of men, he was equally conversant with and piqued himself on his knowledge of the weaknesses of women. To an abbess who said she could keep a secret, he once gave a pretty box, which she promised not to open. Of course she could not help raising the lid, and a linnet which the pope had placed inside took flight.[2] So he got a laugh out of the abbess, too, and to be old and merry is certainly no sin.

Although a money lover, he founded a library at Avignon, and his attitude to De Bury, author of

---

[1] Piers Plowman.
[2] Rabelais, Bk. III., chap. 34.

Philobiblion, whom he appointed Bishop of Durham
is to his credit.   A right called *jus spolii* allowed a
pope "in certain circumstances " to divert the estate
of a deceased bishop into the papal treasury, and
John took care that these " certain circumstances "
should be in pretty frequent evidence.   By these
and other honest means he steadily thrived, and
when in 1334 he died, at the age of 84, he is said
to have left five million golden florins,[1] weighing
" two hundred and fifty tons."   Every man should
lay up against old age, otherwise he may become
a burden to his relatives.

The shoes of the reign of **Edward III.** were
highly decorative. The design on one of them,
which is shown in a fresco in St. Stephen's chapel,
Westminster, resembles the rose window in the
transept of old St. Paul's, and reminds of
Chaucer's parish clerk,[2] who had " Paul's window
carven on his shoes " [Pl. 18].   Another figure
in St. Stephen's wears a black boot with a top of
lattice work, and a third has on one foot a black
shoe over a blue stocking, and on the other a
white shoe over a black stocking, all of which, to
use a phrase of the day, were made by " gode and
kunnynge felawis.[3]

An early rendering of St. Mark i. 7 runs, " I am

---

[1] See, however, article in *The Month*, July, 1921, where the sum is
whittled down to one million.

[2] Miller's Tale.

[3] Good and skilful men.

not worthe . . . to loose ye thongs of his chaucers,"[1] illustrating the fact that shoes in those days were generally so-called; and the poet Chaucer (1340—1400) was no doubt of shoemaker stock.[2] His " Wife of Bath " wore a " foot-mantel or overall " [Pl. 18]. It was in this period that the Flemish weavers introduced into England the *klomp*, a wooden shoe something like the French sabot, from which has descended the modern clog[3] (used in the cotton mills), though it bears little resemblance either to its progenitor or even to the clog of birch or alder of our grand-fathers.

38. This too was the age of the **Poulaine,** a long toed shoe diapered with flowers or covered with designs that were usually bizarre and some-times obscene. At the end of the toe were *grelots* (hawk bells), and the women (the fine lady of Banbury Cross, for instance, who had bells, that is to say, *grelots*, on her toes, and made music wherever she went) were as eager as the men to be in the mode [Pl. 18].

Similar to the Poulaine was the **Crackowe** [Pl. 19], introduced from Cracow. A prince's

---

[1] From the French *chaussure*.

[2] His grandfather was " Robert Malyn, surnamed le Chaucer," and his father kept a tavern at Ipswich, and probably combined ale selling and shoe making.

[3] See *Footwear Organiser*, January, 1921 : " The Evolution of the English Clog " by Frank Omerod. There are six thousand cloggers (clog makers) in the cotton counties.

crackowes might measure 2½ feet from heel to toe, hence the saying, " to be on a great footing in the world." If a suitor, with scarlet toes a foot long, overtook, on his way to his lady, a rival whose toes, also scarleted, stretched half across the street, he felt keenly the disadvantage at which he was placed. Piked pattens which crooked upwards were sometimes worn with them, and the combination received the name of Devil's Claws [Pl. 21]. To walk with these long toes was attended with difficulty, until at last some inventive genius hit upon the charming expedient of fastening them to the knee with silver chains.

The fashion which succeeded (1350) was more ungodly still, for it consisted in having the toes turn outward instead of upward, and made people look knock-kneed and **Splay-Footed.** The ladies, of course, followed suit, and those who had the good fortune to be born knock-kneed and splay-footed triumphed it over their friends in a way that was far from Christian. This fashion, however, gave the coveted appearance to even the most obstinate leg. Sighs ceased, tears were wiped away, and there was joy and gladness in every home. Not content with looking splay-footed in their lifetime, these good folk must needs be so portrayed after death in their memorials, one of the most striking being the Peacock Brass of Robert Branche, of Kings Lynn [Pl. 16].

39. Though **Buckles**[1] were at earlier dates occasionally worn, they did not come into general use till about 1376, when they were made at Bolsover.   The fashion, which went out in Mary's reign, when the rose shoe-tie took its place, came in again in 1675.

40.   The first reference to the **Northampton Company** seems to be the entry in the borough's *Liber Custumarum* concerning the ordinance made Oct. 16th, 1401, which imposed a fine of 6s. 8d. on anyone setting up as a shoemaker, half of which had to go to the Mayor and half to the craft for "torches and lights."   The shoemakers worshipped in the White Friars' (Carmelites')[2] church, and were allowed the use of the monastery for their "drinkinges," a custom that continued even after the Dissolution, when the fees went to the town chamberlain.   Their   burial   ground   was   that

---

[1] The renderings of St. Mark i. 7 throw light on the fashions at different periods for securing the shoe.   They may be tabulated thus :

Anglo-Saxon	Ic his sceona thwanga bugende uncnytte.
Wyclif, about 1380 ...	I . . am not worthi for to vndo, or vnbynde, the thwong of his schoon.

MS. of a little later date :

i. and ii.	Unbynde the thwong.
iii. and iv.	Unbynde the lace.
Tyndale, 1525	Whose shoe latchett.
Geneva, 1557	Whose shoes latchet I am not worthy to . . . unloose.

Homilies of the Church of England, 1574 ...	Unworthy to unbuckle His shoes.
Authorised Version, 1611	The latchet of whose shoes I am not worthy to . . . unloose.

[2] There were three religious houses within the walls of Northampton : those of the Grey Friars (Franciscans), site indicated by Greyfriars Street ; the Black Friars, in the Horse Market ; and the White Friars, near Wood Street.

Plate   13

BIRTH   OF   JOHN   THE   BAPTIST.

From a painting in the Chapel of the Crypt of Canterbury Cathedral.   The Latin at the top is from Luke i. 15, "The child shall be great in the sight of the Lord   .   .   and shall be filled with the Holy Ghost."   *On   the   left*, Elizabeth saying, "He shall be called John."   *On the right*, dumb Zacharias writing, "His name is John" (Luke i. 60 and 63).

Taken from engraving in Northampton Public Library.

Photo Coldham & Son, Northampton.

Plate 14

PILGRIM'S SIGN.

Sir John Shorne with devil in boot.

Found in Thames at Queenshithe, London, in 1866.

From *Records of Buckinghamshire*, Vol. 3, No. 8 (1869).

ARMS OF LONDON CORDWAINERS

SIR JOHN SHORNE, 1314.

From a Rood Screen at Causton, Norfolk.

See p. 73.

adjoining St. Catherine's chapel, and every member paid 12d. a year towards the maintenance of the officiating priest. In 1465, at a common assembly held at the Guildhall, rules were drawn up and charges fixed. The records of Daventry go back to 1574, and the provisions are similar to those of Northampton. At Coventry, the craft joined with the other companies in the Lady Godiva procession.

41. As regards the **Continental Guilds**, we hear of corporations at Ghent in 1304, at Namur and Bruges [Pl. 25] about 1376, and at Brussels in 1489. The *Confrerie des Compagnons Cordonniers* of Paris dated from 1379. Most of the French and Flemish corporations of *tanneurs, cordonniers* and *savetiers* (cobblers) had banners, arms and seals, and some used presence counters—the figures of Saints Crispin and Crispianus [Pls. 17 and 18], either in the cauldron or carrying palm branches, being a popular form of ornamentation. In some of the arms are displayed the circular knife and boots of various kinds, but the tanners invariably preferred the *couteau à revers* or double-edged, two-handled knife.

42. To turn from Europe to the East, the **Hindu Girl,** like her Western sister, is fully alive to the seductive power of attractive footgear. "Colour," says the *Uttaradhyazana*, "attracts the eye, it is the pleasant cause of love;" and in the *Sutrakritanga*, we see how it may prove the un-

G

doing of a monk. The artful Savitri, say, comes along with her rose-tinted feet encased in munga-grass sandals with turned up toes. She talks to him both with her tongue and her feet. The holy man, if he were wise, would regard her words "like wild rue" (with which pigs are decoyed), but he is not wise and, like the softy in the Book of Proverbs, he falls into the trap. His end is an affecting one. Secure in her toils, he becomes her slave. She orders him about. " Fetch me the collyrium box," she says. He meekly complies. " Now the pin."[1] " Now my munga-grass slippers " (those very slippers that had caused all the mischief)—and lastly she even makes him—hold the baby ! What a warning to us all !

In Lafcadio Hearn's *Some Chinese Ghosts* occurs the pathetic story of the beautiful **Ko-Ngai.** Her father, the bell-maker, Kouan-Yu, was ordered to make a bell, " strengthened with brass, deepened with gold, sweetened with silver," and of such a size that it could be heard for one hundred *li*. But the metals refused to mingle. Again the bell was cast, but the result was even worse. Then word was sent to Kouan-Yu, " If thou fail a third time, thy head shall be severed from thy neck." Ko-Ngai, on hearing this, sold her jewels and sought the help, at a great price, of an astrologer. Said he, " Gold and brass will never meet in wed-

[1] For applying the collyrium to the eye.

lock until the flesh of a maiden be melted in the crucible." The awful hour for the final casting arrived. The workmen wrought at their tasks in silence. Kouan-Yu prepared to give the signal to cast. "For thy sake, O my father!" came a voice, and Ko-Ngai, even as she cried, leaped into the boiling lava of the furnace. Of the lovely girl no trace remained except a little shoe, which was left in the hands of a slave who had endeavoured to hold her back. And to this day does the bell, whose tones are deeper, mellower and mightier than the tone of any other bell, utter the name of Ko-Ngai; and between the mighty strokes is heard a low moaning, a sobbing of "Hiai!" It is Ko-Ngai crying piteously for her little shoe.

43. Very beautiful sandals and "pattens of gold purfled with pearls" were worn by Omar Khayyam's[1] Heart's Desire and **Hafiz's**[2] **Shireen**, a young lady who knew how to give two hundred kinds of kisses. It is a question which made most havoc, their green[3] cheeks or their henna scented feet peeping out of their pretty boat-like shoes. Not that their feet were the only parts that were perfumed, for these inventive young ladies were fragrant all over, it being their habit to hold a lighted censor fed with aloes wood under their skirts so that the whole of their person

---

[1] Khayyam died in 1122. [2] Hafiz died in 1388.

[3] The tiny hairs on the face of a Persian girl are of a brown or, as the Persians call it, a green colour. There are many songs in praise of these green cheeks.

might be odorous.   The Persian lover—Hafiz, for example, thought it a privilege to be allowed to kiss his lady's shoe :

> " He only, dear, can kiss thy shoe—that pretty
>   shoe you tread on—
> Who daily haunts thy portal, and by hope
>   and fear is led on."

But even after obtaining this favour the poor poet was often flouted.   So provoked on one occasion was he that he said :

> " From Shiraz I'll flee and I'll dwell in some
>   other city instead.
> She laughed and, ' Go Hafiz, thy feet, who is
>   it that holds them ! ' she said."

That was all the comfort *he* got.

Omar Khayyam paid a charming compliment to Heart's Desire when he said :

> " To kiss, dearest Saki,[1] thy shoes' pretty tips,
> Is better than kissing another girl's lips."

I hope this came to the ears of her shoemaker, for when you come to think of it, it was a compliment to him too.   The custom, however, was never very popular in England, where the girls were inclined to sympathise with Robert Greene's Carmela,[2] who exclaimed,

> " Ah, leave my toes and kiss my lips, my love."

Notwithstanding English prejudice, however, I incline to the belief that kissing the shoe is

---

[1] Girl cup-bearer.
[2] *Merry Eclogue.*

attended with far less risk than the other habit.
The lady in Marston's *Dutch Courtezan* was also of
this opinion, for her lover's bristles "stroke
through" her "lippes," and she had to spend
"ten shillings on pomatum" to "skinne them
againe." Next time, no doubt, she either made
him give the low-down salute or pay the apothe-
cary's bill.

Specimens of beautiful Oriental shoes may be
seen in our museums, and they carry us to *The
Arabian Nights*, and remind of musk-smelling and
ensorcelled princesses, and of the consuming
passions which burnt in the travelling litters of
red gold, and beneath the lac and ebony of
Asiatic palaces. "How beautiful are thy feet with
sandals, O prince's daughter!"[1]

Like their brothers of Rome, the **Persian
Shoemakers** were fond of birds, and especially
parrots, which they taught to talk by placing their
cages before mirrors (of polished metal), behind
which the shoemaker, being hidden, said what he
wished the bird to repeat. Of the cobbler's love
for flagon and song I have several times spoken,
and as it was in the West, so it was in the East.
John Payne tells us[2] of " a cobbler of Baghdad
[Pl. 35], who every spring time was wont to shut
up his shop and station himself, with flagon and
cup and bowl of roses, by the wayside, where he

---

[1] Solomon's Song, vii. 1, Revised Version.
[2] Footnote to his *Omar Khayyam*, p. 71.

would remain till the end of the rose season, refusing to do any work, and singing at the top of his voice Bacchanalian ditties, with the invariable refrain :

> " Drink ye wine in the season of the rose,
> For the petals fall fast and the time soon goes."

44. With **Henry V.** buskins laced at the side came in, those of Abbot Ingon (St. Germain des Prés) being of dark violet-coloured silk ornamented with polygonal designs, upon which were worked greyhounds and birds of prey in gold. The military shoe of this period and later was an articulated solleret. The *Liber Albus* of the City of London (1419) mentions such leathers as cordovan, nonpier,[1] bazein[2] and Godelmynges, some of which were dressed with tan and others with alum.

45. The great shoemaker of Henry the Sixth's reign was **Sir Simon Eyre,** a native of Brandon,[3] Suffolk, shoemaker, " upholster " and draper,[4] who drifted to London at an early age. It was the custom of the prentices in his boyhood to go to a place " near the conduit " in order " to break their fast with pudding pies."[5] When it came to his

---

[1] Nonpareil.   [2] Basil or dressed sheepskin.

[3] *Gentleman's Magazine*, February, 1821, page 126.

[4] Register of St. Mary Woolnoth, where occurs the entry : " 1442. Joan Eyr to be buried '*in cancello*' by her husband Thomas Eyr." In those days the occupations of shoemaker and draper or mercer were sometimes combined. Thus there is a Coventry token : Obverse, " William Gilbert " ; centre, a wrinkled boot between two staves. Reverse, " Mercer, in Coventry " ; centre, " W. G." See *Gentleman's Magazine*, August, 1851, p. 164.

[5] Puddings with meat baked in them.

turn to pay, he had no money, whereat he merrily
said, " My faithful friends, . . . excuse me.
I do here vow unto you that if ever I come to be
Lord Mayor of this city, I will give a breakfast
unto all the prentices in London." " We do take
your word," quoth they, and so departed. Some
time after Eyre had started in business, it chanced
that a ship laden with lawns and cambrics was
wrecked on our coast. These commodities were
then very scarce in London, and Eyre told his
wife—who was soul of his soul—that if he could
purchase the cargo, he could gain enormous profit.
This put her into a violent hurry of thought, and
she told him that by passing himself off as a rich
alderman he could, by means of a small deposit
and the promise of full payment in three weeks,
accomplish his end. Though at first reluctant to
move, owing to the audacity of the proposal, he
eventually took courage in both hands and secured
the cargo at a cost of five thousand pounds.
Within the three weeks—so quickly were his goods
disposed of—he was possessor, after having paid
off the ship owner, of thirteen thousand pounds.
When chosen Sheriff, he expressed the opinion
that his wealth was insufficient for the honour.
At this a grave commoner arose and observed, " I
have often heard Master Eyre say that he hath
a table—a little table—in his house, whereon he
breaks his fast every day, that he would not give
for a thousand pounds." After this objection was

useless. An alderman and some other of the citizens having accompanied him home, the alderman asked to see the table which Eyre valued so extraordinarily. Mistress Eyre, who wished, as they had guests, to use a big table, at first demurred, but her husband said, " Good wife, despatch and prepare the little table, for these gentlemen would fain have a view of it " [Pl. 20]. Whereupon she came in according to her wonted manner, and setting herself down on a low stool, laid a fair ' napkin ' over her knees, and set the platter with the pasty of venison thereupon ; at which " Master Alderman " said with a sudden and hearty laugh, " Why, Master Sheriff, is this the table you hold so dear ? " And the fame of it spread all over the city.

In 1445, when Eyre became Lord Mayor of London and was knighted,[1] he was able to keep his promise made to the prentices. The day chosen was Shrove Tuesday, and it was ordered that the festivities should begin at the ringing of a bell.[2] All the city made gala, and cloth of scarlet hung from the upper windows. Preceded by the whifflers and accompanied by the sheriffs and aldermen, the Lord Mayor rode in state through the streets. The bells rang backward. Seated at tables furnished with pudding-pies, pancakes,

---

[1] He belonged at this time to the Drapers' Company.

[2] According to Deloney, this was the origin of the Pancake Bell, which was formerly rung in every parish.

wine and ale, the prentices, radiant with happiness, ate and drank, while drums and trumpets sounded, and the Lord Mayor and his lady went in and out among their guests. The festivities over. the prentices "flung up their caps, giving a great shout, and incontinently they all quietly dispersed."

Sir Simon is also remembered as the builder of Leadenhall, which he erected in order that there should be " a Market place kept every Monday for leather, where the shoemakers of London, for their more ease, might buy of the tanners without seeking any further." On the east side of the " quadrant " he built a " fayre and large chapell," over the porch of which " hee caused to be written, ' *Dextra Domini exaltavit me* ' " [The Lord's right hand exalted me]. This fine old Englishman, who " ended his life in London with great honour " on Sept. 18th, 1459, was buried at St. Mary Woolnoth's, and left " by will five thousand marks to charitable uses."[1] His fame fired the imagination of every shoemaker's apprentice, and eclipsed even that of Whittington. A poor country boy who came up to town on a Lord Mayor's Day to be bound to a cobbler, said when asked, " Is not this

---

[1] Towards a Brotherhood of our *Lady* in St. Mary Woolnoth's he left " The *Cardinal's Hatt* Tavern in *Lombard Street* with a Tenement annext on the East part of it, and a Mansion behind the East Tenement together with an *Alley* from *Lombard Street* to *Cornhill* with the appurtenances, all of which were by him new built."—*Registers of S. Mary Woolnoth*.

a brave show ? " " Ay, 'tis this we must all come
to." [1]

Under **Edward IV.,** poulaines came in again,
and even boys had toes " a quarter of an ell long,"
but eventually Parliament stepped in, and pro-
hibited " beakes " " longer than two inches beyond
the toe." As nobody regarded the injunction,
application was made to the Pope who, in 1468,
sent " a bulle for the cordyners and cursyd thos
that made any longe *pykys* passynge ij yenchys of
lengthe . . . and thys was proclaymd at
Pouly's Crosse. And sum men sayd that they
wolde were longe pykys whethyr Pope wylle or
nylle, for they sayde the Popys curse wolde not
kylle a flye." In poulaines walked Jane Shore
(" Shore's wife hath a pretty foot ").[2] At one time
she lived at Northampton, a town where pretty
feet are prettily accommodated, and no doubt her
poulaines were made to match in colour her " long
hayre of a dark yellow."[3]

46. The cordwainers of Exeter are heard of in
1378 and those of York in 1398. The Lincoln men
received their charter in 1399, but their hall was
not erected till about 1549. The Nottingham
Company (founded 1410) owned " Shoemakers'
Close," a property near Kennel Hill; the Dublin

[1] *Epigrams of Sir John Harrington*, 1633.
[2] Shakespeare, *Richard III.*, Act I., Scene i.
[3] Chap-book.

"Gild" (founded 1426) had a hall in Cork Street; and the Aberdeen[1] cordwainers are heard of in 1480. The **Edinburgh** Company was probably formed about 1449, but their records go no further back than 1475. Their arms were on a blue ground, a clicker's knife with a crown above it—an allusion to King Crispin—[Pl. 20] and there was a crown among their regalia. Among those who took part in one of the Crusades were a number of Edinburgh craftsmen who carried a banner popularly known as **The Blue Blanket,** bearing the inscription, "*In bona voluntate tua ædificentur muri Jerusalem;*[2] and on returning home they placed it above St. Eloi's altar in St. Giles's Church. Of the fourteen companies who in later years rallied under this banner, the cordiners were, in point of order, 11th. At the head of each craft was a Deacon, and over the Deacons was a Convener, whose duty it was to call the crafts together on important occasions. When a master of one of these companies took an apprentice, he had to pay twenty shillings to the altar of St. Eloi, where a "chaplaine" did "divyn service dayly." In addition, every master had to pay his "oukly[3] penny," and every servant "ane halfpenny" to the altar. Whenever the crafts believed that their

---

[1] The history of the Guild is contained in the *Aberdeen Crafts Guild.* The present Deacon is Mr. Alex. T. Morrison, of Aberdeen.

[2] From Psalm li. 18.

[3] Weekly.

rights were being infringed, out came the Blue
Blanket, and the craftsmen rallied round it with
great shouting. In the reign of James V.,[1] the
Crown became debtor to the town in vast sums,
and as payment could not be obtained, the magistrates and merchants in concert raised a mob and
gave instructions to the ringleaders. Later, as the
king was passing through the streets to the parliament house, this mob insulted him, and after
putting the guards to flight, they violently seized
him and thrust him within the walls of their
" common jail." The Convener—a certain Cuthbert—having heard of the happening, ordered out
the Blue Blanket. The craftsmen hotly rallied
round it, made for the prison, stormed it, and
rescued the king. The magistrates and merchants,
who began to dread the consequences, then won
over Cuthbert to their interests " by a lusty purse
of gold."

Next day the king intimated his intention of
conferring some token of favour on the crafts, and
Cuthbert, instructed by his new friends, cunningly
made the request that the trades " in all time
coming might be free of that toilsome affair of
being magistrates of the burgh," and that " the
disloyal merchants be henceforth loaded with the
office," which, of course, was just the opposite to
the wishes of the crafts. The king, though

1 He reigned from 1531 to 1542.

astonished, gave a smile and said, "Cuthbert, it shall be done." The crafts, however, on hearing what had happened, applied to the courtiers, requesting them to represent how villainously they had been betrayed. On being a second time commanded to set out their demands, the crafts drew up a short memorial in which they craved that "his Majesty would be pleased to confirm all their ancient privileges of the Blue Blanket." The king not only granted their request, but considerably enlarged their authority. That abject thing, the Convener, suffered for his treachery by being murdered at the North Lock near a spring, which was subsequently known as Cuthbert's Well. On many other occasions the Blue Blanket was brought out, and the cordiners, who were never behindhand when a broil seemed likely, were among the first to rally to it. The crown and clickers' knife appear on several Edinburgh houses that were connected with the Guild.

The seats of the stalls in some mediæval churches form, when tipped back, smaller seats on a higher level, called **Misereres,** which were used by aged priests during long services. In Rouen Cathedral are two dating from the 15th century, with carvings representing shoemakers at work [Pl. 20]. In Wellingborough Church, Northamptonshire, is one which is usually known as "the Bootmaker's Seat," and in spite of the pronouncement of antiquaries, who consider the figure to be that of a sculptor, I like to think that after all it does represent a shoemaker with his tools. Has he not, on the right of him, the shoemaker's bird —the crow ? [1] Perhaps he combined the two crafts, and so was a carver both in wood and in leather.

[1] See pp. 1 and 35.

CHAPTER IV.

THE TUDORS.

47. UNDER Henry VII., **Birmingham** became a market for leather, but by 1700 the trade was extinct. Two salaried sealers, however, upon whom it periodically devolved to eat a good dinner (a duty which they performed conscientiously), continued to be annually appointed. The cordwainers of Norwich and other towns were in the habit of working on Sundays, and both the local authority and Parliament attempted, though unsuccessfully, to stop the custom. In 1546, Edward Bretten, a Norwich shoemaker, was "sent to Master Maier" to be punished for a crime of a different sort. It appears that the wretch had been caught in the very act of reading the Bible in the cathedral, and trustworthy witnesses proved that it was not the first time either that he had committed this serious offence. The quaintest wear of Henry the Seventh's reign, if not the quaintest of any period, was the **Two-horned Shoe**[1] [Pl. 24], which was followed by the Duck-Billed toe, the Slashed Leather shoe [Pl. 24], and the Shallow Toe, the prevailing fashion under

[1] There are good examples of the Two Horned and other Tudor Shoes in the London Museum (Stafford House), and also in the Guildhall Museum.

Henry VIII. Montezuma, King of Mexico, wore sandals ornamented with pearls and a green stone called chalchivitl.

48. To this reign belonged three of the shoe-maker magnificoes whose exploits are recorded in the absorbing pages of Deloney, namely, Richard **Castelar,** Peachey, and the Green King of St. Martin's. Castelar, named "the Cock of Westminster," because he started work at four in the morning, was married to a comely Dutch-woman, who "could doe divers pretty feates to get her own living," and his shop in Whitehall, thanks to his industry and skill, was famous throughout London. Some of the nobility passing by "did many times heare the shoomaker's journeymen singing, whose sweet voices and pleasant songs were so delightful that people hung about the doors to hearken." When the king invited Castelar's men to court, they attended in doublets and hose of crimson taffety, black velvet caps decorated with white feathers, yellow stockings, and fair swords, which hung by their sides. After they had sung "The Song of the Winning of Bullen" (Boulogne, 1544), the king cast them for a reward "a purse with fifty angells," and they spent the money in feasting their master and mis-tress. Castelar and his wife lived together many years, and "he did divers godly deeds," one of his benefactions being the gift of land to Christ's Hospital.

Plate 15

SIR JOHN SHORNE.
Figure on the Rood Screen at Gately, Norfolk.

SIR JOHN SHORNE.
Figure on a Rood Screen Panel, once in
the possession of a Mr. G. Dupont,
Sudbury, Suffolk.   See p. 73.

PILGRIM'S SIGN.
Sir John Shorne with devil in boot.

PILGRIM'S SIGN (Sir John Shorne).
Both Signs found in the Thames at Queenhithe,
London, in 1866.

All these plates are from *Records of Buckinghamshire*, Vol. 3, No. 8 (1869).

Plate 16

THE PEACOCK BRASS, KING'S LYNN.

Robert Branche, Mayor, entertaining King Edward III., *circa* 1350. See p. 79.

Peachey, "the shoemaker of Fleet Street,
kept all the yeere forty tall men on worke, besides
Prentises, and every one he clothed in tawny coats,
which he gave as his livery to them." On
Sundays, when he went to church "in his black
gown garded with velvet," all his men—each with
sword and buckler—were expected to wait upon
him. Among those who entered into his service
was Sir John Rainsford, a knight who had got
himself into trouble " for burying a massing priest
alive," his object in turning shoemaker being to
avoid " misery " by following " misterie."[1] When
the French landed in 1545, Peachey at his own
cost "set forth " thirty of his men including Sir
John, who behaved so valiantly that his treatment
of the " massing priest " was discovered to be only
a little wildness of youth, and it was felt, moreover
that one priest fewer in a country where priests
were so numerous did not really very much matter.
Consequently the knight was restored to royal
favour, while Peachey was appointed shoemaker to
the court.

Many of the craft at this time had—as we have
seen (p. 70)—their stalls in St. Martin le Grand's,
and among them was **The Green King**, so called
from the colour in which he and his threescore
journeymen were accustomed to strut on great
occasions. He never went abroad "without a two-
handed sword on his shoulder or under his arm,"

[1] Latin, *ministerium*—service, employment.

H

and that "which made him more happie" was
that God blest him with a good wife. Being too
fond of pleasure, however, he neglected his business; and when he came to grief none of his
friends would help him, save an old fiddler nick-
named Anthony Now Now, who used to sing a
song beginning:

> " When should a man show himself gentle and kinde ?
> When should a man comfort the sorrowful minde?
>   O Anthony, now, now, now !
>   O Anthony, now, now, now ! "

The Green King then determined to go into
hiding, but while he was away his wife managed
the business so well that it grew great again; consequently when he returned, he found awaiting
him not only two loving arms but also a heavy
purse. He made her, however, owing to his love
for practical joking, only an ill return for her
goodness. When she urged him to take her out
on a Sunday, as the other shoemakers took their
wives, he said he would go to St. James's Fair if
she would accompany him. She, supposing that
he meant St. James's Fair at Westminster, readily
consented, but it transpired that he meant the one
at Bristol, and he made her walk every step of the
way with him. After performing a hundred other
" merry feates," at last, " being aged and blinde he
dyed, after he had done many good deedes to
divers poor men."

49. The Emperor **Charles V.** was given to

wandering about Brussels at night in disguise, although, owing to a conspicuous nose, he must have taken great pains in order to hide his identity. During one of these rambles, his boot required immediate mending, and he applied to a cobbler. Unfortunately it happened to be Oct. 25th, and the cobbler, who was drinking with his "pew-fellows," exclaimed : "What ! mend a boot on St. Crispin's ! Were it Charley himself I wouldn't. But come in and wet your whistle. You're welcome ! Luck to all ! Drink about ! Here's to Nosey ! "

Emperor : " Then you love the Emperor ? "

Cobbler : " Certainly ; though I should love him better if he'd tax us less. But what have we now to do with politics ? Fill, fill ! "

The Emperor, having drunk a long glass, expressed thanks and took his leave. Next day he sent for the cobbler, who was dismayed at finding himself face to face with sovereignty, and still more dismayed when asked, " And what did you mean when you said you wouldn't do a stitch even for Nosey ? "

As the poor man made no reply, but only fidgeted, the Emperor said, " Well, I thank you for your hospitality all the same ; and now, tell me how I can recompense you." The cobbler requested that his craft might be heraldically represented by a boot and the imperial arms. " It is granted," said the Emperor, " but as you are so moderate, ask further." " Henceforward then," said the cobbler, " let the company of cobblers take precedence of the company of shoemakers." This too was granted, and the cobblers of Flanders have exercised their privilege and spoken patronisingly of the shoemakers ever since.

50. One of the most attractive figures of the Reformation era was **Hans Sachs,** [Pl. 23], a gentle, humorous, lovable soul who made sunshine wherever he trod. Born in 1494 at Nuremberg, he became a shoemaker, but he used the pen as frequently as the awl. The versatility of his genius was amazing. He wrote—and writing made him extraordinarily happy—1,700 merry tales, besides plays and songs. He found mirth in almost every occurrence, if it was not there he put it in. Nothing could ruffle his temper, and even age could not detract from his cheerfulness. Though he had more misfortunes than most men, he knew how to enjoy, as Evreinov would put it, the illusion of happiness. By 1560 he had lost his wife and all his children. Next year, at the age of 67, he indomitably made a new start by marrying Barbara Harcherin, a girl of 17. His life, which was one long tra-la-la-la, ended in 1576.

In Tudor times, the Scotch and the Irish wore brogues, made from deer-hide with the hair side outward. On the island of Aran (Galway Bay), these shoes were called **Pampooties,** in the Scottish highlands **Cuarans,** and in the lowlands

Plate 17

Arms of the Cordwainers of Arras, France.
Saints Crispin and Crispianus.
See p. 81.

Arms of the Cobblers and Tanners of
Pouzolles, France. Two two-handled double-
edged tanner's knives and a cobbler's knife.
See p. 81.

Arms of Cordwainers of Toulon, France.
Saints Crispin and Crispianus in the
Cauldron. See pp. 52 and 81.

Arms of the Cobblers and Cordwainers of
Mauriac, Department of Cantal, France.
See p. 81.

Presence Counter of the Tanners of Ghent·
These counters served as admission tickets
at the meetings of the Corporation. On
fête days they ensured free refreshment.
See p. 81.

Seal of the Cordwainers of St. Trond,
Belgium. Two pattens, a paring knife, an
awl, etc. Legend : Sigillum . . . tery
opidi S . . . Trudens. See p. 81.

All these illustrations are from Lacroix. *Historie de la Chaussure.*

Plate 18

Shoe, reign of Edward I.
See p. 70.

Paul's Window Shoe.   See p. 77.

The Wife of Bath, showing " footmantel."
Ellesmore MS.   See p. 78.

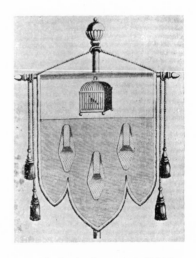

Banner of Cordwainers and Cobblers at
Amboise, near Tours, France.
See p. 81.

From *Lacroix*.   *Photo Mr. G. Avenell.*

Shoe with *Grelot* (Hawk's Bell).

" Rings on her fingers and bells on her toes,
She shall have music wherever she goes."   See p. 78.

Revilins. The Scotch gashed their cuarans, "though new made," in order that the water might run out after they had crossed a river; and it is said that the ornamental punctures in the toe-cap of to-day are a survival of this practice. In the wilder parts people went barefooted; and to wear cuarans was to give one's self airs. One evening a messenger came to Tongue House (Sutherland) from Dunrobin Castle, and showed his importance by placing his cuarans on the dresser. The cook was indignant, but she said nothing. When, however, next morning he asked for them just before leaving, she enquired how he liked his breakfast. "I never enjoyed a better," said he. "Then you have the satisfaction of knowing that you carry your cuarans inside, instead of outside, this time. And never you again take upon yourself to place your upstart Gower cuarans on the dresser of gentlefolk." The "clouted brogues" of *Cymbeline* (IV., 2) were shoes studded with nails (clouts), the sewing being done not with thread but with horse-hide thongs. Spurs were then called "rippons," from the town in which they were made, and if a person wearing them entered a church, the beadle would be sure to demand a fine called "spur-money."

51. In the reign of Mary the "broad toe" became broader and broader, toes of seven inches across being common. Velvet "moyles" (heelless quarterless slippers, ancestors of the latter-day *mules*) and "slip-shoes" (slippers) were also extensively worn.   The murder of Arden of Feversham was brought home to his wife by the discovery of rushes in his "slip-shoe." We hear much of the **Pantofle** (or pantable), which was of a slovenly appearance, notwithstanding Sidney's phrase, "pantable of Pallas." "How should they be handsome," says Philip Stubbes, "when they go flap, flap up and down in the dirt, casting up the mire to the knees of the wearer!" A little later (1586) Stubbes, who had written so bitingly against the shoe fashions, married Katherine, daughter of William Emmes, cordwainer grandee of London. She was only 15, and his quaint but affecting account of his love for her, and of her death four years after, is one of the curiosities of literature.

Pinsnets and **Pinsons**[1] were worn by women, and when the country girl "in stammel red" came to a town, a pair of cork soles[2] was almost her first purchase; and then she would go "trip, trip, trip, over the market-place, holding up her petticoats"[3] to show her fine coloured stockings and new foot-gear.

Among the many who suffered during the Marian persecution were several shoemakers, one of the saddest cases being that of **John Kurde,**

---

[1] Thin-soled shoes. French, *pincer* to pinch.

[2] Dekker calls women " the cork-heeled sex."

[3] *Willy Beguiled*, a play, 1623.

who in 1557 was tried at Northampton for deny-
ing the doctrine of Transubstantiation. The
whole world might go wrong, but John Kurde
would not swerve. Some people talked, he acted.
" How beggarly," says Whitman, "appears argument before a defiant deed ! " He was led through
the Northgate, and burned at Kingsthorpe in the
presence of a great crowd [Pl. 24]. Not all
came out of cruelty or even out of curiosity.
Some, no doubt, like timorous John Rough, who
watched the burnings at Smithfield, attended in
order "to learn the way." The same year
occurred the martyrdom, at Laxefield, of the
Suffolk shoemaker, John Noyes, one more out of
the many who, in this violent manner, were hurried
from their " houses of sticks and dirt " to one of
their Father's many mansions.

52. In Elizabeth's time, the shoe trade of
Norwich gave place to weaving (introduced by the
Huguenots), and it was not until the 19th century
that the shoe again asserted itself there. Thetford,
Stratford-on-Avon and Great Grimsby had shoe
corporations in the 16th century. At St. Albans
all the crafts and occupations were originally
divided into four companies—the Mercers, the
Inn-holders, the Victuallers, and the Shoemakers,
each of whom had two wardens ; and in 1587,
when the Armada sailed, each company had to
provide a man, a corslett, and a " quallever." [1]

---

[1] Caliver. A gun smaller than the musket. It was fired without a
rest.

There was a company of the " jornemen of scho-makers " at Leicester, in 1531-2, and by a regula-tion of 1589, " Boots made contrary to statute " were " forfeited on presentment of a jury of corvisors," but Leicester did not become an important shoe centre till about 1840.

53. At **Inverness**[1] the " cordiners " had, at an early date, formed themselves into a " craft " with a deacon at its head, and in the parish church before the Reformation was an altar to St. Crispin. A large trade was done in the skins of goats, which were brought into the burgh by the Highlanders ; and at the head courts, held thrice a year, " stallangers and booth-holders "[2] were authorised to trade, and prices of shoes fixed. " Forestalling[3] and making shoes of horse leather " were a common offence.[4] In 1576 James Tomson admitted that he had sold boots which he himself had made out of worn-out smithy bellows. Witches and harlots were allowed neither to buy nor sell.

54. When speaking of **The Plague**, we are apt to think only of the great sickness of 1665, but there were serious outbreaks in London long before, one of the worst being in 1581, when the

---

[1] *Life in Inverness in the 16th Century*, by William Mackay, 1911.

[2] The lowest class of cordiners.

[3] That is, buying up goods before they were exposed for sale, so as to obtain command of the market.

[4] So it was in England. At Bristol, in 1726, the magistrates burnt at the High Cross a number of shoes which, in contravention of regulations, had been made of seal and horse skins.

doors of infected houses were marked, and
searchers had to carry a " Redd Roode " (cross).
In vain the people drank " mithridatum and
dragon-water," and stuffed their noses with worm-
wood. Anybody might come out like a zebra, only
the stripes were black and blue ; and the " nastie
gravemaker was the busiest man in town." Dekker
tells some queer stories of this terrible period.
One is of a virtuous and very innocent cobbler
whose wife was down with the stripes, " she wiping
her cheekes with the corner of one of the sheets,
and he his sullied face with his leather apron."
Thinking she was dying, she confessed that she had
been unfaithful to him, and he nervously strokes
his beard. She recovered, however, and the story
here breaks off, the poor man being left nervously
stroking his beard. Another story is of a cobbler
mated to a shrew. Weary of her tantrums he
applied to a doctor, saying, " I am struck—I have
a plague upon me." The doctor bade him show
the sore. " Wait a moment," said the cobbler,
going out, and presently he returned with his wife,
borne " on his backe like a sowe new scalded on the
backe of a butcher, and for all her kicking, rayling,
cursing and swearing, yet to the Doctor he came
with her, crying, ' Looke you here, Maister Doctor,
this is my plague, the sore that so torments me.'
' That can soon be cured,' said the doctor, picking
up a cudgel, ' This is what you need.' " The
cobbler tendered his thanks, made use of the

medicine, which he took care should be "well shaken," and lived thenceforward in peace and quiet.

55. In 1582, Thomas Price was brought before the Lord Mayor and fined £10 for shipping old shoes beyond seas, contrary to statute. However, by request of Queen Elizabeth the fine was remitted on account of his poverty. In this affair the Queen shows to advantage, but in another otherwise. Although search and allowance of leather had been granted to the city she, in 1592, took away this privilege, and bestowed it by patent upon a certain **Darcie.** The Lord Mayor and the aldermen having resented this encroachment on their rights, Darcie made an assault on them. This came to the ears of the prentices. In an instant cries of "Murder! Clubs! Clubs!" rang through the streets. Tools were thrown down, goods dropped into the dry-fat,[1] and hundreds of delighted prentices in blue cloaks, white breeches and flat caps streamed through the city, armed with their favourite weapon, shouting and gesticulating. But for the Lord Mayor's intervention, Darcie would have been dealt with "sowterly," and perhaps killed. In no wise grateful for the service, Darcie then cast into prison "the wives of certain leather-sellers," whereupon the Lord Mayor petitioned that the women might be released, and the patent revoked. Then occurred a characteristic action on the part of the

[1] A sort of basket.

Queen. In granting the patent she had both wronged the city and broken her own laws; but she was willing, she obligingly said, to revoke it on condition that a fine was paid to her of £4,000—a trick worthy of our artful old friend John XXII.

Late in the reign was introduced from Italy the **Chopine,** a lady's shoe on a painted wooden stand which raised it from three or four inches to a foot from the ground. Certainly this outlandish " machine" kept the shoe from the dirt, but the wearer found it impossible to walk abroad unless supported by two maids, and even then it was necessary " to deliberate cautiously" every step she took. Sometimes a gentleman would be called upon to lend an arm, or to lift her about as if she were a mummy or an inverted flower-pot, which in her " vardingale" she much resembled. Some gentlemen, especially if the lady was pretty, complied readily, causing her to blush to the roots of her fashionable red hair; but others, including, I grieve to say, the husband variety, spoke sarcastically both of the chopine and its wearer, calling the former " a scaffold," and the latter a " Half-er" [half woman half timber], which cruel and unnatural conduct sometimes reduced the poor lady to tears. Men patronised the *Startup*, a high shoe that opened at the side.

In 1588 began the famous Pamphlet War, known as the **Marprelate Controversy**, waged against

Episcopacy by the Puritans, whose principal writers were John Penry and John Udall. The agents in the distribution of the tracts were two courageous cobblers, Cuthbert Cliffe and Humphrey Newman, who " jerked out their elbows " in every meeting-house, and " wore out three or four pulpits with the unreasonable bouncing of their fists." Brilliant as were the Marprelatists, their arguments were no match for those used against them—the jail and the rope. Udall died in irons in 1592; Penry was hanged in 1593.

56. In 1590 appeared anonymously a collection of Tales (a little *Decameron*), **The Cobler of Canterburie,** supposed to be told by a merry party as they proceed by barge—a ship of fools, as Nashe calls it—from Billingsgate to Gravesend, the moving spirit being a tall, bald-pated, facetious cobbler, whose philosophy is summed up in his " Lives not a merry man longer than a sad ! " A second edition appeared in 1608, and in 1630 it was again issued, but with a new title, **The Tincker of Turvey,** the Introduction being slightly altered, while the last two tales gave place to others. In Turvey, a Bedfordshire and formerly a shoe-making village, was an inn called the Tinker of Turvey, and its signboard, showing the Tinker, his doxy (old Nell), and his dog is still preserved. A spring in the village has time out of mind been known as Nell's Well. However, as I have just shown, *The Tincker of Turvey*

Plate 19

POINTED TOE OF SHOE.

Found in London. 14th Century. Guildhall Museum, London. See p. 78.

Photo Mr. Geo. Avenell.

WOODEN PATTEN.

Found in Temple Gardens. 14th Century. Guildhall Museum, London.
See p. 72.

Photo Mr. Geo. Avenell.

CRACKOE. English 15th Century.

Victoria and Albert Museum, South Kensington. T. 391—1913. See p. 78.

Plate 20

ARMS OF
EDINBURGH CORDWAINERS.

From *The Blue Blanket*,
2nd Edition, 1780, p. 153.

See p. 91.

Az. their cutting knife
in pale, and in chief a
ducal crown, or.

"The Little Table that was valued at over a thousand pounds." See p. 83.
From Copy of *The History of the Gentle Craft*, preserved in Cordwainers' Hall, London.

MISERERE (Shoemaker and his wife), Rouen Cathedral. See p. 93.
All these from photos by Mr. Geo. Avenell.

is only another name for *The Cobler of Canterburie*, the protean hero having merely cropped his
hair, removed his hand leathers and exchanged his
lapstone for a kettle. We voyage in the same old
lumbering barge, with the same old careless wags,
and listen for the most part to the same old im-
proper stories. In England formerly the itinerant
cobbler went from village to village with his kit in
a basket on his back. On getting a job he would
drop down on the doorstep, and while at work, he
and his customer would strike up with a song, or
talk politics. If the Cobbler of Canterbury kept
loose company, and was none too pious himself,
on the other hand there were shoemen just then of
quite a different cast; for example, we read of the
cobbler of Norwich who, " being one morning at
St. Andrew's, stept up, as the Vicar was not to be
found, into the pulpit very devoutly, and made a
good thriftie exhortation on the praise of plain
dealing." Naturally, the negligent vicar became
the subject of sympathy, and naturally, too, the
obliging cobbler was bundled off to prison.

57. On February 26th, 1564, had been
christened at Canterbury, **Christofer Marlowe,**
a shoemaker's son, who was destined to hold high
rank in the realm of the spirit. His fiery
Tamburlaine was first acted in 1588. All the town
flocked to see it, and watermen on the Thames
sang snatches from his *Hero and Leander* as they
plied their sculls. With him were associated

Robert Greene (1558—1592) and Thomas Nashe
(1567—1600). Fluctuating between the tavern
and the stew, they drowned their souls in strange
passions, and yet both had "seen Pan sitting in
his bower of delights." They were huge feeders
on those rare occasions when they had anything to
eat. We know **Greene**, son of a Norwich shoemaker, by his "great shock of hair," "the jolly,
long, red peake like the spire of a steeple," which
he called a beard, and his "faire cloake with
sleeves of greene." His works, and those of Nashe,
form a perfect atlas of shoe life under the Tudors.
In one he tells how shoemakers came to be thrift-
less. The god Mercury being "passing hungry,
came upon a company of shoemakers who were
regaling themselves on powdered beefe and
brewesse. Before he could ask almes they said,
' Wellcome good fellowe, wilt thou doe as we do,
and taste of beefe ? ' " Mercury sat down with
them, ate his fill, "dranke well of good double
beere," and then went home to his master—Jupiter,
who asked him, " What news ? "

" ' I have lighted,' he replied, ' amongst a crue
of shoomakers, the best fellowes that ever I met
withal ; they have frankly fed mee without grudg-
ing, and therefore grant me a boone for them.
Grant that for this good turne they have done
mee, they may ever spend a groat afore they can
yearne twopence.' ' It shall be granted,' " replied
Jupiter. Mercury, "as soone as Jupiter said the

word he bethought himself and sayd: 'Nay, but
that they may yearne a groat afore they spend
twopence, for my tongue slipt at the first.' 'Well,
Mercury,' quoth he, 'it cannot be recald, the first
wish must stand;' and hereof by Mercury's boone
it grew that all the Gentle Craft are such good
fellowes and spendthriftes."

Of the three writers Greene was the first to go.
Early in August, 1592, he, Nashe and their friend
Monox indulged in a banquet of wine and pickled
herring, and Greene, who fell ill, turned for shelter
to the house, near Dowgate (London), of a poor
shoemaker named Isam, to whom he was previously deeply indebted. Isam's kindly wife—" a
bigge, fat, lusty Amazon" who could bang people
who offended her "abominationly," offered him
hospitality and lent him her husband's shirt while
his own was washing. Greene, in a pathetic letter
written on his deathbed to his wife Doll, begged
her to see Isam paid, "for," he concluded, "if he
and his wife had not succoured me I had died in
the streets." When the end drew near, Greene,
who had hungered for, and who by his sweet songs
(which have the scent of honeysuckle), his plays
and prose works, had deserved literary fame,
turned to Mrs. Isam and asked her "to crown him
as he lay dead with a garland of bays." "This
she did, for she loved him dearly." Few incidents
in literature are more moving; and I can always
see poor Greene lying there on that humble pallet,

with his long hair about his pillow, his "jollie long red peake" of a beard, "like the spire of a steeple," above the coverlet, Isam and his ample wife standing by—and lastly the coronation.

If Greene's death was the result of a debauch, Marlowe's was even more shocking. In 1593 the plague raged again in London, and Marlowe with many others sought refuge in the village of Deptford where, in a bawdy house, he became involved in a wretched quarrel about a harlot. Daggers flashed. He fell. "Christopher Marlowe," runs the entry in the burial register, "slain by ffrancis Archer the 1 of June, 1593." He was only twenty-nine. What a tragedy! Peele, Chapman and Nashe paid eloquent tributes to the genius thus terribly cut off. He is the "dead shepherd" of *As You Like It.*

58. The literary activity of **Thomas Nashe** —"one of the wittiest knaves that ever God made"—commenced in 1589, the book in which he is most daringly himself being *The Unfortunate Traveller,* and his loveliest song, "Spring, sweet Spring," in which he expresses the rapture of a delicious moment. Despite, or by reason of, his feverish unrest, he wrote superbly. His vocabulary is rich, his narrative rapid. He did not marry; "Women," he said, " what an yrksome kind of people they be!" His works are crowded with illustrations from the shoe world. For example, we have in *The Anatomie of Absurditie,* "It

Plate 21

Devil's Claws (Long Piked Patten).

Henry VI.　See p. 79.

Child's Hinged Patten.

15th Century.　Found in Finsbury Circus.

Guildhall Museum, London.

See p. 72.

Photo Mr. Geo. Avenell.

Mailed Footwear.　Sir David de Esseby
slain at Evesham, 1265.
Albert Hartshorn Collection, Northampton
Public Library.
Photo Coldham & Son, Northampton.

Hinged Wooden Patten with Leather Straps.

Found in 1921, in Finsbury Pavement, on the site of the Marsh of Moorfields.　15th Century.
Guildhall Museum, London.　See p. 72.　*Photo Mr. Geo. Avenell.*

Plate 22

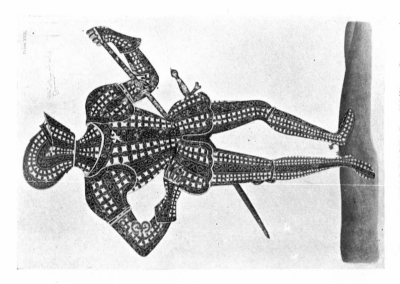

SIR HENRY LEE.
Knighted, 1553.

EARL OF WORCESTER (William Somerset).
1526—1589.
Footgear to match the armour.

delighteth them to put their foote in another man's
boote " (i.e. to borrow from other writers), which
by the by Nashe himself, one of the earliest com-
pilers of a phrase book, continually did; and in
The Unfortunate Traveller we meet with, " I would
never have gone so farre over the shoes, to plucke
you out of the myre," and " Their shoes shined as
bright as a slike-stone." [1] In the same story he
makes his noble Lord " sell cheese which he cuts
with a shoemaker's knife in little pennyworths ; "
and he tells the lurid story of Cutwolfe, the
" wearish,[2] dwarfish, writhen-faced cobbler of
Verona," who bartered his " bristles, pritch-aule,
and punching yron " for a rapier and a pistol.
This brought him to the wheel, on which he died,
not, however, before delivering himself of such
notable sayings as, " My bodie is little, but my
minde is as great as a gyant's," and " Cobblers are
but men, and kings are no more." The name,
" The Red Herring's Kinsmen," given by Nashe
to the shoemaker fraternity, means, as may be
inferred from his *Lenten Stuffe*, that as the son of a
king, the shoemaker is related to the king of fishes.

59. When **Shakespeare** was writing *Henry V.*,
he was boarding with a Huguenot family named
Mountjoy, in Silver Street, London, within a few
yards of the St. Martin shoemakers, and he often
passed their stalls while they were singing at their

[1] A stone used for polishing anything.
[2] Wizened.

I

work. It is not surprising, then, that the play should contain references to the shoemakers, and the stirring words put into the mouth of Henry on the morning of Agincourt, fought on St. Crispin's Day. Shakespeare was instrumental in bringing about the union[1] of Mountjoy's daughter with her father's apprentice, Stephen Bellott, and no doubt the young lady's broken English (interrupted by kisses) was responsible for the amusing love scenes between Katherine and Henry.

60. Thomas Deloney, already several times alluded to,[2] was born in 1543 at Norwich, and life through, he divided his affections between the weavers and the shoemakers—the two sorts of craftsmen who had brought prosperity to his native city. On removing to London he took to ballad writing, but it is on his historical romances, especially those complimentary to the lapstone, that his fame chiefly rests. He found it difficult to earn his bread, and at the same time to express the god within him, for he was hindered at every step by circumstance and dullard—even Strype, who ought to have known better, referring to him as "one Deloney, an idle fellow." As he occupied himself with ideas that are foreign to the minds of most men, everything he wrote has the piquancy of novelty. He loved books, and could from the

---

[1] The marriage took place at St. Olave's, Silver Street, Nov. 16th, 1608.

[2] See pages 48, 54 and 96.

poorest extract thoughts that the author never put there. He wrote as he liked, and therefore creatively. It was for brightness that he chiefly looked, consequently he stored up in his pleasant nature, or deflected into his tales, every beam of sunshine that stole upon him ; and he had also the ability, by his alchemy, to lift and ennoble characters in themselves not really poetical. As a rule he provides them with excellent wives. He had noticed that it is to the sterling qualities of the wife that many a shoemaker had owed largely his success in life ; and at the present day it is not unusual for the manufacturer, when asked the reason for his prosperity, to press somebody's hand and say, not without a break in his voice, " It's all through her ! " In spite of his difficulties, Deloney, with his delightful temperament (for our riches are within us) must have led a happy life.

61. If Deloney is the shoemakers' novelist, **Thomas Dekker** (Ben Jonson's "Crispianus ") is pre-eminently his dramatist. Dekker's breezy play *The Shoemakers' Holiday* (1599), does not hold us as does Deloney's story, *Sir Simon Eyre,*[1] upon which it was founded, but its good humour and its joyousness are as exhilarating as a morning in April. " Hum," says Sir Simon, " let's be merry whiles we are young."—" I had rather than a thousand pound," says Oately of Eyre, " I had a heart but half so light as yours." There is plenty

---

[1] See pp. 86.

to eat and more to drink in this play, and the
rollicking " Three Men's Song " goes with a rare
swing :

> " Trowl the bowl, the jolly nut-brown bowl,
>   And here, kind mate, to thee ;
> Let's sing a dirge for Saint Hugh's soul,
>   And down it merrily."

Ben Jonson was unwise enough to twit Dekker
with being often out at elbows, whereupon Dekker,
whose hair fell in glorious curls about his handsome face and on his shoulder, replied politely that
it was better to have a frayed coat than a face
" punch full of eyelet holes like the cover of a
warming pan."[1]   After that Jonson left " Crispianus " severely alone.

A charming custom alluded to in *The Shoemakers'
Holiday* is that of pinking on the uppers of shoes
the name of sweetheart or wife, and of inserting in
the shoe some pretty **Posy**.   The journeyman
Hodge, who had been pressed, made for his wife,
just before setting sail, a pair of shoes as a parting
gift.   " They are," he says :

> " Made up and pinked with letters for thy name.
>   Wear them, my dear Jane, for thy husband's sake."

Favourite posies were : " The shoe maketh me
woo," " Heigh-ho ! tread off my toe," and " God
for me appointed thee."   If very far gone in love,
the poor gentleman would as likely as not beg one

---

[1] Jonson was marked by small-pox.

of his lady's shoe-strings, and carry it about (looking very forlorn), hanging on his ear.

In another play of Dekker's, *If it be not good, the
Devil is in it*, (1612), there is a reference to
St. Monday. "They say Monday's shoemakers'
holiday. Ill fall to that trade." "This is not
St. Crispin's Day," remonstrated somebody, one
Monday, to a shoemaker who was sitting at his
cups. "Sir," was the arch reply, "the anniversary of St. Crispin is the first Monday in every
week." Contemporary with Dekker was Richard
Robinson, leather-seller, versifier and translator of
the *Gesta Romanorum*.

62. The study of the stars has in most ages
attracted shoemakers, and in Tudor times some of
them were adepts in judiciary astrology. Many
were real seekers after knowledge—mortal men,
they sought immortal joys—and when they "cast
a figure," it was with no intention to deceive. In
Don Quixote and other contemporary works fun is
frequently poked at the predilection of the cobblers
for their "vain science," and perhaps the saying,
"Cosgrove is the place where the moon changes
in the barn," glances at the Northants astrologers.
To magic also—to anything indeed that seemed to
give wings to the mind—the fraternity were also
attracted, and they held that men had yet to learn
the alphabet of the soul. They culled night-
herbs, disturbing the owl and the eve-jar, and
burnt scrolls covered with "strange cipherings"—

which led the profane (who had no use for geomantic tablets) to call them **Devil cleperes**—invokers of Satan. The French cobblers claimed that they possessed a " spirit debonair "—a mentor similar to the " daemon " of Socrates; and Whittier, in his " Cobbler Keezar's Vision," has dealt with the craft's hankering after curious knowledge.

63. In **Rabelais,** as translated by Urquhart in 1654, we find among the titles of books, " The Pantofles of the Decretals," and " The Gamashes alias the Boots of Patience." The word gamashes, or gamashoes (Old French, *gambe,* a leg—high boots or spatterdashes worn by ploughmen), corrupted to "gambages," ultimately resolved itself into " gambadoes " [Pl. 33], the name also given to mud-boots—large leather cases which were fixed to the saddle.

CHAPTER V.

THE STUARTS. SHOEMAKERS' TOKENS AND SIGNS.

64. In Gorlitz, Germany, flourished from 1575 to 1624 the shoemaker and mystic, **Jakob Boehme** [Pl. 34]. When he was an apprentice, a grave and reverend stranger called to him in a loud voice from outside his master's shop : "Jakob, Jakob, come forth." The boy obeyed in a great fright—amazed that a stranger should call him by his Christian name. The man then, taking him by the right hand, said, "Jakob, thou art little, but thou shalt be great and become such a one as the world shall wonder at; therefore, fear God and reverence His Word." The prediction made on the boy—and he often recalled that marvellous moment—a lasting impression. Thenceforward he could never sufficiently study God's Word and the book of nature, in which he saw characters unperceived by normal vision ; and few men have obtained more inspiration from either. At times he was bathed in a divine light, and trees and flowers disclosed to him their hidden mysteries. In these moments of excitement he said more than he knew, did more than he could, and became more than he was. A little lean, hawk-nosed man, his blue, thoughtful eyes were the windows of a soul absorbed in God. His conversation was a string of audacious felicities, and ecclesiastic and sage listened in dumb amazement. He loved every man, and therefore was able to multiply himself indefinitely. His books created more wonder even than his speech. All the time he worked hard at his shoemaking, and saved enough to buy a house. He was often subjected to persecution, but this had no effect upon his modest, gentle and forbearing spirit. There was a divine circle around him in all his dangers. On his death-bed, when those blue eyes which had seen what no other eyes—blue, black or brown—ever saw had become dim, he heard " excellent music." " Hark ! " he said, and then, after taking a tender leave of his wife and his son, " Now I go into paradise ! "

The fop of the day affected fantastical boots in Spanish leather with wide tops (which were fringed [Pl. 28], or turned down in order to display the lining of rich point), and spurs with " large loose rowels " that looked like " forerunners of wheelbarrows," and made a " pestilent gingle ; " and thus shod, toothpick in mouth and carnation behind ear, he stuck out his elbows and sauntered —the Oscar Wilde of his day—down Cheapside and through " Poules." Cavaliers affected broad, Puritans pointed, toes, consequently your boots

revealed your politics [Pl. 26]. In this reign
Philip Kirtland, a shoemaker of Sherington,
Bucks, driven away by religious persecution,
emigrated to **Lynn,** Massachusetts, and founded
the enormous trade in boots and shoes for which
that city is famous.

From 1560 to 1632 flourished the French
antiquary, **Beniot Baudouin** (Balduinus), son of
a shoemaker of Amiens, who, while principal of the
theological college at Troyes, published (in 1615)
his *Chaussures des Anciens* (Shoes of the Ancients),
subsequently (1667) issued as *De Calceo Antiquo*—
a work crowded with curious lore. And another
Frenchman, Henri Michel Buch, is remembered
as having established at Paris, in 1645, a religious
order of shoemakers.

65. In 1638 appeared William Rowley's comedy,
A Shoomaker a Gentleman, founded on the old
Crispin and Maximinus story. There was a Shoe-
maker's Corporation at Salisbury in 1634, and both
Stamford and Higham Ferrers were then shoe
centres. To **Nathaniel Ward** (1578—1652),
Puritan Divine, who in 1634 emigrated to America,
and in 1646 returned to England, we owe the tract,
The Simple Cobler of Aggawam (1647), and the
epigram :

" The world is full of care, and much like unto a bubble,
  Women and care, and care and women, and women
    and care and trouble."

66. In the Civil War, gigantic boots played a

conspicuous part.   The boots of the Cavalier, Sir
Lewis Dyve, which hang at Bromham Hall, Bedford, have a terrible spike two inches in length
projecting from the toe, and those [Pl. 26] of John
Lilbourne, leader of the Levellers, had tops so
broad that he could not walk in them without
straddling ridiculously.

The aim of the **Levellers** was " to build
Jerusalem in England's pleasant land."   But
reformers are always in a hurry, and no one could
have been more in a hurry than Lilbourne.   Even
when being whipped from the Fleet prison to the
pillory, he flung his pamphlets among the people,
and when gagged in it so that he could not speak, he
stamped his foot.   As the leader, so the led.   They
wanted the millennium, and they wanted it the
same afternoon.   Their numbers increased daily.
Their badge of sea green was displayed in every
town.   " You must cut these people in pieces,"
said Cromwell, " or they will cut you in pieces."
He shot one as an example (Nov. 15th, 1647), and
clapped their leader in the Tower.   It made no
difference.

Northampton was particularly affected, but its
inhabitants had always been restive.   In 1648
Thomas Pendleton, the first shoemaker Mayor of
the town, and others obtained an army order for
" 4,000 pairs of shoes and 600 of boots."   General
Douglas said they were " the best and cheapest
boots he had ever seen "—which, as they were

never paid for, was probably the truth. It must have been similar shoes of Northampton make that his contemporary, Christian, wore when Apollyon straddled over him on the highway and threatened to spill his soul, for they were " shoes that would not wear out."

While this business was afoot, trouble broke out with the Sea Green men in the camp of Salisbury where their leader was Cornet Thompson, and in that of Banbury, where they were headed by his brother, **Captain Thompson**, "a very stout man."[1] Hearing that Cromwell was hurrying to Salisbury, Cornet Thompson, with 1,000 men—a number that swelled to 5,000—marched north-east to Burford, where he was joined by his brother. A fight with Cromwell followed, the Levellers were defeated, and Cornet Thompson and others were sentenced to be shot (May 17th, 1649). Capt. Thompson managed to escape ; and then occurred an amazing series of events. Aware of the temper of Northampton, he resolved to take the town. Yet of his many followers, there remained to him only fifteen. That fifteen musketeers could capture a town the size of Northampton may seem impossible, but it was done. Having marched in, they made for the Guildhall—a solid-looking, rectangular and turreted block on Wood Hill, and bluffed the Mayor into the belief that 700

[1] In a pamphlet, *England's Standard Advanced in Oxfordshire,* May 6th, 1649, Captain Thompson sets forth his grievances.

more would follow. That accomplished, Thompson opened the gates of the jail and freed the prisoners. A tun of a man, he made promises proportionate to his size, telling the people in the market-place, in an orgy of words, that they were no more to be burdened with excise or tithe ; and having raided the Tax Office, he seized the money there, and distributed it broadcast, while the poor distracted Mayor looked on, helpless. A number of the townsfolk flocked round Thompson and prayed for him, but within twenty-four hours, finding that his hopes for large support were not realised, and fearing to be entrapped by the troops of Cromwell, who were approaching, he retired to Walgrave, where he was overtaken. His men having been scattered, he fled thence to a wood, whither he was followed. A corporal with a carbine charged with seven bullets fired at him ; he fell, and with him perished the last hopes of the Levellers. They laid him on a horse and brought him to Northampton. It was Saturday —market day—and in and out among the people and the booths moved that strange cavalcade— corsleted troopers and a dead fat man—with a terrible countenance—slung over the back of a horse. The simple folk, who had supposed only three days previous that the millennium had really come, stared in stupid wonder. On the Sunday morning the corpse was buried in All Saints churchyard. To this strange event there was a pathetic sequel—one that recalls the sad old story of Phinehas's wife. Mrs. Thompson was at the time in the hands of her nurse, and " hearing of her husband's death she fell in labour, and both she and the child died."[1] As a punishment for going sea green, Northampton had to find free billets for 800 horse soldiers, but the shoemaker Mayor escaped scot free. Perhaps that was on account of the little bill owing to him by the Government. If so, for his " 4,000 shoes and 600 boots," he did after all, in a sense, receive payment in full. John Lilbourne—John Trouble-World, as people got to call him—was set free, but his career was over. He died on August 29th, 1657, and the millennium is still to come.

67. Another prominent figure in the War was **Sir Samuel Luke**, commander of the garrison of Newport Pagnell, and original of Butler's Hudibras, who also figures in *The Tale of the Cobler and the Vicar of Bray*. The pair, it seems, were hobnobbing together in a tavern " that far exceeded all Bedfordshire for ale and landlady," when the cobbler ventured to say that he could repair soles and under-prop backsliders. This being a flagrant case of encroachment on the monopoly of the clergy, the Vicar was naturally indignant, and in less than no time the two had their fists in each other's faces, while the bystanders took sides and egged them on. When Sir Samuel arrived, the

[1] Perfect Diuruall.

Vicar, in giving evidence against the cobbler, said angrily,

> " The rascal had the insolence
>   To give himself the lye,
> And to aver he had done more good,
> And sav'd more souls than I."

However, the impartiality of Sir Samuel settled the matter by locking the combatants face to face in the stocks, where they continued to argue and shake fists at each other till they were tired.

The burly, one-eyed and gifted Colonel **John Hewson,** the Cerdon of *Hudibras*, who rose from the cobbler's bench to membership of Cromwell's House of Lords [Pl. 26], was the subject of a host of lampoons, in which his single eye was not forgotten.   His enemies, by way of joke, pelted him with old boots, which usually missed ; he, also by way of joke, replied with new bullets which invariably hit.   At the Restoration, a gibbet intended for him was set up in Cheapside ; but he went into hiding and, though his enemies again and again courteously invited him to come forward and put his head into the noose, he, for some unaccountable reason, held back,   So they hung up his effigy which, however, proved to be a poor substitute for the original ; and his lack of consideration for them was very generally commented upon.   Until recently there used to be sung at wine parties in Oxford a coarse song which began, " My name is old Hewson."   For chorus a burring noise was made "with the lips, while the doubled fists were rubbed and thumped upon the thigh as if the cobbler's lapstone had been there."

Even more prominent, however, was his colleague, Praise-God Barbon—changed by the enemy to **Barebones**—Independent Minister and leather-seller, of London. In a wood-cut which illustrates the ballad, *A Word to Fanatics*, Barbon and his friend Greene are represented preaching— the latter in a barrel—on Dec. 19th, 1641 [Pl. 26]. A man of means and grit, and a tenacious supporter of Cromwell, he became the most conspicuous figure in "Barebones' Parliament," which sat from June to October, 1653; and he held staunchly to his principles even after the Restoration and right on until his death in 1679. He had a brother named If-Christ-had-not-died-thou-hadst-been-damned Barbon—which the opposition prettily abbreviated to "Damned Barebone."

A very different character was **Luke Howard,** shoemaker, Baptist preacher and pamphleteer. When the War began he, wishing to be in it, bought a high horse and offered his services to the Parliament, but they were declined. Another man would have been discouraged. Not so Howard. He meant to be in the mellay somehow. Nothing daunted, off he galloped to the king, and was accepted. He and his high horse were the gladdest creatures in the world. He changed a good many times after that, caring little to what, provided he was given something to do; and when the cannons had ceased to grumble and everything was done in the world, he and his old horse decided that it was time to get out of it. They did.   They died.

68.   When **Cromwell**, one Sunday in 1650, attended the High Kirk in Glasgow, the preacher bitterly attacked the principles of the Independents, and in the middle of the diatribe one of the officers whispered to Cromwell, who seemed to answer him curtly.   Among the worshippers was a shoemaker to whom Cromwell, who recognised in him an old acquaintance, endeavoured after the service to speak.   To the surprise of everybody the man took to his heels, but he was followed and brought back, when Cromwell enquired, " Why did you run away ? "

Shoemaker : Because my father was in the service of the Royal Family.

Cromwell (placing gold in his hands) : Pooh ! what did that matter !

Shoemaker : As you are so kind, I should like to know what the officer said to you in church.

Cromwell : He proposed to pull forth the minister by the ears, and I replied, " The preacher's one fool, you're another."

While the Parliamentary army was encamped before Perth (July, 1651), a soldier named Monday hanged himself, and Cromwell having offered a

Plate 23

HANS SACHS.
Plate from *Hans Sachs Sein Leben und seine Dichtung*, 1874. See p. 100.
British Museum, 10708 A 1.

SS. Crispin and Crispianus arrested by the Roman Soldiers.
From sculpture by Francois Gentil, end of 16th Century, in the church of St. Pantaleon, Troyes,
France. See p. 70. *Photo (from print) Mr. Geo. Avenell.*

Plate 24

Martyrdom *of* John Kurde, *in the* Stone Pits, *near* Northampton.

John Kurde, of Syresham, 1557.
From Plate in Northampton Public Library.   See p. 103.

Two-horned Shoe, portion round
heel missing.   See p. 95.
Guildhall Museum, London.   *Photo Mr. Geo. Avenell.*

Slashed Leather Shoe.   Henry VIII.
(1509—47).   See p. 95.
Victoria and Albert Museum, S. Kensington.   37850 B.

reward for the best lines on the event, a shoemaker sent in the very original verse:

> " Blessed be the Sabbath day,
> And cursed be worldly pelf ;
> Tuesday will begin the week,
> Since Monday's hanged himself."

69. A picturesque figure in these troublous
times was **George Fox**, founder of the Quakers
(1624—1690), who at an early age was apprenticed
to a shoemaker at Drayton, Leicestershire. Clad
in a leathern suit of his own making, he set out to
pull into shape a very distorted world. The Lord
" forbade him to put off his hat to high or low "—
for he never quailed before any man—and his zeal
and boldness subjected him to continual persecution, which, however, made possible that fascinating book, his *Journal*. Among his friends was
Solomon Eccles, who in early life had been a
musician. Convinced, however, that love of
music was a snare of Satan, he burnt his instruments, turned to shoemaking, and joined the
Quakers, who in those days seized every opportunity of showing their disapproval of and contempt
for ceremonialism. One Sunday morning, when
the citizens of Cheapside were entering the church
of St. Mary, Aldermanbury, they were amazed to
hear the sound of hammering proceeding from the
pulpit. It was Eccles who, seated there, was
calmly and industriously engaged in making
shoes. When ordered out, he assumed an injured

K

air, but in spite of his protests he was forcibly ejected. Next Sunday he was found noisily at work in one of the pews, and probably would have gone on hammering during the whole of the service if he had been let alone. This time, however, constables were called in, and Eccles, shoe in hand, hopped over from pew to pew in order to escape them. Finally he was captured, and although he expressed indignation at being interfered with when he was so usefully employed, he was flung into Newgate. Out again, he stripped himself to the waist, fixed a pan of fire and brimstone above his head, and strode from street to street in London, calling, with lungs of brass, upon all men to repent unless they coveted for their city the fate of Sodom ; and amid the roar of the Great Fire of 1666 his pan and his prophecy were re-called. Thomas Traherne (1636—1674) author of *Centuries of Meditations* and other works, was the son of a shoemaker. In 1656 a shoemaker, Sir Thomas Tichborne, became Lord Mayor of London.

70. Very pretty, no doubt, were the shoes worn by the mice-like feet of the lady of Sir John Suckling's song, but prettier still were those of a Miss Langley, which were of silk trimmed with point [Pl. 27]. It is not stated whether she herself was good looking. It was an age, however, not only of beautiful shoes, but also of beautiful women. How good was God—how good is God

—to bestow on the world so much loveliness! He might have made it full of ugly men. Many of the ladies' laced shoes were green, a colour that was supposed to work great havoc in the male heart; and Steele in *The Tatler* (No. 143) reads quite a sermon on the perils of looking in a shoe-maker's window (" The Laced Shoe " was a sign in Chancery Lane), which, he archly said, created "irregular thoughts and desires in the youth of this nation."

Nicholas Lestage made in 1660, for Louis XIV., among other wonders, a pair of boots without a seam, which led all France to exclaim, " How the devil did he do it! " and his portrait was hung in the royal gallery above a verse which may be rendered:

> " Great the fame of him portrayed
>> Was, and none and naught could dim it;
> When his wondrous boot he made,
>> Mind and art had reached their limit."

There used to be a language of shoes as well as of flowers, though it was difficult to learn. " Mr. Spectator," runs a well-known letter, " I am a foot-man in a great Family and am in love with the Housemaid. We were all at Hot-cockles last Night in the Hall these Holidays; when I lay down and was blinded she pull'd off her shoe, and hit me with the Heel such a Rap as almost broke my Head to Pieces. Pray, Sir, was this Love or Spite? "

We were just then fighting the Dutch, and among our admirals were two from the lapstone, Sir Christopher Myngs, killed in the sea fight of June 4th, 1666, and **Sir Cloudesley Shovel.** Knighted by William III., Sir Cloudesley won, by his intrepidity, new laurels at La Hogue and Malaga, only, however, to perish by shipwreck off the Scilly Isles on the foggy night of Oct. 22nd, 1707.

71. Northampton had by this time become a very important shoe centre. " You knew when you were within a mile of it by the smell of the leather and the noise of the lapstones."[1] As old London vanished and new London rose owing to the fire of 1666, so old Northampton gave place, owing to the " dreadful **Fire**" **of Sept. 20th, 1675,** to a better-built and more convenient town. It " did begin in a lane near the castle, by a poor, infamous and common woman " carrying " a few live coales in a fire shovell from her neighbour's house to her own in ye lane to warme her dinner. Ye wind, which was from the west, being very high and strong, blew some of ye coles upon the thatch of her house." In a few minutes whole streets were burning. Cries of " Fire ! " mingled with the weird sounds of the alarm bells, which jangled from every point. A cherry orchard seemed to bar its further progress, but the roaring flames leaped it like tigers, and within an hour the

[1] *Proverbs of Northamptonshire,* by Major C. A. Markham.

greater part of the town was alight. The falling houses made reports like thunder. The terrified people piled their goods in the Market Place, but blebs of fire fell continually over them, and in a little while they too were threatened by the flames. All Saints' Church—lantern, nave and aisle—burnt furiously. A man brought out of his cellar a barrel of gunpowder, and carried it safely up Gold Street, though that thoroughfare was flaring on both sides and yellow flames were licking round him. Next morning the ruins were still crackling. One solitary blackened block—the Guildhall—stood out practically intact, Kaaba-like, amid this sea of ruin. The wind was still blowing high and hard. The rest of the town seemed doomed. Perhaps some terrified watcher (his soul well nigh scared out of his body), behind the Guildhall turrets, could, while the sparks blew over him, have seen, like Sister Anne in the story, a little speck in the distance, furnishing hope. In any case it was a deliverer coming. The speck grew in volume and developed into ink black clouds which rolled towards the town. Three rainbows—three dazzling and splendid concentric curves of red, yellow and green—arched the sky, and the falling of a deluge such as memory had never known ended the great Fire of Northampton.

72. Among the articles of the Cordwainers' Company of **Duns** (1665) is one that lays down " that none of the trade be absent from preaching upon the Sabbath under the paine of four shilling the maister and two shillings the prentis." Others relate to the election of officials. It was ordained in 1673 that " none should go forth to sell until the searchers[1] had been through the market;" and in 1727 that " non in ye said trade shall be found out after ten of ye clock at night being ye Fastern week ; " that no one was to "give more than ten sh. ster. for ye football," and that no man was to be compelled to give. Other entries concern the mor-cloaths or palls, bearing out the statement on p. 41 that all down the ages the companies were also funeral societies.

Under William III. " roses " went out and **Buckles** came in again, most of them being made from a metal called tutania, after its inventor one Tutin. Very often they were troublesome. A master one day overheard a worker cursing the man who was to wear the buckles upon which he was busy. " But why ? " enquired the astonished master. " Because," was the answer, " I know when he wears them he will curse the maker, and I thought I would be beforehand with him."

73. On November 5th, 1709, Dr. Sacheverell preached his precious sermon on the advisability of harking back to the system of religious persecu-tion which prevailed under James II. As his head was absolutely empty, he was naturally listened to with awe and wonder, and soon had a large

---

1 "Insufficient shoes " were confiscated and the maker was fined.

following. His "lovely"—that is to say, smug and expressionless—image in mezzotint stared out of every print shop. Opposed to him was the party led by the Rev. Benjamin Hoadly. Of course the shoemakers, like other folk, had to take sides, though they shouted **"Church and Cheverel"**[1] (instead of Sacheverel) as they naturally would. An outcome of this commotion was a racy tract, *Crispin the Cobbler's Confutation of Ben H [oadly]* by Dr. William Wagstaffe. Crispin describes himself as a sober, trusty fellow, who " now and then cry'd ' Huzza, Church and Cheverel! ' " Persuasion, however, brings him over to Hoadly's side; and with the zeal of a new convert he goes from coffee-house to coffee-house endeavouring to influence others. " If anybody wanted a pair of shoes to be soled, all he could talk about was the necessity of Resistance," with the result that his business deserted him. His wife told him bluntly that when he followed his cobbling his family were better fed, and she strengthened her arguments by the use of a ladle. Then his son Jack seized a poker, and with the observation that Resistance was lawful upon such occasions, " gave him such a baster upon his head that it was two months before he perfectly

---

[1] A soft leather made of kid-skin. Thomas Blount *(Glossographia,* 1656) after mentioning that " cheverel " is usually derived from the French *chèvre*, a goat, observes quaintly : " Others hold that it takes its denomination from the river Charwell or Chervel . . . running off the east side of Oxford, the water whereof is famous for tawing or dressing leather, than which no leather in the world is more soft, white and delicate." See pp. 63 and 64.

recovered " [Pl. 28]. This affectionate treatment
led him to return to his earlier views, and eventually, no doubt, prosperity again visited him.

A quieter and more thoughtful shoemaker was
John Bagford (1657—1716), whose bent may be
gathered from the fact that when a young man he
walked all the way from London to Bedford on
purpose to see John Bunyan, who received him
" very civilly and courteously." An ardent book-
lover, Bagford was able to preserve from destruction many valuable relics of early literature. He
still loved his trade, however, and from his pen
came *Shoes and How to Make Them*, although he is
best remembered by his collection, *The Bagford
Ballads*. A cobbler contemporary, Henri Sellier,
of the Rue Coq Héron, Paris, was author of *Les
Lundis du Réparateur des brodequins d'Apollon* (The
Mondays of Apollo's cobbler), 1701, in which
appeared the popular song, " Belle duchesse de
Bourbon."

74.   The quality at this time wore **Clogs** [Pl.
32], with a well to receive the heel, which, however, owing to their beauty, really needed protection as much as the shoes themselves [Pl. 29];
but the middle classes clung to the old-fashioned
pattens which, on a wet day, covered the streets
with circles, giving them quite an ornamental
appearance. The pattens, however, made a terrible
clatter on a pavement. Within living memory
there hung in the church porch at Wanborough,

near Swindon, a board with the lettering:—
" LADIES ARE REQUIRED TO TAKE OFF THEIR
PATTENS BEFORE ENTERING ; " and one recalls Dr.
Darwen's ludicrous lines, in allusion to the diffi-
culty the ladies then had in negociating the dirty
London streets:

> " Pretty ladies, how they talk !
> Prittle prattle, prittle prattle;
> Like their pattens when they walk,
> Pittle paddle, pittle paddle."

The trade of patten-making fell into desuetude in
the 19th century, but in 1918 new life was given to
the Patten-makers' Company by the admission
into it of the leading British manufacturers of
goloshes and other rubber footwear. On rocks of
the old red sandstone in the Teme Valley,
Worcestershire, may be seen the impressions made
by the patten rings of the legendary maid who is
said to have stolen St. Catherine's mare and colt.

To the 16th and 17th centuries belong three
Shoemaker Painters, Gabriel Cappellini,
Francesco Brizzio (1574—1623), and Ludolph de
Jong, born in 1616.

75. For long, tradesmen had been greatly
hampered in their business transactions owing to
the shortage of small change, halfpennies being
almost unprocurable ; but at last somebody hit on
the expedient of providing them himself. The
idea was copied, and in a little while every tradesman had his private mint. Some of the tokens

were made of leather ; but, if we are to believe old writers, **Leather Money** was used centuries before. In Sir William Davenant's play, " The Wits " (1633) occur the lines :

> " Bury her old gold with her !
> 'Tis strange her old shoes were not interr'd too
> For fear the days of Edgar should return
> When they coined leather."

And in Deloney's " Thomas of Reading " (1597) we read, " From thence they went to the Tower of London," and " there they saw the money that was made of leather, which in ancient times went current amongst the people."

Leather tokens were issued from three of the Coffee Houses, " Robins in Old Jewry," the " Chapter " in Paternoster Row, and the " Union " in Cornhill.

76. Among the **Metal Tokens** [Pl. 30] issued by shoemakers, the following are the most interesting :

> O. IOHN HARDY OF Cordwainer's Arms.
>
> R. STAMFORD 1667. I. M. H. ¼.

As regards " I. M. H.," I stands for John, M for his wife's Christian name, and H, of course, for Hardy.

> O. JOHN . FARRAH . SHOEMAKER.   A cat fiddling and three men dancing.
>
> R. IN TVLEY . STREETE. 1667 = HIS HALFEPENY.

This interesting token has reference to the Three Tailors of Tooley Street, who had the confidence to address a petition of grievances to the House of Commons beginning, " We, the people of England."

O. Sibbi^l . Theam^e . Christ = A shoe.
R. Aspetal . Sho . mak^{er.} = S. T.

The issuer of this token was shoemaker to Christ's Hospital, Newgate Street.

O. John . Corne = A lady's shoe.
R. In . Martines . Le . Grand = I . C . C.

O. Thomas Gawthorne. T.E.G.
R. In Grendon.[1] The Cordwainers' Arms.[2]

O. Thomas . Avery . 1667 = The Cordwainers' Arms.
R. In . Meriden [3]. Shoo . maker = his half peny.

77. Of **Tavern Signs,** many relate to the shoe trade and its patron saints. " *The St. Hugh's Bones,*" as a token of 1657 shows, was once the sign of a house in Stanhope Street, Clare Market, London. We find the *Crispin, Crispin Inn,* or *St. Crispin* at Ashover (Notts), Aldershot, Christchurch (Hants), Burnham (Bucks), Chesterfield, Harwell, Windsor, Wokingham (Berks), Lutton (Lincs), Newport (Isle of Wight), Stourbridge, Sherburn Hill (Durham) and Worth (Kent). At Morpeth is a *King Crispin Inn,* at Strood a *Crispin and Crispianus,* at Southampton a *Crispin and Bear,* and at Northampton *The Crispin Arms.* We hear of *The Boot* at Chester (1643), *The Golden Slipper* at

---

[1] Northants.   [2] Engraved in Baker's *History of Northants.*
[3] Warwickshire.

Goodrange (Yorks), and *The Boot and Slipper* at Smethwick, near Birmingham. Norwich has *The Goat and Kid*, and there are many other Boots and Goats. Oddly enough, there is not a single *Shoe* in all Northamptonshire. In Smithfield used to be *The Shoe and Slap*, the slap being a lady's shoe with a loose sole; and in Prescott Street, Goodman's Field, *The Five Clogs*. Who has not heard the story (apocryphal probably) of the rival cobblers, one of whom placed over his stall the motto from Virgil, "*Mens conscia recti*,"[1] which led the other to affix over his door that wonderful piece of Latin, "Men's and Women's conscia recti!" A shoemaker at an inn near Liscard, Cheshire, had for his sign *The Last*, with the legend:

> "All day long I have sought good beer,
> And at The Last I've found it."

Over a shoemaker's door at the Hague was a couplet which may be translated:

> "This is St. Crispin, but my name is Stoffel;
> I can make you a boot, a shoe or pantofle."

Some verses by Ronsard are addressed to the hostess of *The Sabot*, a tavern in the Faubourg, St. Marcel, Paris.

Northampton has a St. Crispin's Church, a Crispin Street and a Crispin Ward, and London has a Crispin Street and a Cordwainers' Ward.

---

[1] "*Mens sibi conscia recti*." A mind conscious of its own rectitude. *Æneid*, i., 603.

CHAPTER VI.

THE FIRST THREE GEORGES. THE HARDY TRIAL. LATE TOKENS. 1714—1793.

78. UNDER the early Georges a square-toed, buckled shoe was worn by gentlemen. Of ladies' shoes of the period there are fine collections in the London, Victoria and Albert [Pl. 29] and Northampton Museums, including specimens of painted kid; of silk damask ornamented with silver thread and gilt metal buckles; and of peacock green silk with cream-coloured heels. Demiclogs of green kid and other materials, and shoes made of calamanco, a woollen stuff from Holland, were in common use.

In 1716 was produced at Drury Lane, Charles Johnson's farce, **The Cobbler of Preston,** which was derived partly from Christopher Sly in *The Taming of the Shrew*, and partly from an old ballad, " The Frolicksome Duke." Kit Sly, of Wigan, is conveyed while drunk into splendid apartments, where he is dressed in Spanish costume, and on waking learns that he is a Grandee who has been asleep for 15 years. The object of the farce, like that of Wagstaff's tract, is to cure " Crispin " of his democratic prejudices.

79. At this time flourished the brilliant lyric poet, **J. B. Rousseau** (1670—1741)—a shoemaker's son, with whose red bristling hair, carbuncled face, white eye-brows, squinting eye and over-large mouth we have become familiarised owing to Voltaire's *Crispiniad*—and also the gifted actor Thevenard. One day when Thevenard was passing a cobbler's stall in Paris he noticed a girl's slipper, which struck him by its remarkable smallness. He could not forget it, and the cobbler, when questioned, could give no clue, except that the owner had left it with him to be repaired. Thereupon Thevenard's passion for the unknown girl became so extravagant that he lapsed into melancholy. But then, he was just at the tender age of 63. Daily he watched at the stall in the hope that the owner of the slipper would return. Eventually his patience was rewarded, and he discovered her to be a poor girl who was, however, very pretty. After making her acquaintance he became passionately attached to her and, with the consent of her parents, made her his wife. Such was the story of Cinderella the Second.[1]

Contemporaneously, a romance of another kind was taking place in London—**John Came**, the benefactor of the Cordwainers' Company, being on his way to fortune and fame. Apprenticed in 1732 to a cordwainer of Cheapside, Came in 1746, when his master died, took over the business and

[1] See *Mirror*, Vol. 10, p. 408.

married the widow, a comely woman of reasonable wealth who, in the phrase of the day, "had cast a very good countenance upon him." His continued success led him to seek larger premises, and he transferred his business from one side of the street to the other. I's and J's were in those days the same, and Came who, like most shoemakers, was a wag, inscribed upon the fascia of his new shop front :

I. CAME FROM OVER THE WAY.

He died in 1796, leaving £37,000 for charitable purposes.

80. Naturally the Georgian shoemaker and his family were subject, like other mortals, to various **Ailments,** and for the treatment of them they usually turned to Culpepper, whose witticisms alone acted as medicine. The cobbler could cure sore fingers with felonwort,[1] tetters with mandrake,[2] agues with sengreen,[3] and gravel with gold-of-pleasure[4] ; and if his child fell with chin-cough[5] he was also equal to the occasion ; but the imaginary defect of " head-mould-shot "[6] nearly broke his heart. He himself might be laid up with tymphany[7] or, more terrifying of all, "strongullion."[8]

---

[1] Woody nightshade.
[2] Their name for the White Bryony.
[3] Houseleek.   [4] *Camelina sativa.*
[5] Whooping cough.
[6] The overlapping of the bones in an infant's skull. They right themselves in a few days.
[7] Dropsy.   [8] Strangury.

If it was only a cold or a stiff leg, his wife, after hinting that his life was in danger, laid hold of the burnished copper warming-pan, and, after filling it with sugared coals, ordered him to bed, rather pleased than otherwise at having the opportunity of domineering over him. If he grew worse, she did not call in medical aid, being of the opinion that a man could die just as well without a doctor as with one, but dosed him with amber, then regarded as a cure-all. If he died, and she did not know of what, she unhesitatingly called it "strongullion," and the relatives who did not in the least know what strongullion was, were emphatically of the same opinion. The cobbler's habit of dealing with every emergency himself, instead of calling in the physician or surgeon, is touchingly dealt with in a broadside of 1798. The good man who, "like the great Doctor Galen could cure the most obstinate ailing," thus describes how he exercised his art on his sick wife :

> " My lancets were out of the way,
>   Yet my Awl did the business as well ;
>   She died, as a Body may say,
>   But the Reason I never could tell."

It would, however, be very wonderful indeed if every operation was successful.

When a shoemaker was hanged (and occasionally a member of the fraternity did, as it was prettily said, " die upright in the sun "), his friends liked to keep an affectionate eye on the **Gallows,**

Plate 25

VOLET DE LA CORPORATION DES CORDONNIERS.
(Wing of the picture, The Corporation of Shoemakers.)
Bruges—The Cathedral.
By Anthonius Claeisins, 1608.   See p. 81.

Plate 26

Praise-God Barebones and his friend Greene preaching, Dec. 19th, 1641. From a hostile ballad entitled *A Word to Fanatics, &c*

This was reproduced in *The Mirror*, Vol. 2 1827, p. 137. See p. 127.

Barebones' Parliament, the "Little Parliament" summoned by Oliver Cromwell, met July 4th 1653. It consisted of 139 persons, "faithful fearing God, and hating covetousness." Barbon (Barebones) died in 1679, and was buried at St. Andrew's, Holborn.

COLONEL JOHN HEWSON.

Subsequently one of Cromwell's Lords,

See p. 126.

From print in Northampton Public Library.

CAVALIER'S BOOT.

See p. 121.

JOHN LILBOUUNE'S BOOT.

See p. 122.

lest the body should be appropriated by the wicked surgeons. In April, 1739, some highwaymen, among whom was a shoemaker, " died longitudinally " at Kennington Common. The surgeons having seized the body, some of his mates, who had been preparing for eventualities, promptly rescued it, and carried it off in triumph to the widow. The woman, however, who secretly approved of the course which the law had taken, and who, moreover, strongly objected to be unnecessarily saddled with the expense of black candles, a pall and other luxuries, refused to take it in, and slammed the door in their faces. Their indignation can be imagined. One seems to hear them saying: " What wicked things are women ! It is surprising that they should be suffered in a Christian country ! " However, they had no means of compelling her to their wishes, so not knowing what other course to take, they hawked the corpse from street to street among the apothecaries who, however, were not buying ; and as everybody else unaccountably held back, the shoemakers, who heartily wished they had left their brother in the air, were obliged to dig a grave in order to get rid of him, but the words which they used on the occasion were not those provided in the Book of Common Prayer. At that time corpses were left to hang on the gibbet till they dropped to pieces. The charitable William Andrews, of Denton, was so distressed by the sight of the faces dented by

L

bird pecks and the skin dried up by the sun or sodden by the rain, that by a deed of March 20th, 1620, he granted an annuity of £3 for the burial of executed prisoners in the churchyard of St. Giles, or as somebody deliciously put it, "to provide ropes to hang the shoemakers of Northampton and to decently bury them after."

81. In the great revival of religion under Whitefield and Wesley, two shoemakers, **Thomas Olivers** and Samuel Bradburn[1] took prominent parts. Olivers, whose soul had been released and set on fire by a sermon, fell, when a young man, with smallpox, which left him stone blind for weeks; and, life through, he was easily known by his deeply pitted face. On one horse he travelled 100,000 miles to preach. "A rough stick of wood," he after a while (without parting with his horse) found himself installed in the Book Room at the Foundry, Moorfields, the Methodist centre. His hymn, "The God of Abraham praise," is in every important collection. An acceptable preacher (notwithstanding a raucous voice) and an intemperate and vigorous penman, he was never idle. Red hot pamphlet followed red hot pamphlet. "Cobbler Tom" indeed, as Toplady called him, continued to battle year in year out for his cause, and but for the fact that he is well covered up by Wesley's side in the graveyard in

[1] Olivers (1725—1799), Bradburn (1751—1816).

the City Road, he would still be crusading at the Foundry or on his hundred thousand mile horse.

If Olivers was the controversalist of the movement, **Samuel Bradburn,** at one time a dissipated shoe apprentice at Chester, was its orator. As with Olivers, it was a sermon that woke him to repentance, and gave force and glow to his spirit. His conversion was followed by a call to the ministry. On week days he made shoes, and on Sundays he preached. Wesley, who knew he was poor, once said to him: "Beware of the fear of man! Apply to me when you want help." On one occasion Wesley sent him several five pound notes and the words: "Trust in the Lord and do good . . . and verily thou shalt be fed." Bradburn replied, "I have often been struck with the beauty of this passage of scripture, but I must confess that I never saw such useful expository notes upon it before." He fell in love. Her name was Betsy. She had a cherry lip. She always has. She was perfect. She always is. One night when he and a friend occupied the same bed, he arose quietly, and believing that his companion was asleep, he knelt down and prayed aloud for divine guidance in reference to the selection of a help-meet, finishing with the words, "But, Lord, let it be Betsy!" "Amen!" came in a clear voice from the supposed sleeper. Bradburn married his Betsy, and lived happily with her. As a preacher he held his hearers spellbound. " My hair," said one, " seemed actually to stand on end." He, too, lies by the side of Wesley in the City Road—quiet enough now, and disturbing nobody's hair.

82. James Lackington (1746—1815), Somerset lad and maker of stuff shoes, was first set thinking by a copy of Ellis Walker's translation of Epictetus. In 1774 he and his newly-married wife settled in London. One Christmas Eve he went out with half-a-crown to purchase the next day's dinner. A copy of Young's *Night Thoughts* so tempted him that he was led to secure the book instead of a piece of beef. Next day, after a dinner of plain bread, he observed to his wife, " If, my dear, we had bought beef, it would have been eaten by now and gone, but if we live for fifty years we shall have *Night Thoughts* to feast upon." His next step was to borrow five pounds in order to set up as a bookseller, and ultimately he settled in a huge building in Finsbury Square where he laid himself out to make a fortune and succeeded. He then returned to Somerset with the object of spending it, but that was beyond him, though (and his charity became a proverb) he did his level best.

Another amazing career was that of **Johann Joachim Winckelmann**, son of a shoemaker at Stendhal in Prussia. Owing to assiduous application, he was able to advance until he became curator of the Vatican Museum at Rome. But though a Catholic in name he had with a view to attaining the great end of his life—the penetration of antiquity—become a pagan. *The History of Ancient Art*, the greatest of his works, appeared in 1762. At Trieste an ill planet caused him to make the acquaintance of a fellow traveller named Archangeli, to whom he showed some gold medals. Next day (June 8th, 1768) Archangeli, who said he was about to leave for Venice, entered Winckelmann's room, and having bidden him an affectionate farewell asked for one more sight of the medals. Winckelmann gladly turned to his portmanteau and knelt in order to unlock it. In a moment Archangeli threw a cord with a slip knot over Winckelmann's neck, drew his dagger and plunged it into his victim's heart. That his object was merely to obtain possession of the medals is unlikely. What was it then? The question cannot be answered. There are in the human heart recesses which it is impossible to explore. A brilliant, kindly, gentle, guileless character, Winckelmann deserved a better fate. Too early he joined "the innumerous generations of the dead."

83. The distinction between the shoeman making for his own shop and the wholesale maker was by this time complete, and the custom of sending **Basket Work** (boots and shoes in hampers) by wagon to London had become general. The manufacturer followed in a coach, did his business in some tavern, and when it was done walked (or was carried) up to bed.

John Smart, cobbler of Kettering, who died in 1774 at the age of 84, was one of the earliest advocates of limitation of families. He was strongly of opinion that no man ought to have more than thirty-four children ; and furthermore he carried his theory into practice, for this was the exact number he himself had by his five wives. A little after Smart's time Kettering became an important shoe centre, among its earliest manufacturers being Thomas Gotch (1748—1806), afterwards of the banking firm, Gotch and Sons. In 1785 **William Carey** was working as a shoemaker at Moulton (Northants), where he attracted the notice of Mr. Gotch, who gave him a weekly sum so that he might leave shoemaking and devote the whole of his time to study. After two years preparation under Sutcliffe at Olney, Carey embarked for India where, as missionary and translator, he laboured till his death in 1834. In that same year died also Dr. Robert Morrison (at one time a maker of lasts and wooden clogs) the apostle of China. As the result of the impetus given to the shoe trade, Kettering, Rushden, Higham Ferrers and other Northants centres grew and expanded with fungoid rapidity.

The custom of wearing shoe buckles continued till 1790, when they gave place to shoe-ties. The buckles had a tiresome habit of getting out of

order at all sorts of inconvenient times. One
evening while the poet **Cowper** was adjusting a
buckle [Pl. 31] on the step of a stile, the village
post-woman—an honest dumpy soul—came along
without his noticing her. Having mounted the
stile, she placed her big flat foot on what she
supposed to be the step on the other side, but
which turned out to be the back of the poet's head.
Cowper, wondering what had happened, tossed his
head up suddenly, and up went the astonished old
woman, making, in Cowper's words, "a rotatory
somersault in the air." Profuse apologies were
tendered on both sides, but needless to say, when
Cowper told the story, as he did in his own comical
way, to his friends at Weston Hall, the company
was convulsed with laughter. When about to get
over a stile you should always look first to see
whether there is a poet on the other side.

84. At the end of the 18th century there
was again a shortage of small change, and
tradesmen once more began to issue their own.
Unlike the old tokens, which were small and thin,
those of the latter date were as large and thick
as a present day penny. Among the earliest was
one associated with a stirring event—the trial for
High Treason of **Thomas Hardy**,[1] **Thomas
Holcroft**[2] (both of them shoemakers), John
Horne Tooke and John Thelwell. Hardy, a
friend of Thomas Paine and an admirer of *The*

[1] and [2] See Plate 34.

Rights of Man, had a fashionable boot-shop in Piccadilly. Holcroft's father had been a maker of " chairmen's shoes "—a wear which enabled the buyers to tread their way safely when carrying the fine folk of London about in their sedan chairs; but Holcroft himself, like Hardy, worked chiefly for the quality. All four were patriots, and most of the reforms for which they contended have long since been conceded. Tooke took the lead, but Hardy had to bear the brunt of the trial. The excitement of the country was intense. The trial was the one theme of conversation, and when the result, " Not Guilty," was known, a roar went up in London such as had not been heard since the acquittal of the Seven Bishops. Crabb Robinson, who then lived at Colchester, rose at six in the morning in order to be one of the earliest to obtain a London paper with an account of the trial. The first words that met his delighted eyes were " NOT GUILTY," in letters an inch in height. He ran about the town like a maniac, knocking up no end of people who were peacefully sleeping in their beds (and who, moreover, were quite uninterested in the event), and screaming, NOT GUILTY! The shorthand notes of this trial were taken down by Manoah Sibley (1757—1840), shoemaker and linguist, and published in two volumes in 1794. Sibley's brother Ebenezer (1752—1817), also at one time a shoemaker, became a physician and an astrologer, and his fame is alluded to in a contemporary adaptation of *Horace*, Book I., Ode XI. :

" I advise, my dear friend, that you never demand
What limits the gods have prescrib'd to our days;
Nor consult Mr. Sibley, that notable hand
At nativity-casting—believe me, 'tis base."

Tokens, both pence and half-pence, were struck to commemorate the Trial. The penny token reads:

O. Full-faced bust of Hardy. THO⁸ HARDY, SECRETARY TO THE LONDON CORRESPONDING SOCY. Inner legend: NOT GUILTY, Novr 5, 1794.

R. BY THE INTEGRITY OF HIS JURY WHO ARE JUDGES OF THE LAW AS WELL AS FACT.

In the middle are the names of the jurymen. Holcroft, who is also remembered on account of his novel, *Hugh Trevor*, and his song, " Gaffer Gray," died in 1809, and his autobiography edited by Hazlitt appeared in 1816. Hardy lived till 1832.

85. Other Tokens associated with shoe-makers are those of John Carter, Barnet Guest, Thomas Hatfield, William Allen [Pl. 32] and the Denton-Prattent series, the following being the wording of Carter's :

O. CARTER 32 JERMYN STREET LONDON 1795. In the middle a lady's shoe.

R. LADIES SHOE MANUFACTORY. A floral ornament above and below the word SHOE.

A particularly interesting token is the Denton-Prattent :

O. Cordwainers Hall Built 1790.   Picture of
Hall and small shield of arms of the Cord·
wainers' Company.

R. London and Westminster Penny 1797.
Arms of the City of London and Westminster
on a spade-shaped shield; a mural crown above.

Edge. I Promise to pay on demand the Bearer
One Penny.

86. The rise of **Stafford** as a shoe town
dates from about 1767, the founder of the trade
there being William Horton, friend of Richard
Brinsley Sheridan the dramatist, who had offered
himself to the borough as a candidate for Parliament. It is said that Sheridan's previous dealings
with shoemakers redounded little to his credit.
According to the story, which his opponents cir-
culated freely, once when he had (as usual) no
money, he contrived to get a pair of boots in a
very original way. He went to two bootmakers,
neither of whom would trust him for a pair, and
asked each to let him take home one boot to try
on. Thinking that they ran no risk they obliged
him, but from the one man he took a left boot and
from the other a right, and so got himself inexpen-
sively suited. It is, however, nothing but fair to
add that precisely the same story, in reference to
somebody else, appeared in *Scoggin's Jests*, 1626,
that is just one hundred and fifty years previous.
In any case, Sheridan was returned, and his
influence brought large orders to his friend Horton.

When he faced his constituents, his vivacity and his exhaustless wit made the town overflow with merriment, and he is credited with the toast, " May the staple of Stafford be trodden underfoot by all the world."

On several occasions he was pecuniarily indebted to Horton, but one day he came down to Stafford with the amazing statement that he had a balance at his banker's. " I want," said he, " to pay off my debt," and he wrote out a cheque for £1,000. Horton accepted it, twisted it up, lighted his pipe with it, and threw the burnt paper on the fire. " By ——! Will," said Sheridan, and his black, brilliant eyes emitted new sparks, " you are the king of cobblers." Perhaps Horton was actuated solely by kindliness, and perhaps he flatly disbelieved the marvellous story of the balance, and was of opinion that this particular cheque was no better and no worse than other cheques that had proceeded from the same source. Horton employed many village shoemakers, who brought their work into the town in long wallets thrown across the backs of donkeys, and he issued tokens worded :

O. STAFFORD. 1801. A shield bearing the arms of the borough (a castle between four lions passant).

R. W. H. (in cypher). PENNY. The Stafford shoe knot.

EDGE. Payable by Horton and Company.

John Cartwright, of Stafford, also issued tokens.

Black Spanish or Morocco leather was introduced into England by John Brown, of Abbey Holme, Cumberland, who died about 1798. The **Hessian** boot with a tassel worn over light pantaloons, which was part of the outfit of the English officer in the French War, was popular with civilians till the middle of the 19th century. The ugly Clarence boot, which was blocked like a Wellington and laced at the side, had a short vogue during the reign of William IV.

87. Samuel Taylor Coleridge as a boy, sadly wished to enter Shoe Lane. Near Christ's Hospital, where he was educated, resided an old shoemaker, and Coleridge, who desired to become apprenticed to him, prevailed on him to see the head master, the Rev. James Boyer. " Odds ! my life, man ! what d'ye mean ? " burst out Boyer in a fury, and pushed the scared shoemaker out of the room.[1] Coleridge, however, all his life was indebted to leather, one of the pleasantest friendships in literature being that between him and Thomas Poole (1765—1837), tanner, of Nether Stowey.

Very amazing was the career of the madcap **Nat Pearce** (1779—1820), leather mercer, of Smithfield. Every country was his home. Nothing came amiss to him. His leather shop being unable to hold him, off he went voyaging with no object except adventure, which he had to his

[1] *St. Crispin,* Vol. I. p. 33.

heart's content. He was taken prisoner by the French, and put in irons. His jailer's daughter— a pretty girl—fell in love with him. He revelled for a time in her smiles, but constancy was a word he did not understand. We find him subsequently in Amboyna, in China, at the Cape, at Mocha—in the moon. He is shipwrecked. He is lashed for desertion. He turns Mohammedan. He is pre- pared at five minutes' notice to turn anything that your purse might suggest. He finds favour with the Ras of Tigré, whom he treats judasly. The Ras's wife falls in love with him, "and gives him the full enjoyment of her favour and countenance." He is a model of faithfulness for three whole days. He is gone. He marries a Greek girl. He leaves her. How many other Greek girls, or girls of other nationalities he married, he never precisely knew. He was not good at arithmetic. He starts home, and dies at Alexandria, June 20th, 1820. His Journals were issued in 1831. He continually shocks, but what life he gave to life!

88. The revival of the Shoe Industry in **Norwich** took place in 1792, when John Smith, a leather-seller, who had abandoned the old practice of taking the measure of every foot, began to make up boots of different sizes. His grandson, C. Winter, perfected the idea, and laid the founda- tions of a great business. The manufacturers of Norwich devoted their attention almost exclusively to ladies' wear, but during the War (1914—1918) they made thousands of boots for the Allied Armies. To-day the Norwich trade has reverted to its pre-war status, and it produces the lightest and daintiest footwear which the mind of man can devise, many of its shoes being of the turnshoe or sew-round variety. Among the well-known Norwich firms are those of Howlett and White (Norvic Shoe Co.); Henry Sexton and Sons; Sexton, Son and Everard; Philip Haldinstein and Sons (founded 1799); James Southall and Co. (founded 1792); Arthur Chittock and Sons; Ramsbottom Bros. and S. L. Whitton, some of whom specialise in children's shoes, as well as in other wear. Mr. H. N. Holmes [1] (of Edwards and Holmes) was Lord Mayor of Norwich in 1922 [Pl. 51]. Mr. G. E. White (Howlett and White) said recently in an article in *The Daily Mail*: " Fashion looks to Norwich and Stafford as its interpreters of style in women's fine shoes, but Norwich is something more than an interpreter, it is a creator of fashions."

The first shoe shop in Glasgow was opened in 1749, at a position west of " The Tron Church," and its first warehouse, that of Gavin Williamson, in 1762. The firm of Adam and William Paterson celebrated its centenary in 1920.

---

[1] See *Footwear Organiser*, Feb., 1922, p. 104.

CHAPTER VII.

THE OLD STITCHMEN.   1800—1850.

89. **Robert Bloomfield,** who was born in 1766, at Honington, Suffolk, and found his way, at the age of 15, to a London garret, was taught shoemaking by his brother George. Just then there was a dispute in the trade as to whether those who had not been apprenticed could work as journeymen, and George, as instructor, was threatened with prosecution. In order to allow the storm to blow over, Robert returned to Suffolk, and while there the rural sights and the fragrance of the flowers gave him life, and led him to express himself in verse. Thenceforward his soul in all her higher moods thought and spoke in poetry. When God wishes to set a man on fire, He employs whom He will to apply the spark, and usually it is an adversary. Few men sufficiently value their enemies. On Bloomfield's return to London he became an apprentice. A slender, dark-complexioned lad, he toiled at his work, haunted the book-stalls, and took a wife before he had anywhere to put her — as a poet naturally would. His *Farmer's Boy* appeared in 1800. After a false step [1]—and yet to a good man (and Bloom-

---

[1] The acceptance of a post (in the Seal office) for which he was unfitted.

field was a good man) no step can be a false one—he turned to shoemaking again, and died at Shefford (Beds) in 1823.[1]

William Gifford (1757—1826) who had worked as a shoe hand at Ashburton, Devonshire, was editor from 1809 to 1824 of *The Quarterly Review.* He further served the public by translating Juvenal and by editing Massinger and other dramatists. His attack on Dr. Walcot drew the retort, *A Cut at a Cobler*, but he also struck, as little vipers sometimes will, at big quarry—at Hazlitt, for example, who turned and gored him.

A peculiarity of Tom Brown the shoemaker, of Garstang, Lancashire, was that he would never work except for women; and he left in 1811 the whole of his property to his female relations, thirty-six of whom, with white handkerchiefs held correctly to their eyes, followed at his funeral. I believe there is a tombstone to his memory with a misleading inscription. But of that no one can reasonably complain; if it told the truth, it wouldn't be a tombstone. As a foil to Tom Brown, the lover of women, must be mentioned another Tom—Morris, a crabbed Welsh shoemaker, of Berriew, Montgomery (born in 1794), a

[1] Other shoemaker writers of verse were Joseph Blacket (1786—1810), John Bennet (died 1803) of Woodstock, John Struthers (1776—1853) of Glasgow, James Woodhouse (born 1733) of Rowley Regis, William Edward Hickson (son of William Hickson, boot manufacturer, Northampton) 1803—1870, hymn-writer; David Service of Colegram on Clyde, author of *The Village Cobbler*, 1814, Rev. James Nichol (1769—1819) and Edmund Gill, York.

Plate 27

A SHOE-SHOP IN THE STUART PERIOD.

From *The History of the Gentle Craft*, 1676, copy preserved in Cordwainers'
Hall, London.   The figure is Sir Simon Eyre.   See p. 86.

Photo Mr. Geo. Avenell.

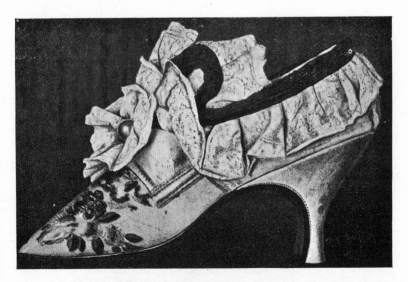

LACED SHOE

that belonged to a Miss Langley, time of Charles II.

It is made of pale yellow silk, tastefully embroidered and trimmed with lace. The ribbon at the
top is green, the sole is brown. From the *Book of Illustrations of Collections of Ladies' Old-
Fashioned Shoes*, by T. Watson Greig. For permission to use it we have to thank the Committee of
the Northampton Public Library.   See p. 130.

Plate 28

To show FRINGED BOOTS. Time of James I. See p. 120.

From Philip Stubbes's *Anatomy of Abuses in England* in 1583. See p. 102.

Crispin the Cobbler being chastised with a poker by his son Jack. See p. 135.

From Frontispiece to *Crispin the Cobler's Confutation of Ben H[oadley]*, by Dr. William Wagstaffe, 1726.

hater of women, who emigrated to Nebraska. As
statistics show, married men live much longer than
bachelors, and Morris, who obstinately refused to
marry, was cut off in his hundred and twenty-sixth
year. If he had taken a good wife—or a series of
good wives—he might have lived to a ripe old age.

90. The amazing **William Huntington**, S.S.,
a labourer's son, preached—after studying, mending shoes, and starving—to vast audiences, and
married as his second wife Lady Sanderson,
widow of a Lord Mayor of London. His works
teem with terse and weighty sayings (for he put a
snap and a sparkle into everything he wrote), such
as : "Half a grain of faith moves the world,"
"Grace carries many rays of majesty with it,
though it takes up its abode in a beggar," "Fortune, Luck and Chance are the trinity of fools,"
"Nature should not be forced, nor will Providence
be hurried." His *Bank of Faith*, one of the raciest
and most stimulating books in the language, is a
glowing record of God's loving-kindness to him
both spiritually and temporally. People occasionally vexed him by throwing stones at his summer-
house. One day, while a friend, Mr. John Over,
was sitting with him there, a stone crashed through
the window. In a moment Huntington, who was
a powerful man, ran out and with the words, "You
villain, I have you at last!" felled the culprit at a
blow. On returning he said, troubled, to Mr. Over,
"The moment I struck the man, the word of God

M

struck me: ' No striker.'¹ Here are two guineas.
Go and find him ; I dare say he is in some ale-
house hard by, and on his promising never to
throw stones again, give them to him." The man
after taking the money said, " You tell Mr. Huntington he may knock me down as often as he
likes, provided he gives me two guineas every
time." When Mr. Over returned to the summer-
house, he found Huntington on his knees confess-
ing his sin." The day Huntington was buried (at
Lewes) a great and strange silence fell on the city
of London. So many persons had attended the
funeral that the streets were carriageless.² A force
among the Quakers at the time was the shoemaker,
Thomas Shillitoe (1754—1836) who, in the spirit
of George Fox, made visits of mercy to haunts of
vice, and delivered his message personally to
crowned heads.

91. The Napoleonic wars gave a great impetus
to the Northampton trade, for during part of the
period the town was represented by Mr. Spencer
Percival [in 1809 Prime Minister] who worked
hard in its interests. It was owing to William
Hickson, who left London and settled in
Northampton as a manufacturer in 1867, that the
Basket Work method gave place to the Exhibition
system—the first show place in London being a
warehouse in Smithfield. The fame of Hickson,

¹ 1 Timothy iii. 3.

² See my *Life of William Huntington* (C. J. Farncombe & Sons, Ltd.)

however, pales before that of that grandee of the
shoe world, **" Hoby the Great,"** of St. James's
Street,[1] London, shoe-maker and Methodist
preacher, the panels of whose doors were em-
blazoned with the names of monarchs whom he
had fitted. When the battle of Vittoria (June
21st, 1813) was won, the Duke of Kent walked
into his shop to impart the news. " I knew," said
Hoby, " that Lord Wellington would be victorious,
for my boots and "—he was pleased to add—" my
prayers bring him out of all his difficulties." Sir
John Shelley once showed Hoby a pair of top
boots that had split in several places. " Good
heavens ! Sir John," was the comment, " you've
been walking in them."[2] Other customers of his
were the well-known men of fashion, Beau
Brummell and Horace Churchill. " See here,"
once said Churchill, " I am thoroughly disappointed in these boots, and I will never employ
you again." " Close the shutters, John," cried
Hoby, in affected distress, to an assistant, " It is
all over with us. Ensign Churchill is withdrawing
his custom." No man stage-managed his life
better than Hoby, who, moreover, " clapt up
Fortune in a cage of gold," made her turn her
wheel as he thought best, and died worth a
hundred and twenty thousand pounds.

---

[1] There was another Hoby who lived at 12 York Street, Covent
Garden.

[2] Top boots are made specially for riding, of course.

In the British Museum is a collection of Shoe-makers' Trade Cards, including specimens lettered, " Bloomfield, Ladies' Shoe-Maker, No. 14 Great Bell Alley, Coleman Street ; " " Tho⁵ Berry at the Patten and Crowne, Fleet Street ; " and " Ralph Aldersey at the Crown and Slipper, Minores."[1]

The battle of Waterloo was won, we are told, by the Northampton boot. It is true there were on the field some minor elements which conduced to the victory—for instance, Wellington was there, and the British soldier was not an altogether negligible quantity—still, had our army been worse shod, Bonaparte's last days might have been spent at Windsor instead of Longwood. With the signing of peace (1815) came trouble to the trade. Wages went down, inferior materials were used, and anything was considered good enough for the bottom filling. Indeed, things came at last to such a pass that in high class London shops it was announced in bold lettering, " No Northampton goods sold here." The best all round work had drifted to London, ladies' to Stafford, children's to Norwich ; and Bristol, Leicester, Leeds, and other towns also profited. By 1850, however, an improvement had set in. Every year new progress was made, and Northampton work now means work that is

[1] Illustrations appeared in *The Footwear Organiser* for Sept., 1920.

unsurpassable ; those who praise it most being the manufacturers of rival towns.

In 1817 a London shoemaker delighted his patrons by screwing thin **Plates of Brass** to the heels of their boots, and the click they made as their owners, swollen with satisfaction, promenaded down the sunny side of the street, provoked the lines :

> " Both Learned and Dunces are vain, it is said
> (Each in turn oft betrays what he feels),
> And they who no notice can gain by their head,
> Make a noise in the world with their heels."

The successors of these brass plates—tips of horse-shoe shape with a flange on the inner side, drilled with holes to receive nails, and iron plates with perforations forming an arabesque design, —ultimately gave place to the modern boot protector.

92. From 1819 to 1839 **John Pounds**, the Portsmouth cobbler, was gathering round him and teaching the ragged boys and girls of his neighbourhood. With massive forehead, bushy eyebrows, gleaming, benevolent and spectacled eyes, he might any day be seen with an old shoe between his knees, his canary on one shoulder, his cat on the other, and his ragged pupils about him. At first the children were shy of him, but gradually, by means of hot potatoes and other educational requisites, he won their confidence. He loved to talk to them about God, who, he told

them, saw everything. " Put gladness," he said,
" in one another's lives. That is pleasant to Him,
the only Being who really counts." The children
listened with open mouths and tears in their eyes.
Nobody had talked to them like that before. To
be in his company was like strolling through a
happy garden. His example being copied—so
quickly do kind and disinterested actions fire the
mind—in a very few years every considerable town
could boast of its Ragged School; and so the man
who had never coveted the toys of human glory
became glorious. On the morning of Jan. 1st,
1839, while looking at a picture of his shop, drawn
by a friend, he reeled and fell dead.

The shoemaker career of **Thomas Cooper**
lasted from 1820, when he was 15, to 1828. He
first worked under a cultured master, Joseph Clark,
of Gainsborough, and later was assisted by a
certain " Don Cundell," who taught him to make
women's shoes. After studying Gibbon and
teaching himself several languages, he became the
recognised leader of the Leicester Chartists. His
efforts in behalf of the masses had the natural
result of bringing about his arrest, and he was
imprisoned in Stafford jail, where he wrote tales
and verses which became popular. His autobiography appeared in 1872, and he died in 1892.

93. Among the best workers of Hoby the
Great was **James Dacres Devlin,** a native of
Dublin, who drifted first to Dover and afterwards

to Holborn, where he contributed to *The London Journal*, edited by Leigh Hunt, *The Daily News*, and *Notes and Queries*, and accumulated material respecting the history of the trade upon which he hoped to write monumentally. After travelling on the Continent, he published *The Boot and Shoe Trade of France* (1838), in which he pointed out that English leather was then not equal to French leather, that the roans with which English boots were lined could bear no comparison with the French article, and that we had "a very inferior manner of blocking[1] or turning the front-piece of the Wellington boot." "Let the English," he continues, "spend more time in the lecture room and less in the skittle alley—then we can beat our rivals at all points and, instead of importing from them, we shall export to them." This golden advice fortunately entered into receptive ears. It could scarcely do other, for its author's whole-hearted enthusiasm carries one away. In 1839 Devlin contributed to Knight's *Guide to Trade* (and there is a warmth and gladness about everything that he wrote) *The Shoemaker*, re-issued in 1862; and in 1848, *Helps to Hereford History, with some account of the Mordiford Dragon.* He also founded *The Cordwainers' Companion* and other short-lived periodicals, in which the richness and liberality of his temperament constantly

[1] Blocking or shaping the instep (and blockers were the best paid men in the trade) was done after the clicker had been at work, but blocking has now died out.

displayed themselves. A voracious student himself, he was never tired of urging his fellow craftsmen to acquire a taste for letters. The words, " Learn, read, see," were continually in his mouth. " Double your life," he said splendidly, " by having a mental as well as an animal existence." At the same time his enthusiasm for his trade is quite delightful. " Stitching is a handsome operation," " the English boot closers are the best in the world," and similar phrases glitter like gold in his pages. He insisted that shoemakers, instead of keeping their secret methods—" crans "—to themselves, should share them with their mates. His garret—a cabinet of enchantment — in Holborn was crowded with scarce and curious books ; but his passion for literature did not hinder him from distinction as a workman. He was one of the best closers in London, and sometimes put in, by hand, 60 stitches to an inch. One pair of riding boots which he made had the tongue (the fancy part of the vamp which extends a little way up the front of the leg) designed in the form of a shamrock leaf. At the end of his thread he used, instead of the customary hog's bristle, a hair from his daughter's head.[1] Among his friends were John Blackman, author of *The Bard of Anningsly*, and John O'Neill, a burly, flashing-eyed giant, whose lines, *The Drunkard*, subsequently altered to *The*

[1] T. B. Leno, *The Art of Boot and Shoemaking*, 1889, p. 72.

Blessings of Temperance, were illustrated by Cruik-shank. The friends—and all were shoemakers and Temperance workers — usually spent their Sunday evenings together, talking on great themes, in O'Neill's lodging off Tottenham Court Road, where they were sometimes joined by two other flaming souls, T. B. Leno and Cooper the Chartist. They regarded literary conversation especially as a sea of new delights. O'Neill, whose story is told in " Fifty Years of an Irish Shoemaker," a series of papers which appeared in *St. Crispin* [see Chapter IX., Section 140], died in a garret in St. Giles's on February 3rd, 1858 ; and Devlin, who knew so much, yet did not know how to distil gold from ink, was soon to follow him. Circum-stance brayed him alive. In a well-known passage in *The Shoemaker*, he refers to Don Speirs, the last of the great stitchmen to make shoes with white rands, who, though he once swaggered gorgeously in gold buckles and a cocked hat, ended his days in St. James's parish workhouse. Pathetically enough, Devlin himself died in that same sad sanctuary. James Dowie and J. Sparkes Hall also wrote popularly on boots and shoes.

Of shoemaker **Naturalists,** three in particular are remembered, Richard Buxton (1786—1865), who devoted his leisure to botanical research ; Thomas Edward (1815—1888), the subject of Smiles's *Life of a Scotch Naturalist* ; and John Younger (1785—1858), a sketch of whose career appears in his book, *The Light of the Week* (1849).

94. The first volume by **John Askham** [Pl. 33] of Wellingborough (1825—1894), *Sonnets on the Months*, appeared in 1863. He dearly loved the familiar objects of the countryside—the blades of grass because they were blades of grass, and the brook, because it was a brook. Often he would, if no paper were handy, pick up a leather sole and scribble a verse upon it. Genial and humorous in his conversation, he possessed "the inner light that fadeth not," of which he himself sings—"the sunshine of the heart." His second book, *Descriptive Poems* (1866) was composed in the ceaseless din of a large factory, where even the windows rattled. To some there was no music in the rustling, restless monotone of the machines; but even in that song Askham found harmony—

> "You may deem them harsh, but their notes to me
> Are sweet as the softest minstrelsy,"

for they brought him his little bit of daily bread. He reaches his high water mark in that arresting little poem, "The Inner Life":

> "Each has a secret self—an inner life
> Of hopes and fears,
> High aspirations, doubtings, calm and strife,
> And joys and tears."

Two other volumes entirely in verse left his pen, *Judith, and other Poems*, 1868, and *Poems and*

Sonnets, 1875 ; *Sketches in Prose and Verse* appeared in 1893, and he died on Oct. 27th of the following year. His uneventful career contrasts strikingly with that of his fellow townsman, Ernest Leech, packer to a boot and shoe manufacturer of Irthlingborough, who ran away to sea, met with adventures in every land, and returned home to write *On the Banks of the Nene* and *Where the Ise Brook Flows.*[1] Of the poems of John Gregory[2] (1831—1922), the Bristol shoemaker, the best are " St. Crispin's Bell," " Grandfather Hoare," and " Saint Monday."[3]

95. The early 19th century stitchman, like his forefathers, began and finished a shoe throughout,

---

[1] He died in 1921. A sketch of his life, by Mr. Harry E. Moore, appeared in *The Wellingborough News*, of March 4th of that year.

[2] See *Footwear Organiser*, Sept., 1921. One of his sons is Sir Richard Gregory, editor of *Nature*.

[3] Connected with the shoe trade also were Hans Christian Andersen, author of *Fairy Tales;* Timothy Bennett of Hampton Wick (1676—1756), defender of the rights of the people ; John Burnet (1789—1862), philanthropist ; Seth Berridge of Wakefield, politician ; Nehemiah Coxe (fl. 1685), linguist ; Thomas Cooke (1807—1868), astronomer and optician ; Samuel Drew (1765—1833), metaphysician ; John Fellows of Birmingham (ob. 1715), hymn-writer ; Sir Henry Jones (ob. 1922), Professor of Moral Philosophy at Glasgow ; John Kitto (1804—1855), Biblical scholar ; Richard Savage (ob. 1743), minor poet ; William Sturgeon (1783—1833), electrician ; John Sirgood, founder in 1850 of the sect called the Dependent Brethren, whose centre is the village of Loxwood, Sussex ; and George Shergold of Gloucester, maker in 1880 of the first safety bicycle, who embodied in a home-made machine the five leading principles of construction which may be seen in the present day model, namely, Front Steering, Rear Driving, Chain Transmission, Gearing-up, and Back-wheel Brake. After riding on iron tyres for a year, Shergold substituted rubber, but unhappily, though he made millions for other people, he himself (he died in 1903) never benefited to the extent of a single penny. The Rev. Dr. Alexander Whyte, preacher and Boehme student, who died in 1921, was also in his early days connected with the trade. Among American shoemakers who distinguished themselves in other walks of life were : Noah Webster (1758—1834), lexicographer ; William Greenleaf Whittier (1807—1892), poet ; Noah Worcester (1758—1838), reformer ; and William Lloyd Garrison (1805—1879), abolitionist.

and even at the present day a few workers make the whole shoe. The **Principal Operations** were and are : 1, Cutting out the uppers; 2, Closing the uppers, that is, attaching the linings[1] and stitching the various pieces together ; 3, Lasting the upper, that is, moulding it to the last with tacks ; 4, Sewing on the welt[2] (which is the foundation of the handsewn shoe) ; 5, Putting in shank[3] in order to strengthen the waist ; 6, Filling the bottom up, that is, the space enclosed by the welt.[4] (In old days shavings from the curriers' shops were used.) 7, Stitching on the outer sole ; 8, Making the heel, which consisted of piece-sole, split-lifts, lifts and top-piece (the portion that touches the ground).

When **Children** were sent to the shoemaking, their first work was to boil the pitch, resin and tallow in an old saucepan, and pour it into a pail of water. Then, after pulling it, they made it into balls of " wax." Next, taking several strands of hemp, they would wax them and roll them on the knee in order to make Cobblers' or, as the Olney people call it, Codgers' End (thread) for sewing on the welt.[5] For stitching on the sole,

[1] Linings were generally of jean, but sometimes leather was and is used, as for heavy boots.

[2] A strip of leather round the shoe, between the upper and the sole.

[3] Shank—that which is put under the waist of the sole to give it its rounded shape.

[4] A middle sole would be put for some heavy boots, but most hand-sewn boots have no middle sole.

[5] See also " Making a Wax End," by J. W. Andrews. *The British Shoeman,* Sept., 1921, p. 85.

flax was always used. The thread having been
made, the bristles were attached to it. The
sewing was done with flat awls bent at the end,
the stitching with square awls with a sharp point,
so as to go easily through the leather. The heel
awl was like the sewing awl, only larger.[1]

96. A boy, says Devlin, writing in 1839, "after
having learned how to make his threads and use the
awl, commonly gets to closing children's shoes,
using the *clams*—those two tall nipping pieces of
stave-like timber—which he holds pressed hard
together between his knees; or holding the work
on the block—that somewhat half-round clump of
wood, which he lays along his left thigh, held down
by the *stirrup*. . . The *Stabbing* is a different
process again; the portions of leather being in
this case stitched directly through, either in
straight or curved lines, as may be necessary. The
work is held either in the clams or between the
knees, and receives the awl at the right side,
piercing through to the left or inner side, from
which the left hand hair should at once be pro-
truded, the right hand hair being put in afterwards
and the stitch drawn smartly in. This is called
Blind Stabbing [Pl. 35], and . . it is certainly the most beautiful process in the whole
trade . . Quickly in goes the awl, and as
quickly it is out again ; but not before the hair

[1] These notes are almost word for word as they were given me by John
Field of Lavenden, in March, 1920. He was then about 80.

from the fingers of the left hand has found the passage, *without being at all directed by the sight, but literally in the dark,* hence the term. . . The ability to do this is alone the acquisition of the British shoemaker — one Brown, who lived in Whitcomb Street, and who worked for the elder Hoby, being probably the earliest of our boot closers to use himself to it, about 60 or 70 years ago.[1] Now there is not a closer in the kingdom but can blind stab."

Those who made the uppers sat with their clams round the **Candleblock**—a heavy stool, three feet high, with a hole in the middle into which was inserted a holder that could be raised or lowered as occasion required. Of the candle itself, " Little Jack Dandiprat,"[2] it used to be said :

> " Little Jack Dandiprat, in a white petticoat,
> The longer he lives the shorter he grows."

Occasionally the candle would burn down to the hole and set the candleblock on fire.

97. Of all the work turned out by the old stitchmen—and it is still done by a certain number of men employed by the firms Frederick Cook of Long Buckby, G. M. Tebbutt & Son,[3]

---

[1] That is, they did not practise feeling for the hole previous to this date.

[2] Because originally it cost a dandiprat, a coin worth three-halfpence, minted by Henry VII. The dandiprat is mentioned in *Nashe*, McKerrow's Ed., ii., 212.

[3] Of Clare Street. The founder of the firm was Thomas Tebbutt of King Street, who commenced in 1843, and the business is now superintended by his grandsons, Albert Edward and Alfred. See also p. 31.

and Charles Smith,[1] of Northampton—the most extraordinary and perhaps the most fascinating is what is called **Long Boot Closing**, or Flat Seaming—the making of the seams for riding and hunting boots. In this very fine handwork sixteen stitches to the inch are usual, but old time men, who revelled in the operation, have been known to put in, as we have seen (p. 168), as many as sixty. " Long Boot Closing," observed Sir James Crockett to me, " is one of the fine arts." Speaking of long work in Jockey boots and Napoleons, an old stitchman, Mr. Thomas Matthews, said, " The finest workmen (taught when very young) did it, and it is the cleverest and most delicate work turned out by the craft, the most difficult operation being the ' closing in ' of the tongue,[2] which is done by hand." Mr. H. F. Swann, while showing me some splendid specimens of the " long boot " made by his firm (Charles Smith), observed with justifiable pride, " It's something when you've finished." The boots are made of wax calf,[3] willow calf, box calf, and patent leather. Polo boots are always brown. The old Long Boot men were the aristocrats of the shoe world, and as aristocrats usually are, they were haughty

---

[1] Founded by Smith and Dawson, who were succeeded by William Smith, who about 1885 was followed by his brother, Charles Smith, the present head.

[2] The tongue can of course be " laid on," but most ladies and gentlemen would not look at a boot made in this way.

[3] Wax calf is dressed on the flesh side, hence its smoothness; other leathers are dressed on the grain side.

to, and regarded patronisingly, the rank and file.
One evening old Paddy Smith, a London long
closer, graciously took an ordinary closer home
with the object of sharing a bottle with him.   As
they were ascending the stairs towards Paddy's
attic, his landlady screamed out from somewhere,
" Who is it ? "   " Old Paddy Smith," was the
reply, " and an inferior craftsman."

98.   Nobody could mistake **The Old Stitchman.**   He had the temperament of an Epictetus,
and everything he wore, did or said, was stamped
with the peculiarity of his race.   Like his Roman
predecessors who copied their god Apollo (though
may be it was the god, persuaded by the sculptors
and painters, who copied them), he wore his hair
long, rolled up behind, and kept back by a band
of leather, called at Leicester the Brain-band
[Pl. 35], and at Northampton the Brow-band—an
unhappy name, since it gave Leicester the opportunity to say (and Leicester men can be very
provoking), " We have brains, you have only
brows."   Among the last in Northampton to wear
a brow-band were Jim and John Ward, both of
whom had raven black hair which fell in luxurious
ringlets on their shoulders.   The last in Olney to
wear it was old Samuel Wright, who lived in the
house now occupied by another shoemaker, Mr. W.
Barnes.   One day Samuel's wife received from a
relative at Leicester a parcel of what she supposed to be tarts.   Being unable to get her teeth

Plate 29

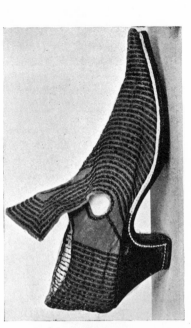

SHOE, SILK BROCADE.
English; Late 17th Century. 37849 B. T. 435—1913. See p. 141.

LADY'S SHOE. Leather with applied Silk Braid.
English; Time of Charles II. 47494. T. 107 and A—1917.

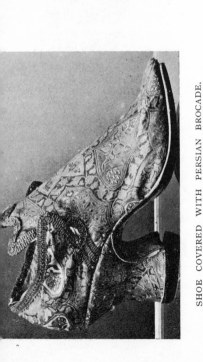

SHOE COVERED WITH PERSIAN BROCADE.
Probably made in England about 1700. 37849 A. T. 444—1913. See p. 141.

SHOE, LEATHER, WITH LATCHETS.
Time of Charles I. (1625—1649). 37845 B. T. 420—1913.

All the above are photos from Shoes in the Victoria and Albert Museum, South Kensington.

Plate 30

TRADE TOKEN OF JOHN TOMSON AND HIS WIFE M. TOMSON. See p. 138.

TRADE TOKEN OF EDWARD LEGG, YORK.

See p. 138.

From rubbings by Mr. S. H. Hamer, Halifax.

SHOE. Time of Charles I.

Footwear Organiser, Nov., 1919, p. 541.

JACOBEAN POMPOM SHOE.

Footwear Organiser, Nov., 1919, p. 541.

BOOT, Leather, with broad Top.
17th Century.

Victoria and Albert Museum, South
Kensington. 37852 A. T. 425—1913.

into them, she called in my mother. " I'm sure
they're good," she said, " or Mrs. Lebutt would
not have sent them. I think they want a little
more cooking ; perhaps you can tell me what to
do." " Why, Mrs. Wright," said my mother, as
she picked one up, " they're not tarts, they're
fire-lighters ! "

But for the brain-band, the stitchman would
have looked like Ibsen or an angora rabbit, and
his hands would have got hopelessly entangled
when making his stitches. His beard, which was
as long as Zeno's, he tucked into the bib of his
apron ; his spectacles had circular eye-pieces ; on
the wrist of his left hand was the Hand-leather [or
as the French, in honour of King Crispin, charmingly call it, the *Gant Royal* (Royal Glove)],
and he looked more patriarchal than Abraham
himself. The possession of which he was most
proud, however, was his top hat, which seems to
have passed as an heirloom from father to son.
Often he could be seen (and his haunt in North
ampton was in the neighbourhood of Narrow-toe
Lane) wandering down the street for wax, hemp
and bristles, his " black flag " (apron) before him
and his aged, moulting hat above. It was not
only a hat ; it was also a portmanteau. After its
owner had collected at the grindery shop his wax,
bristles, hemp, heel-ball and other sundries,[1] he

---

[1] In those days he reckoned to get five articles for a penny : a ball of
wax, heel ball, glass for a scraper, rye flour for his paste horn, and a
couple of bristles.

N

would, as often as not, take off his hat, put his purchases inside it, lay a red handkerchief over them, and return the hat with its contents to his head.   If a gust of wind caught it, down, of course, came the bristles, the heel-ball, and all; and a stranger in the town happening to meet him had the surprise of a lifetime.   Some of the old Northampton hands used to go to Yardley Chase for boxwood, and also to search for bones of the deer[1] for rubbing the welt, &c., though never, of course, for bones (with meat on) of the hare or the pheasant.   With the boxwood they were able, on account of its peculiar curves, to make a stitch-man's spokeshave—a combination of rubbing stick and press, with which to remove inequalities in the sole.   In Beard-in-bib's home, owing to his cynical attitude towards religion, there was sometimes friction, especially when a new baby came.   The wife wanted it "to be done" (christened); he, seeing no good in the ceremony, objected.   The air then became electric.   The contention, how-ever, usually ended in a compromise.   He gave way on condition that it should be called George (after Odger)[2] or Charles (after Bradlaugh) but preferably Charles; so both Church and Schism were satisfied.

The clicker,[3] in the early days of machinery, was

---

[1] See p. 51.

[2] George Odger (1813—1877), shoemaker, reformer, orator.

[3] Clicking—the cutting of the upper—was accomplished by the use of patterns, cut in early times from cardboard, and later from zinc, sheet-

better paid, and consequently better dressed, than the rivetter and the finisher, on whom he looked down—even going to the length (and to what lengths will not pride carry a man!) of wearing a white collar. The rivetters and finishers, on their part, could not conceal their dislike of the men who gave themselves these provocative airs. But when you come to think of it, there is excuse for being proud, when you are wearing something that nearly chokes you.

In Devlin's time all men's shoes, and in the north women's also, were stitched with the square awl, called in England " The French Blade," and in France "The English Blade " (*Alêne Anglaise*), the reason being that although it came from France, an Englishman perfected it.

Wellingtons and Bluchers were worn in the army, the former being a knee-reaching boot, the tops of which were covered by the loose military trousers, the latter a half-boot. With civilians it was customary to wear Wellingtons on a Sunday and Bluchers on weekdays. Queen Victoria once asked the Duke of Wellington what kind of boots he wore. " People call them Wellingtons," he

iron or fibre-board with a narrow brass binding. The pattern is laid upon the leather by the clicker, who then runs a knife along the edge of the pattern. In doing this he often, although unconsciously, made a clicking noise with the knife, which is said to account for his denomination.

Bailey's *Dictionary* (1721—1800), however, quoted with approval by Devlin [*The Shoemaker*, Pt. 2, p. 67], says " clicker, to click or clack, as shop-keepers do at their doors " [Fr. *claquer*]. From this we judge that the clickers at certain times of the day stood at their doors soliciting custom.

replied. " How absurd ! " commented the Queen,
" where, I should like to know, would they find a
pair of Wellingtons ! "

99.   The bootmaker to George IV. was John
Postill, who removed from London to Newark,
where he founded a great business, which is to-
day superintended by a John Postill, the fourth of
his line.   The shoe industry began to make headway in **Leicester** about 1830, owing to the efforts
of Mr. Thomas Crick, who married a Miss Martha
Throne.   In time he became a "translator ; " in
other words, he " bought old boots and," as it was
prettily said, " converted them into new ones."
For twenty years people had been experimenting
with rivets, and his method was to screw an iron
plate on to the wooden last and then to rivet new
soles on to the old shoe.   In 1853, his son Thomas
took out a patent for " Inside Rivets," that is for
shoes which were rivetted and then turned.   The
heads of the rivets were, of course, inside the
shoe, but he hid them by pasting over them a
parchment slip stamped with the words " Crick's
patent."   The sole was attached afterwards.   The
real makers of the business of D. Crick and Co.,
were Thomas Crick's son John Throne, and his
cousin and successor Throne, who retired in 1896.
The Leicester event of 1894 was the opening of
the Wheatsheaf Works (Co-operative Wholesale
Society), and that of 1921 the completion of the
new Liberty Works — two of the finest of the

many fine factories in that city. Other great Leicester firms are George Hincks, T. Roberts and Sons (Portland Shoe Works), and John Cooper and Sons, Ltd. (Beehive Works). North Evington, Leicester, a modern industrial district, contains many magnificent boot factories, including the "Anchor,"[1] Smith, Faire and Co., Joseph Leeson and Sons, George Durston and Co., and D. Henderson and Sons.[2] The Co-operative development in Leicester has been dealt with in *Co-operation in Leicester*, 1898, and other works. The Leicester Co-operative Distributing Society (President, Mr. Amos Mann, author of *Democracy in Industry*, 1914) has a membership running into scores of thousands.

100. The fame of **Bristol** as a shoemaking centre commenced about 1845, when Messrs. Derham Brothers, previously of Wrington, started business in the neighbourhood of Castle Green. In 1910 the business, which had removed to Soundwell, passed into the hands of the present directors, Mr. Percy Steadman and Mr. Clifford Steadman, under whose control—and their ideas are vast—a rapid extension has taken place. A branch for the manufacture of heavy nailed goods of the better grades occupies premises at Staple Hill, near the head offices. The specialities of the firm are attractive and fine grade ladies' foot-

---

[1] In 1907 the workers began to build for themselves a model village at Humberstone. [2] See also *Footwear Organiser*, July, 1922, p. 47.

wear, and solid working boots, its most famous brands being " Lady," " Ariel " and " Sound." The next oldest Bristol firm is that of Cridland and Rose, though the Cridlands were connected with leather long before the inception of the Bristol business. The founder of the house was Henry Cridland, a tanner of Totnes, and son followed father in the business for several generations. About 1870, Arthur Cridland removed to Bristol and bought the present factory in King Square, and in 1916 he was succeeded by the present head, Mr. Henry Cridland. During the war the firm supplied boots for the Italian army, and its goods now find their way everywhere. Another famous Bristol firm is that of Coe, Church and McPherson.

In Bristol proper there are 12 boot manufacturers, all turning out best-class goods for both men and women. In Kingswood—the hub of the nailed boot trade, there are about 80 manufacturers who make chiefly heavy nailed goods. The first to introduce sewing machines into Kingswood was the late Daniel Flook. For long, little was done beyond heavy wear, but as the result of improvements in road construction there arose among the working classes a demand for medium heavy boots, which was first met by E. W. Pratt and Co. and G. B. Britton and Sons. The heavier boots which are still made are chiefly for the South Wales miners. The firms of Isaac Pow and Sons,

W. J. Edwards and Co., and A. Lovell and Co. have also a great reputation.

Early in the 19th century Sunderland was a shoe centre, and about 1840 Newcastle called itself " The Leather Metropolis of the North." The trade of these towns, however, steadily drifted to Yorkshire, and particularly to Leeds. Aberdeen does a great trade in every kind of foot-gear, and especially in heavy goods.[1] Among notable London houses are those of Britten and Bannister, James Branch and Sons, and Petch and Co. C. and J. Clarke, of Street near Glastonbury, are a very old firm. Somervell Bros. of Kendal,[2] founded in 1842, have a world-wide reputation as makers of mountaineering boots, though they put out every kind of foot-gear. They supplied boots for the Mt. Everest Expedition (1922), in which Mr. T. H. Somervell, a son of one of the directors, took part. Ski boots are made by Thomas Mann, of Cogenhoe, for the London firm of Dowie and Marshall.

---

[1] See also p. 91.

[2] See *Shoe and Leather News*, July 15th, 1920. Article by F. W. Higgins.

CHAPTER VIII.

SHOEMAKERS' HOLIDAYS, SONGS, CHAP-
BOOKS AND PROVERBS.

101. In old times **St. Crispin's Day** (Oct. 25th)[1] was kept by the shoemakers almost everywhere as a holiday. The morning usually saw a grand procession of cordwainers with banners and music, some of them being dressed to represent Crispin, Crispianus, the Princess Ursula, and other personages of the legend. The cordwainers of London, however, outdid those of all the other towns in gaiety. The whole livery assembled in the hall (which was spread with rushes), every man in a new gown, and then proceeded to church, led by singing clerks chanting as they went. On their return they seat themselves to a banquet. A log fire in which is thrown a scented Indian wood called sanders burns on the hearth. All the freemen of the company are present, with their wives and sweethearts. They have met to have a good time, and they have it. The table groans with beef and game pasties. Sausages are served sizzling. Gispens and peg tankards are emptied.

[1] For general account of the Livery Companies and their festivals see *The Saturday Magazine*, Vol. 24, supplements to March and May, 1844.

Metheglin, piping hot, is drunk from "jolly bottom-less cups." The noisy jest goes round. They "birle" to one another (drink one another's health). The women blush and giggle when they are sprinkled with sweet water (scent). The loving cup, filled with generous wine, goes round. Feasting over, the officers for the year are elected. Speeches are made. There is animated talk regarding the condition of the trade. It is clear that in this world nothing really matters except leather. Suddenly there is a braying of trumpets. In come the mummers in comical dresses—some of them, as might be expected at a cordwainers' feast, wearing goats' heads—and they perform a hundred queer antics. So droll are they that the women, ceasing from their affectation and simpering, cannot restrain themselves from screaming, while the men rock with laughter and roll off their settles. The players are begged to desist. It is too excruciatingly funny. The musicians make ready. Citterns and citoles are tickled. Rotes, lutes and rebecs drone, violins wail, songs are sung, and when all is over the revellers turn, laughing, shrieking and joking into the street, where link-boys are waiting to light them home.

The shoemakers of Scarborough celebrated the day by burning torches on the sands; and those of Edinburgh, Stirling and Cuckfield (Sussex) by choosing a king and queen and parading through the town in sumptuous dresses. At Tenby an

effigy of the saint, after being hung from the
steeple, was cut down and carried in procession
through the streets.   At each shoe shop there was
a halt, a document purporting to be his last will
and testament was read, and some article of his
clothing was left as a memento of the visit.   When
nothing remained to be distributed, the padding of
the effigy was rolled into a ball and kicked about
the town.   Having honoured their patron saint in
this affecting manner, the shoemakers retired to a
jovial meal, which the masters washed down with
Peter-see-me and the journeymen with metheglin,
while the musicians played their maddest dance
melodies.   At Dublin the journeymen walked in
procession, to the sound of kettle drum and
trumpet, from their tavern in Fishamble Street to
St. Michael's Church, and the proceedings finished
up, as elsewhere, with a dinner, the very smell of
which was enough to make a man wish to turn
shoemaker.

102.   In hundreds of homes the custom of
Wetting the Candleblock was observed on this
day.   The young men put on their Sunday clothes
and their jauntiest behaviour, the girls their best
frocks and sunniest smiles.   Instead of sitting
round the old chunk stitching uppers, they took
the same position and drank ale or cobblers'
punch[1] piping hot, ate bread and cheese, told tales

---

[1] Warm ale and gin spiced, sweetened and thickened with eggs and
flour.

and sang merry songs, while Little Jack Dandi-prat, taking on his sauciest mood, winked at the girls and flickered and guttered as if splitting his sides at the fun.

At Northampton the glories of October 25th were overshadowed by those of Mayor's Day, November 9th. Time out of mind the Mayor had been chosen by popular voice in St. Giles's Churchyard, the day being given up to jollity. Subsequently the choice was made in the Town Hall in the presence of the public, who heckled both the outgoing and the incoming Mayor, and by their uproarious conduct reduced the proceedings to mere dumb show. Eventually—about 1890 —the public were excluded. These facts explain how it was that Northampton—the very town where on October 25th one would have expected to find the saint especially honoured—was the only considerable town in which there were no public rejoicings. Every workman, however, all the same, received his "Crispin" (eighteenpence).

But although Northampton paid but scant regard to its saint, it had, and still has, a gorgeous Crispin banner, which is preserved in the Trade Hall, Overstone Road. Some years ago it was taken to Belfast and paraded at a Trades Union Congress held there. Unfortunately, as the procession was passing through the streets, the Orangemen took the notion that the long-bearded figure of the saint was their arch antipathy.

Shouts of "To hell with the Pope!" and "other varses o' scripthur" were yelled out, stones and bricks flew, and innocent Crispin I. received in the chest a brick that was intended for guilty Leo XIII. The bearers, terrified beyond words, hastily rolled up their banner and ran for their lives. The saint, however, was none the worse for his adventure, and he still with serene face, bald head and ample beard, looks benignly down as he passes through Northampton's crowded thoroughfares on great occasions.

103. In **Paris** St. Crispin's Day began merrily with bell-ringing, and the cordwainers went in gay procession with wax candles and the banner of their Company to church. After Mass they returned to their hall, where they feasted, drank too much wine, and got quarrelling. If a member happened in the heat of an argument to break another member's head, or to poke a hole in him with a dagger, no particular notice was taken— such accidents being only what might happen at any little friendly gathering; but if in his cups he cursed the Virgin, he was called to order and fined a pound of best white wax.

In the 17th century the cobblers of Paris used to meet, not on October 25th, but on August 1st. At their gathering in the year 1641, after leaving the Church of St. Peter of Arsis, where they had "bestowed all sorts of praises on their patron," they made merry in a tavern, where they feasted on turnip soup, ox feet, fricassees of tripe, cow beef and sparkling wines.   In Plate 38, which is from an old engraving, we have the scene before our very eyes.   The cobbler's wife has a charming face and a graceful manner.   There is music while they eat, and the ear-ringed singer in ruff and ruffles is evidently, to judge by his comical face, a wag of the first order.   The serving man with a spur on one foot and no shoe on the other has, I am afraid, had too much—turnip soup, which, as everybody knows, is a very heady liquor.

104.   April 1st was also a day on which shoe-makers were apt to lose their heads.   Of practical jokes they never tired, and on one occasion at **Grendon** (Northants) they put a donkey on a shutter and hoisted it, amid peals of laughter in which the donkey joined, on to the leads of the church.   But at Grendon anything might happen ; it was the Gotham of Northamptonshire.

One day two of the shoemakers who had been helping in the harvest field saw, after a visit to *The Half Moon* [Pl. 37], the actual moon in the brook which runs close by; and one of them, thinking it was a cheese, said to the other, " Golly! here's a prize; we must get it out."   So they put in their rakes and worked hard but unsuccessfully. They then returned to the inn, and while they were again drinking, the landlord came in with a real cheese under his arm.   " Well, I never ! " said

one man to the other, "there was you and me
sweating ourselves for two hours all for nothing,
while this chap puts in his rake and outs with it
first go. See what it is to be born lucky!"

The quarrel between the people of the parish
and a former rector could scarcely have taken
place anywhere else. The people, who were
captained by the landlord of *The Crown* (and he
was a learned man) said the church was dedicated
to St. James, calendared for July 25th ; the rector
(and he also was a learned man) said that they had
for centuries been in error, and that the church
was really dedicated to St. Mary, calendared for
the 20th ; in short, the rector sought " to antedate
the village feast by a week." The people, determined to resist "this unjustifiable innovation,"
kept away from church ; the rector denounced
them ; the people requested him to resign, and he
replied, in the beautiful idiom of Northamptonshire, that he would see their necks as long as his
arm first. I am grieved to say that as the result
of this unhappy quarrel, the rector ate his pepper-
mint rock and gave himself indigestion on the 20th,
while the people stubbornly refused to eat theirs,
and give themselves indigestion, till the 25th. It
was quite appropriate, too, that it should be at
Grendon that the floor of the church gave way—
as once it did—and allowed a number of people,
" much to their surprise," to drop down a foot or
two to the ground beneath. The surprise was not

that the floor gave way (occurrences of that sort
you would naturally expect at Grendon), the surprise was that they went down no further than a
foot or two. Then again it was quite in keeping
with the spirit of the village that there should have
been what is called " The battle of Grendon," a
ding-dong fight at the brook (the same brook in
which the good men dipped their rakes) between
the labourers of a farmer named Wright and those
of another named Spencer, while the shoemakers
who had gathered round looked on approvingly,
and laid bets with one another. Of course, after
it was over it was discovered that there was not
the slightest necessity for a fight, and that half a
dozen words of explanation would have prevented
the breaking of at least a dozen heads. But that
is not the Grendon way, which is to act first and
give the matter their thoughtful and prayerful
consideration afterwards. Outsiders are in the
habit, when referring to Grendon, of calling it
"that much tried parish." From this it might be
supposed that most of the people die young. It
is not so. They live to an absurdly great age.
This may be owing to the number of cheeses which
are still almost any evening to be found in the
brook by those who have eyes to see. And the
Grendon people have good eyes. And cheese is a
very nutritious food. Another peculiarity of this
village is that it is always summer there—owing to
the sunny disposition of the inhabitants.

Other Northants villages which have a reputation for wisdom almost equal to that of Grendon are **Harpole** and Cottesbrooke. A cobbler of Harpole who was in the habit of frequenting *The Fox and Hounds*, lay down in a field, after a visit to this seductive tavern, in order to hear the grass grow. As he heard nothing, though he lay there half-an-hour, he went home in great distress to tell his wife. Coming upon her very unexpectedly, he so startled her that she dropped a plate of "thrumety,"[1] which she had prepared for his supper, and it struck the flagged floor, making a noise, which the cobbler to his relief heard quite plainly. "That's all through you!" said she. "Oh wife," he followed, "never mind about the thrumety. My hearing's come back, and I can't be too thankful."

In Northants people turn over their money when they first hear the cuckoo, otherwise they are unlucky the rest of the year. A Harpole cobbler once left *The Fox and Hounds* to follow a wagon, the front wheels of which were smaller than the back wheels. He wanted to see the big wheels catch up the little ones. After walking and watching a good while he said, "Of course I shall not see it done this year for, silly-like, I forgot to turn my money over when I heard the cuckoo."

A shoemaker of **Cottesbrooke** once whitewashed his chimney, and as there was a likelihood of rain,

[1] Furmenty. Boiled wheat with spices and raisins.

Plate 31

ARMS OF THE PATTEN MAKERS' COMPANY, LONDON.
See pp. 72 and 137.

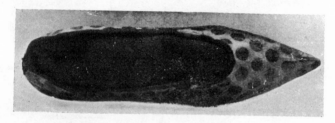

Very striking lady's shoe of kid, painted gold colour with large black spots.
The seams and the upper edge are bound with black silk braid.   English.
Late 18th Century.   Length, 9½ ins. ; width, 2½ ins.   Victoria and Albert
Museum, South Kensington.   Case 339.   1125—1901.

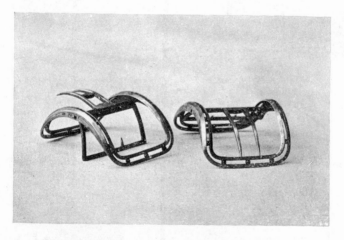

THE POET COWPER'S SHOE-BUCKLES.

Lent by Mr. Henry L. Longuet Higgins, Turvey, Beds.

See p. 151.

Photo Coldham & Son, Northampton.

Plate 32

SHOE AND CLOG with silk damask and brocaded front. Early 18th Century. See p. 136. Victoria and Albert Museum, South Kensington. 37842 B. T. 600—1913.

TOP BOOT.

English. Middle of 18th Century. Victoria and Albert Museum, South Kensington. 37852 B. T. 452—1913.

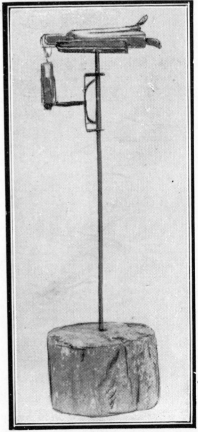

ANCIENT COBBLER'S STAND DISCOVERED AT ISHAM. See Appendix.

Photo Mr. Spencer Percival, Kettering.

he decided to take the chimney indoors. "Stop!"
said his wife, "it would be less trouble to let it
stay where it is, and give it another coat when it's
left off raining." "I never thought of that," said
he, "what a smart sort of people women are!"
When the rain was over, he mounted the ladder
with his pail and brush, and she stood below to
watch him. Unfortunately his hand slipped,
and the contents of the pail fell over her just as it
began to rain again. As, white from head to foot,
she was about to run to the house to clean herself,
he called out, "Stop, missis, it would be less
trouble for you to stay where you are, and let me
give you another coat when it's left off raining!"

105. The great event for the Northampton
shoemakers was **Boughton Green Fair**, which
formerly lasted nine and latterly five days (June
25th to June 29th). It was opened with ceremony
by the bailiff of the Lord of the Manor who, surrounded by his halberdiers, read to a great and
respectful gathering, the statute which commenced,
"This is to give notice to all traders and others
that Buckton, alias Boughton, Fair is to be held
on the day before Midsummer day and also upon
Midsummer day and the three next days after. In
the name of ——." Then followed the name of
the Lord of the Manor (in 1610 it was Earl
Strafford), and the various regulations, ending with,
"God save the King and the Right Honourable
William, Earl Strafford, lord of the ffair."

o

In the 17th, 18th and early 19th centuries nearly the whole country for twenty miles round poured in—and the green was big enough to hold all, seeing that it had an area of 17 acres. The shoemakers were there to a man, resigning themselves wholly to delight. Many would go when the fair was opened and stay night as well as day for the whole of the five days, while their stalls at home were as quiet as the grave. At one time anybody who hung a " welt or gard " (ivy bush) outside his booth was allowed to sell ale, hence the term " Bough Houses." Latterly, however, these houses were licensed, and four were allowed to Boughton village, in addition to *The Old Griffin* inn—the licences lasting five days. The word " welt "[1] (which we are now-a-days accustomed to associate with a boot) meant originally " to adorn with a border," and it could be used in connection not only with a tavern, but also with "a home spunne tale " which might put out a filament at any point.

On the first day the business proper, sales of horses and cattle, took place, and you wanted all your wits at that time in Northampton to dodge the horns of the bullocks that were driven through the streets northward. The Welsh ponies were hurried on by gypsies with old-fashioned whip-

---

[1] Nashe, Works, McKerrow's Ed., III., p. 157, speaks of the " welte of land " at Yarmouth, "a little tong of earth betwixt it and the wide maine." See p. 172.

stocks and red flags at the end of a fishing rod, to
the cry of :

> " Hi ! Hi ! Hurroo ! Hurroo !
> Here's a beauty from Waterloo ! "

—Waterloo being probably Rothwell Fair which
was just over.

On the second day the quality gave their
patronage, purchased at the stalls (in 1772 you
could buy men's boots there at 4s. 9d. a pair and
women's at 2s. 8d.), took part in the raffling,
looked in at the shows, treated their children to
gingerbread, and finished up with a ball at *The Red
Lion*, Northampton.

The third day was given over to matches of
single-stick and other sports. On the fourth there
was wrestling, and on the fifth, horse and foot
racing. According to a libellous declaration,
Boughton Fair was the only occasion in the year
on which a shoemaker put on his Sunday clothes.
In the Stuart period, Crispin having arrived at the
Green, accompanied by his sweetheart in Coventry
blue, treated her to a dinner of salmon and green
peas and bought her a pair of gloves, which she
received with a bashful modesty, and for which
she then and there requited him with " a kisse."
Then they would amuse themselves by " running
the Cobblers' Round "[1]—a Maze which consisted
of sunk paths surrounded by a green sward circle

---

[1] Also called " The Shepherd's Puzzle." It was in existence till about
40 years ago.

[Pl. 43]. It was really an appurtenance of Boughton Green Church, now in ruins. In pre-Reformation times the paths were covered with flints, and people who were ordered, by way of penance, to go to Jerusalem, were allowed, instead of visiting the Holy Land, to make their way on their hands and knees, a sight " pytyous to be seen," to the Jerusalem—that is to say, the centre —of the Maze. In later years the Maze became the scene of trials of skill, which consisted in running it from the outside to the centre in a given time without crossing the boundaries of the path. Crispin usually finished up the day with a glass at *The Old Griffin*, where he and his friends would " sing foolish songs, make great noyses," and play at cards ; and his companions, noticing how boisterous he had become, would comment, " He caps Bogie ! " [1] Late at night he would return home, by his own account, quite sober. Next morning, when he talked it over with the old folks, they would as likely as not say, " Get along wi yer ! That's nothing of a fair ! No doubt you had plenty of he-fools and she-fools. What ye really wanted was the old fools back again." If at the fair a man got too riotous, he might be made to sit " three dayes in the open market " with " a pot [empty, alas !] in his hand and a wryting on his

---

[1] In allusion to the Northants saying " He caps Bogie [an elf], Bogie capt Redcap [a red-haired hairy elf who lived in a cave or a well], Redcap capt Old Nick."

forehead" instead of a brow-band.   And so from
the rapture of the Cobblers' Round he drifted to
the mortification of the Cobblers' Pound.   The
fact that theft was not unknown at Boughton Fair
made possible the following lines:

LEATHER AND THREAD AND TEARS.
A Ballad of Boughton Fair.

With his beard in his bib, the stitchman wrought,
 And his lapstone, leather and awl;
But he sometimes brushed from his clouded face
 A tear—for the tears would fall.

And his hair on his drooping shoulders curled,
 And his band round his brow was tied;
And he said, " 'Tis the eve¹ of Boughton Fair;"
 And he stitched and he stitched, and sighed.

Then he said, " Come in!" to a tap.   She came;
 And her eyes they were borage blue,
And her hair like gold in the sunshine shone.
 " I have scoured, sir, the whole town through.

" So you'll measure me, please, for shoes—and shoes
 That will wear for years and years;
And you'll make me a pair that shall fit me well,
 Of leather and thread, and—tears."

" It is cruel to scoff," the stitchman said,
 " At sorrow that none can allay;
But inform me who, for the wonderful shoes,
 Will, when I have made them, pay ? "

" If it's pay you want, no pay you'll have;
 Yet you'll make, all the same, for me
The finest pair that you ever have made,
 For I read folks' thoughts," said she.

¹ The evening before June 24th (the first day of the Fair).

" 'Twas at Boughton Fair ten years ago
  That you lost what you prized the most."
And the stitchman's face turned white as death,
  Or the face of a sheeted ghost.

" And what did I lose ? " he trembling said.
  " Why you lost me, father, there ;
For I am the girl whom the gypsies stole
  From the stall at Boughton Fair."

And she flew to his arms, and stopped his words
  With kisses. At last he said,
" I shall make them of tears (but they're bound to be
    tears
  Of joy) and leather and thread."

And at dusk they wetted the candleblock,
  And his men their revels made ;
And a loving hand on the stitchman's arm
  While they sang and joked was laid.

And they raised a cup to Crispin old,
  And a cup to Crispin's heir ;
And a cup to the girl whom the gypsies stole
  From the stall at Boughton Fair.

And at dawn the happy stitchman wrought
  As he'd wrought all the ten black years ;
And the shoes were made of leather and thread,
  Of leather and thread, and—tears.

A terrible disturbance was caused at the fair
late at night on June 27th, 1826, by a gang of
ruffians led by **George Catherall** (Captain
Slash). Among the attractions of the fair was
Wombwell's menagerie, an account of the wonders
of which had been freely advertised as far
exceeding " anything the human Imagination can

suggest." It included a rhinoceros, eight lions, "a variety of Bengal leopards," a nilghau, a "noble male panther," and other animals, to say nothing of the birds. The idea of Catherall and his friends was to liberate the lions and, during the panic, to rob the dealers and showmen. Wombwell's, however, were too much for him, and after a fierce fight he and his gang were taken. Some of the show people had gone to bed, for it was late, but the noise of the blows and the shouting, and the report that the lions were loose, woke up everybody. Women screaming and children squealing scattered in all directions, and one woman, with a bag of money in each hand, ran in her nightdress the whole of the way—four miles— to Northampton. Catherall, whose chains were secured by a padlock " weighing two and a half pounds with three bolts," was hanged on July 21st.

106. A line must next be devoted to the terrible event which occurred at the fair on the evening of Wednesday, June 20th, 1850. The darkness which was fast coming on was broken here and there by the flare of a paraffin lamp; the clang and buzz of the day had ceased, for most of the revellers had left, and an uncanny silence had succeeded; when a William Higgins of Northampton saw near Buswell's booth, at the Boughton end of the green, an acquaintance of his—**Joseph Warren** —a powerfully built miller of 54 or thereabouts, loitering with a dark-looking, gypsy-like girl " in a green bonnet with a feather." He spoke to Warren, who wished him good night. At 10.30 a Robert Bilson caught sight of Warren and the girl. They were coming towards him, and he saw Warren kiss her. He looked hard at them and Warren "stared hard at him." Two men—one in a velveteen jacket, and the other—a very stout man—in a white slop—came up. They said something, Bilson couldn't hear what, " but they were swearing," and he believed that they "meditated some act of violence." He then saw the stout man stoop "near some spokes or fellies" as if watching. There was murder in his eyes.

A quarter of an hour later two policemen found " near the beech tree on the Boughton side of the green " the body of " an elderly gentleman," who turned out to be Joseph Warren. They lifted him, he sighed two or three times, and was gone. I do not know anything in the history of crime more harrowing than the mention in the bald police report, of these two or three sighs. On Thursday, the 27th, an inquest was held at *The Old Griffin;* it was proved that death had been caused by strangulation, and the verdict was one of wilful murder by a person or persons unknown. A reward of £100 was offered for their identification, but to this day nobody knows who murdered Joseph Warren. The effect on the fair of this tragedy was disastrous, the quality thenceforward kept away, and it never really recovered its popularity.

The incidents ate themselves into the public memory—the eerie, darkling scene, the heartlessness—the cold indifference—of the decoy, a mere girl "looking for him whom she sought," the judas kiss, the fatuity of the victim veering to his doom, the callousness of the murderers, the two or three sighs ; and, though seventy years are flown, when the anniversary of Boughton Green Fair comes round, the blood-curdling story is still told in cobbler circles to shuddering listeners. The decoy, a velvety yet terrible figure, has in every age had her victims. No chart of the Tender Passions —no Passionate Pilgrim's Progress—would be complete that omitted her. The spot where the murder took place used to be indicated by an inscription cut in the bark of a tree—"the fourth tree before you turn down to Boughton village "— a spot to be passed at twilight in clammy terror. The fair was abolished in 1916.

107. All Northampton naturally turned out at a hanging ; and the most sensational event of this kind was the execution, on August 13th, 1813, of **Huffy White** and Robert Kendall, for robbing the Leeds mail coach. How that robbery was carried out is to this day the puzzle of shoeland. Everything associated with the incident is mysterious. On Oct. 26th in the evening the coach on its journey southward reached Burton Latimer, where John Gardner, the guard, examined the mail-box, found everything in order, and locked it. At a

quarter past six, when the mail left Burton, he
took his place behind against the mail box, but
when going up Burton Hill he got over the coach
and seated himself by the coachman, William
Peach, a not unusual occurrence. On reaching the
windmill near Higham Ferrers he returned to his
seat, and while going through the town he blew
his horn. Arrived at *The Green Dragon*, he stooped
to open the box, when he found the lock
forced and all the bags gone! Suspicion fell on
two men, both notorious characters, Huffy White,
a stoutish man with a face deeply pitted with
the small pox, and his companion Robert
Kendall, of Wellingborough. The empty bags
were found one mile from the Finedon obelisk on
the Higham side, and the trial took place on July
28th. It was proved that both men had had in
their possession some of the contents of the bags,
and the death sentence was passed upon them. At
Fetter Street, on their way to the gallows which
stood on the race-course, the crowd was so great
that the cart was brought to a stand; but the most
unconcerned person on the occasion was White,
who sat on his coffin eating oranges and spitting
the pips at the people, whom from time to time he
considerately, in his squeaky voice, urged to have
patience. "Don't crush, dear friends," he said
mockingly, "there'll be no sport till I get there!"
From the distance came the ominous tolling of the
bell of St. Giles's. The chaplain read the prayers.

"Quick about it," interrupted White, "you're keeping the company waiting." In those days there was no drop, the condemned men were strung up, and the cart drawn from under them. The last public execution at Northampton was that of Elizabeth Pinckard, March 13th, 1852.

About this time *The Northampton Mercury* had (as now) some particularly smart reporters. It would be hard, for example, to improve on the following comment[1] made upon a shoemaker, Samuel Chater, who was charged with being drunk and disorderly:

> "*Cum in arce celebri Bacchus dominatur.*[2]
> Wonderful the uproar is made by Mr. Chater."

"Seven shillings."

108. Many of the Northampton stitchmen were musicians, and there was never any difficulty in providing waits, whether to perform in the snow on Christmas Eve or to meet the judge at Assize time. On the latter occasion they wore long black gowns; two played on violins, one on the hautboy, and another on a "whip and dab" (tabor and pipe).

Every old stitchman had a store of **Songs and Ballads.** We have seen how Hoby the Great[3]

[1] July 13th, 1850.

[2] "When Bacchus has his fling in his famous temple"; or suppose we say, putting it into rhyme:

> "When Bacchus in his temple soaks, a little later
> Wonderful the uproar is made by Mr. Chater."

[3] Page 163.

won the battle of Vittoria (June 21st, 1813). A ballad of the period recounts how, owing to the prowess of **Bob of Kidderminster**, a shoe-maker's apprentice, San Sebastian was on August 31st of the same year taken by storm. The words were sent me by Mr. W. Steward, of Bedford, who committed them to memory when a boy:

BOB OF KIDDERMINSTER.

I'm a prentice boy; my name is Bob—
    The tale I've oft related.
They bound me to a dirty snob—
    A trade I always hated;
The lapstone I did daily shun,
    The sight of a stirrup alarmed me,
So off I run with my master's gun
    To enlist in the Spanish army.

Some balls of wax, with hemp and tacks,
    I thought might be required
To give my foes some precious whacks
    When all the shots were fired;
In battle did I mock their tricks,
    And some of their nobs I twisted;
Thinks I, I'll make them rue the day
    That a prentice boy enlisted.

Oh, General Evans came up to me.
    Says he, " Bob, show no quarter;
You're a valiant man, I plainly see;
    And you shall marry my daughter."
Says I, " The battle will soon be done!"
    Their ramparts then I dashed on,
And with this gun the battle won,
    At the siege of San Sebastian.

Let us hope that when Bob, home again, ventured to claim Miss Evans, the general did not pucker his brows and try to change the conversation.

The reference to the stirrup reminds us that it was used sometimes as a strap for inflicting punishment, and the cobbler when in a dark humour did not lay it on lightly. The Scotch shoemakers favoured the old Border song, " Up wi' the souters of Selkirk," which is said to commemorate the part which this shoemaking town (it made single-soled brogues) took at the battle of Flodden. On the occasion of the conferring of the freedom of the burgh, four or five bristles used to be attached to the seal of the burgess's ticket, and he was expected to dip them in his wine and pass them through his mouth in token of respect for the souters of Selkirk.

Deloney's verses[1] and Richard Rigby's song in praise of the Gentle Craft[2] were favourites everywhere, and the ditty, " To all the good yeomen of the Gentle Craft,"[3] also had its turn. The last, after setting out the virtues of the shoemakers, their charity, love of sport and freedom from malice, runs :—

> " Thus in joy they spent their days
> With pleasant songs and roundelays,
> And God did bless them with content,
> Sufficient for them always sent;

[1] See pp. 49, 50 and 54.

[2] Printed in Mr. S. S. Campion's *History of Ye Gentle Craft* (1876), p. 51.   [3] Ibid, p. 53.

> And never yet did any know
> A shoemaker a begging go."

Books of songs also from time to time appeared, as for example, *The Shoemakers' Garland containing Six Excellent New Songs*, and including "Bold Crispin's Ramble " and " Sweet Poll of Plymouth." At a later period the compositions of Thomas Cooper[1] and Ebenezer Elliott took the place of the old ditties, while still later could be heard at the bench snatches of Whittier's verses, " The Shoemakers." At Raunds they sang " Jim Rayner," but Kettering preferred " The Song of the Mouse " :

> " The little gray fellow
> Who comes in the night,
> Without any light,
> To pilfer our paste and tallow."

Of Metrical Broadsides relating to the shoemaker there are very many. Thus in the Stewart Beattie Collection, Northampton Public Library, are preserved, " The Cunning Cobbler," " Dick Darling the Cobbler," " The Jolly old Cobbler," " The Drunken Cobbler's Wife " and " The Blinkeyed Cobbler." Of these the last, which tells how a knight's son fell in love with Sue, one of his father's maids, and, by the help of a trick, married her, is far away the best.

109. To several **Shoemakers' Proverbs and Sayings** of Greek or Latin origin mention has

[1] See p. 166.

already been made. Others from the Latin are, " Half a shoe fits nobody," and " To have the right foot in the shoe, the left in the bath "—that is, to be neutral in a controversy. From France we get, " Better bare feet than no feet," " Do not laugh at the ill-shod, your own shoes may wear out." Rabelais offers us " As hollow as St. Benet's boots ; " Villon, in his *Greater Testament*, 1461, bequeaths unto the Seneschal, " The right of shoeing ducks and geese," an allusion to an old saying which meant, " to waste time in trifling." " To shoe the gray goose "—to undertake a difficult or impossible task — has reference to a ridiculous libel on Bertha, the beautiful wife of King Robert of France. She and her husband having offended the Church of Rome (A.D. 995) were thenceforward merely carrion ; and as a little bit of extra ecclesiastic revenge, it was spread abroad that she had a goose's foot, while her statue with this distinction was set over the porches of several French churches. At Piddinghoe (Sussex) they shoe magpies. In what language originated the ancient saying, " Waiting for a dead man's shoes," it would be difficult to say. A young man, it seems, was advised to marry a woman of sixty-five, who would leave him all her property. He declined on the ground that she was not old enough. From Spain comes, " In a field of melons tie not thy shoe." Scotland offers :

" Mair whistle than woo' [wool],
    As the souter said when he sheared the soo [sow],"[1]

" The man of the cuarans[2] must rise an hour
before the man of the shoes " (that is, the poor
man must get up earlier than the rich man), and
" Beginning with a shoe may end with a cuaran "
(if you are so extravagant as to wear shoes when
you start in life, it is possible that in old age you
will be reduced to wearing cuarans).

Of genuinely English proverbs and sayings
among the best are, " As right as a bristle,"
applied to anything that is dexterously attached ;
"There's nothing like leather"; Nicholas Breton's,
" Over shoes, over boots " [In for a penny, in for
a pound]; Robert Greene's, " It is hard to hide
Vulcan's polt foot with putting on a straight
shoe," and " The cobbler to his clout "; Thomas
Nashe's, " 'Tis as good to go in cut-fingered
pumps as corke soles, if we wear Cornish
diamonds," and " To put one's foote in another
man's boote"; Stephen Gosson's, " It is not a
softe shooe that healeth the Gowte "; and Deloney's, " To take him down in his wedding shoes "
(said of a wife who determines to keep her husband
under from the very first).   Thomas Heywood
puts the same idea the other way about :

---

[1] Allan Ramsay's Scottish Proverbs. "Souter" [shoemaker] also occurs
in old English authors, e.g., Piers Plowman.   The resemblance of the
word to the Latin *Sutor* is perhaps a curious accident.
[2] See pp. 57, 100 and 101.

Plate 33

TOKEN ISSUED BY WILLIAM ALLEN. See p. 153.

JOHN ASKHAM,

Wellingborough Poet. 1825—1894. See p. 170.

GAMBADOES, The Museum, Northampton.

See p. 118.

Photo Coldham & Son, Northampton.

Plate 34

THOMAS HOLCROFT, Novelist.
1745—1809. See p. 151.

JAKOB BOEHME, Mystic. 1575—1624.
See p. 119.

THOMAS HARDY, Politician. 1751—1832.
See p. 151.

THOMAS OLIVERS.
Hymn-writer and Pamphleteer.
1725—1799. See p. 146.

" In a good time that man both wins and woos,
That takes his wife down in her wedding shoes."

Isaac Bickerstaff (*Love in a Village*) gives us " A hale cobbler is better than a sick king "; George Eliot, " 'Tis hard to tell which is Old Harry when everybody's got boots on "; and I have heard my mother speak of " The pride of the cobbler's dog."

Boys are fond of doing " the cobbler's knock " (tapping the ice with one foot while sliding with the other), a diversion sometimes called " shoeing the cobbler." A few days ago, Mr. Alfred Ager of Northampton, during a game of billiards, noticing that his opponent was getting ahead with the score, said, " My word! he's got his hand leather on ! "— to wit, " He means business." The term, " He's down on his uppers " (out of luck for the time being), refers, of course, to a shoe the sole of which is so much worn that the portion of the upper under the insole is exposed. " He's down on his split lifts "[1] has the same meaning—having reference to the heel being worn down. At Olney, when a man cannot afford a horse and trap, he has to " Go shoe-cart " (on foot). To observe that a person " will die in his shoes " means that he will be hanged. When George Catherall stood on the scaffold at Northampton (see p. 199) he, bearing this saying is mind, pulled off his shoes and threw them among the people, but, as we have

[1] The split lifts are the portion of the heel nearest to the foot.

P

seen, he was hanged all the same. From Thomas
Fuller, the Aldwinkle divine, comes: " Mock not a
cobbler his black thumbs."   There is a saying in
Lancashire, " Clog to clog in three generations,"
and the swiftness with which families have gone
up and come down again in the shoe trade is
common knowledge. A villager with his clicking
knife rolled up in his apron tramps into a shoe
town and, after working for a while under a master,
takes a poky shop in a back street and employs a
few hands. The wheel of Fortune turns. In a
few years he is at the head of a huge factory,
and does business to the tune of thousands
a year. The wheel turns again. Something has
gone wrong, and in less than no time he is
back again in the little poky shop in the narrow
street, waiting for new developments. Even
if all goes well to the end, there is the danger
that the second generation, having come too
quickly into opulence, may misuse it, with the
result that the third generation is back where the
first started. Various theories have been put forward to account for this condition of affairs, but I
think the matter used to hinge on lack of education, with the result that the second generation
used its leisure improperly. Now, however, that
education is compulsory, the family that has
prospered is less likely to misuse its opportunities,
and the saying, " Clog to clog in three generations," may lose its force.

Why that vain-glorious monarch, Nebuchad-nezzar, should be mixed up with leather I do not know, unless it is because "shoes" happens to rhyme with "Jews." However, when the shoes for which he exchanged his wife began to wear (as shoes not made in Great Britain sometimes will), Nebuchadnezzar began to—repent of his bargain. A shoemaker on being asked why he remained at work while his wife was being buried replied, "Business before pleasure."

110. The trade has received particular attention from writers of **Epitaphs**. Callous would be the man who could refuse a tear for the cobbler who died of a fever and was made to say:

> "I waxed young, I waxed old,
> I waxed hot, I waxed cold."

If Dean Swift's epitaph on John Partridge, "cobbler and star-gazer," has been over-rated, and if Byron's punning lines on Joseph Blackett, "late poet and shoemaker," (May 16th, 1811) are piti-fully poor, on the other hand a really smart contribution of the kind appeared in *St. Crispin*, Vol. IV., p. 65, on "William Nott, of Bedlam in Ludlow," the last stanza of which runs:

> "He was *Nott* born of womankind,
> And so it may be said,
> Although within this grave he lies,
> We know he is *Nott* dead."

In Gorki's *Reminiscences of Leo N. Tolstoi* occurs

an epitaphal verse which I make bold to render as follows :

" Beneath this grey stone reclines Ivan, a tanner
Who wetted his hides in the orthodox manner;
Though he worked and was honest the whole of his life,
Yet he died, and his business he left to his wife.
It happened, dear friends, upon Passion Week Saturday;
Since you may go next, give a thought to your latter day."

Commenting upon this epitaph Tolstoi said, in his charitable way, " In human stupidity, when it is not malicious, there is something very touching, even beautiful."

It was formerly the custom, when a person of position died, to fix over his house a Hatchment, which was subsequently re-erected in the parish church. I have never heard of a shoemaker being thus honoured, but in the Dutch Church at the corner of Fulton and William streets, New York, once hung, and perhaps still hangs, the hatchment of J. Herbendinck, a tanner (ob. 1772), who was one of the original purchasers of Shoemakers' Pasture, a plot sold to the tanners of New York with a view to getting them outside the city gates.

111. Superstitions concerning the shoe are numerous. Irish leprechauns made shoes by glow-worm light. In Islay, Scotland, the elves, who " sing songs with a marvellous olden and magical melody," give trouble ; and unless you burn old shoes they may entice pretty girls away

and carry them under the tumbling sea to sunless
caves hung with blobby weeds, the haunt of the
mer-man and the snorting sea-cow. The Norfolk
girls say that if you put a clover leaf in your shoe
the next man you meet will be your husband, or
somebody bearing the same name; and their Staffordshire sister insists that if her shoe comes
untied her lover is thinking about her, which is
very likely. Deloney's contribution is "whoever
puts but six leaves of mugwort into his shoes shall
never be weary, though he travel thirtie or fortie
miles on foot in an afternoon." The same belief
prevailed in Germany where, indeed, the name for
mug-wort is *Beifuss* (near-foot). Fern seed similarly
used enables a man to know where treasure is hid
in the ground. Old boots and shoes are thrown
for luck after newly-married couples. In rural
districts where the boots are of the hobnail variety
the bridegroom is certainly lucky if they miss him.

In the north of Argyle is a fantastic mountain,
Ben Arthur or the Cobbler (2,863 feet in height)
—a giant figure who, with head in the clouds,
mends his shoes in the sight of all Scotland. In
Basedale,[1] Yorkshire, is a great boulder called the
Giant's Lapstone, the property of an enormous
aerial cobbler, which had the power of promptly
convicting any maiden who had deviated from the
path of virtue. If touched by the foot of a true

---

[1] Five miles from Battersby Station, on the Whitby Line. **Sometimes**
spelt Baysdale.

maiden, the hole, it is said, would contract. A newly married woman could, by invoking the phantom and tapping the stone with a hammer, obtain from him almost any favour she desired.

In ancient Greece men involved in a hazardous enterprise often went with the right foot shod and the left bare. An oracle warned King Pelias to beware of the man with one sandal, and when Jason arrived in this predicament the monarch recognised his doom. Perseus wore only one shoe when he went to cut off the Gorgon's head. In short, one shoe off and one shoe on meant death or victory. A Highland form of divination at Hallowe'en is to throw a shoe over the house. The way the toe points when it reaches the ground is the direction you are destined to travel before long. The soles of Arab sandals are made from a number of small pieces of leather. Mr. Roland Gorbold, who was with the British forces in the East during the war of 1914—1918, was told that if the sole of a shoe was made in one piece, one of the shoemaker's sons would die; but though he insisted on whole soles, he " did not notice any undue mortality among the shoemakers' children."

112. Northampton was the cradle of the 18th century **Chap-book**, the first of these fascinating little volumes, *The Force of Nature, or the Loves of Hippolite and Dorinda*, having been issued in August, 1720, by Robert Raikes and William Dicey, founders and editors of *The Northampton Mercury*.

Subsequently the Diceys (William and Cluer) settled in London, and from their warehouses were issued the majority of the chap-books of the 18th century—the special period for this kind of publication. The most popular of the chap-books relating to the shoe were the histories, under various titles, of Saints Hugh, Crispin and Crispianus, all of which were founded on the narratives of Thomas Deloney. The next in popularity was *The Entertaining History of the King and the Cobler*, which tells how Henry VIII., who liked to go about in disguise, called late at night on a cobbler in the Strand, and asked him to "set a heel." They then adjourn to a neighbouring tavern, where the cobbler sings merry catches, at which the king, who calls himself Harry Tudor, laughs heartily. On returning to the cobbler's house, with a view to "nappy ale," they speak softly for fear of disturbing the cobbler's wife Joan, "for," says the cobbler, "if she awake she will certainly make both our ears to ring again." After the king, who says he is in the royal service, has invited his new friend to court, where they get merry in the palace cellar, he and the queen, both in disguise, visit the tavern in the Strand and invite the cobbler and his Joan to dine with them. Next day the cobbler is brought before the king, who is seated on his throne. "You are to die," says the king to the trembling wretch, "but I will allow you the favour of choosing your own death."

" Why then," said the cobbler, taking heart,
" let me die the death of my grandfather."

" How was that ? " asked the king.

" May it please your majesty, on a death-bed of
old age."

The king then alters his tone and, seeing how
" innocently merry " the cobbler was, he settled
an annuity on him.

Other popular chap-books were those of *The
Wandering Jew*[1] and *The Witch of the Woodlands*,
or " The Cobler's New Translation."   The latter
is the story of the adventures of one Robin, who
lived near Romney [Pl. 40].   After misconducting
himself in his native town he made for London,
but got lost in the woodland.   An old witch gave
him lodging, and while in her cottage he heard the
terrifying words, " uttered three several times "—
" Robin the cobler is mine ! "   The old harridan
then went out, but returned after a while with a
bear—her familiar—at her heels; and accompanying
her were three other shrivelled, gibbering hags, one
with a wolf, one with a cat, and another with a
large knife.   The old women turned Robin first
into a hare when they, as dogs, hunted him; and
afterwards into a horse, when all four, who were as
clever riders as M. De Rougemont, got on to his
back and rode him over mountains and through
rivers and ponds.   After various other adventures,
Robin falls in with an old blind beggar who, on

[1] See p. 38.

learning that he is " a gentleman born," which of course he is, being a " king's son," entertains him at an ale-house and eventually leaves him a fortune.

In *Cobleriana* or *The Cobler's Medley* (2 vols., 1768)—a collection of chap-books—is the following anecdote : " A cobbler at a club held at the Bull's Head in the Borough said to another cobbler, ' Don't you pretend to talk about *Religion* . . I'll lay you a guinea you can't say the Lord's Prayer.' 'Done,' said Tom; up he gets, and with an audible voice repeats the Creed from the Beginning to the End without missing a single Word ; at which the other lifted up his hands with great surprise. ' Well,' said he, ' most amazing indeed ; I never thought he could have done it ; but I fairly own I have lost my wager,' and the other cobblers of the party were equally astonished." Among the chap-books of later date the best known is *The Two Shoemakers* by Hannah More.

113. When Christianity triumphed, the old deities, according to mediæval legend, concealed themselves under various disguises on earth. Two modern writers have allowed the lightnings of their genius to play about this subject—Heine and Pater. According to Heine, **Apollo** was reduced to tending sheep in Lower Austria, and Pater depicts him as a " hireling at will " in an old monastery in Picardy, where history repeats itself and he kills accidentally, at a game of quoits, a handsome youth named Hyacinthus, after which he disappears. Whether or not some merry wind subsequently blew him to old England, perusal of the following lines may reveal :

THE COBBLER AND THE LIKELY BOR.[1]
A NORFOLK BALLAD.

A cobbler once in days of yore
Sat musing at his cottage door.

He liked to read old books, he said,
And then to ponder what he'd read.

The day was done, the light was dim ;
A likely bor accosted him—

A stranger, whose gold hair about
His shoulders fell, held, shyly, out

A broken lyre.   A string too tight
Had snapped.   There were no shops in sight.

" Then I can help yeow, cock," said he
[The cobbler]; " Hand yer lyre tew me.

" I tew can play and sometimes sing ;"
And in the lyre he fixed a string.

" How much ? " " How much ? Why, nawthin', brother ;
We're sent on airth tew help each other."

A year flew by, and illness laid
The cobbler low; he lost his trade.

In debt he slid ; his all was spent,
He'd naught for food and less for rent.

He sighed ; then someone tapped the door,
And in there stept the likely bor.

" Drink this," he said ; " I can't explain,
But drink, and yeow'll be well again."

[1] Handsome young man.

Then through the lattice hopped a crow[1]
And dropped a purse of gold, and lo!

Around the stranger's head there grew
A nimbus of cerulean blue.[2]

His heart too full, the cobbler tried
To blurt his thanks. The bor replied

[And vanished], " Why, it's nawthin', brother;
We're sent on airth tew help each other."

It will be noticed that, although not Norfolk born, Apollo had mastered the dialect. But a god can do anything.

Not only do the old deities sometimes come to life again, other notabilities also occasionally return. One day some shoemen near Soissons, who had quarrelled with their employers, downed tools, and sauntered out into the fields. As the principal workman was strolling by the small river Vesle he was, to his surprise, suddenly touched on the shoulder by a stranger in antique dress, round whose neck was a blood-red circle.

" Out of work, friend ? " enquired the stranger.

" No ! " replied the shoemaker, sulkily.

" Come, tell me your trouble," followed the stranger ; " I am in the same trade, and may be able to help you."

The shoemaker explained his grievance, where-upon the stranger took him by the arm and led him along the stream until they came in sight of

[1] See p. 1.   [2] See p. 34.

a tree trunk laid for crossing. Two goats on the tree were approaching each other.

" Here's fun ! " said the shoemaker, " neither will give way, and each will be over in the water."

That, however, did not happen, for one goat lay down on the tree, and the other stepped gently over him.

" My son," said St. Crispin (for it was he, and the red ring showed where the axe had been), " if you would safely journey through life, forget not this lesson." With that the holy man vanished, and the shoemaker and his comrades decided to return at once to their benches. Of course it was the *French* St. Crispin. Had it been the *English* saint, who died snugly in bed, and had the event happened near the Nen instead of the Vesle, the red ring would not have been there. The lesson, however, would have been the same.

114. It was the enthusiasm of the Norfolk shoemakers for **Birds** that brought about the great trade in the Norwich canary. In years past a whole side of a factory would be occupied with cages. The Northampton man is also an ardent bird lover, and he speaks of his feathered friends almost as though they were kinsfolk. Thus the crow is Royston Dick, the woodpecker Jack Ickle, the starling Jacob, the raven Ralph ; and he likes to have a bullfinch or a goldspink (goldfinch) singing above his head while he is at work. Mr.

John Labrum of Grendon told me of a shoemaker who taught a bullfinch a whole song.

To **Animals** the shoemakers are scarcely less attached. Thomas Harris of Olney kept at one time quite a menagerie, which included a leveret which he taught to sit up on its hind legs and play a tin whistle. Mr. E. J. Dawson, a Castleton (Lancashire) shoemaker, obtained a great name in the Fancy for his beautifully marked tortoise and white cavies, two of which, Elektra and Erl King, defeated all rivals at the Shows. He is now a successful breeder of Chow-chow dogs. Mr. J. R. Warkup of Hull was also a breeder of prize cavies; and Mr. Robert Vicary of Newton Abbott, Devonshire, a tanner, is a famous breeder and judge of fox terriers. Mr. Dowling, one of the editors of *Bell's Life*, knew a poor shoemaker who bred a spaniel of surpassing excellence, and although the man was poor, earning only 14s. a week, he had refused one hundred guineas for it.

The association of shoes with **Flowers** is also a pleasant subject. One thinks first of the calceolaria (Latin, *calceolus*, a little shoe). Very charming too is the name, The Lady's Slipper, given to a lovely little orchis found in moist woods in the north of England; and pray notice that it is not *A* Lady's Slipper, but *The* Lady's Slipper—the lady who is above all other ladies—Kupris (Venus) the goddess of love, as is shown by the Latin name *Cypripedium Calceolus*. The Sandal-wort or

Limp-leaved Toad-flax (*Thesium linophyllum*) is also British. The Sandal Flower (*Pedilanthus*) grows in India. With the juice of the Shoe Flower (*Hibiscus Rosa Sinensis*) the Chinese ladies blacken not only their shoes but also their eyebrows.

115. There are fine collections of shoes in the Louvre and in the Cluny **Museums** (Jacquemart's Collection), Paris. In the Victoria and Albert Museum is a collection of snuff-boxes in the form of shoes, and in the Northampton Museum has been arranged an old stitchman's shop with tools, &c., all complete, the work of the late Mr. T. J. George, with the help of Mr. G. G. Jackson, of Great Billing. A photograph of it with four veterans at work or in conversation appeared in *The Northampton Independent*, Oct. 11th, 1913. When the singer Marchesi was in the height of his popularity (1816), the women of Milan wore his portrait as a clasp to each shoe.

Formerly Sussex was famous for its pottery, which included statuettes, one pair (nine inches high) representing a cobbler and his wife (illustration in *The Connoisseur*, August, 1909). The cobbler has a hammer in his hand and a lapstone on his knee, and his wife is reading a book, presumably a Bible.

The Chinese are adepts at hard stone cutting, and in *The Studio*, Feb. 15th, 1913, is a picture of a clear agate, cut by one of them to represent a boy carrying shoes.

CHAPTER IX.

MACHINERY AND THE FOOTWEAR PRESS.

116. THE word machine was in common use in the shoe trade long before anything in the nature of a machine as we now understand it was even contemplated. "The London stitchmen," says Devlin, "used a spindle thread covered with a sort of perfectly white wax which had the name of machine " — a very strange appellation — "**a Haporth of Machine.**" Among the earliest real machines were those invented by Isaac Brunel about 1810,[1] for the purpose of making Army and Navy shoes. Nails of different lengths for uniting the parts of the shoe were used, nothing being sewn except the three pieces of which the upper leather was composed, namely the vamp and the two quarters. The cutting out was performed by large steel punches; the holes to receive the nails were made with great regularity, and the nails, which were shaped by the same machine, were " dropped with unerring certainty into their places, and driven in at one blow."

The year 1844 was marked by the appearance of

---

[1] David Mead Randolph took out a patent for making rivetted boots in 1809. Brunel's machine was patented August 2nd, 1810.

Poems by E. Barrett (Mrs. Browning) which contained a noble outburst that ultimately led to the
emancipation of young children, who for long had
been employed in the shoe and other factories. It
was about this time, too, that the industry under-
went a great development owing to the opening of
the **Export Trade,** one of the principal markets
being that of South America.

The first of the famous **Goodyear Family** of
American inventors, Charles Goodyear, was at
work in the early part of the 19th century on one
of the greatest commercial gifts to mankind—the
vulcanization of rubber, without which the gum is
worthless.   His son Charles, after years of study,
invented and perfected the apparatus that was to
make shoes by machinery, and Nelson Goodyear
(3rd generation) brought additional wizardry to
bear upon the shoe.   Indeed, one recalls almost
with awe the rapidity of the inventive genius of
this marvellous family.   In the twinkling of an
eye, as it were, they one after another, and again
and again, entirely changed the current of, and
gave new impetus to, the industry with which their
name will for ever be associated.

117. By 1857 the use of the **Closing Machine**
was becoming general,[1] and at first intense bitterness of feeling was created among the operatives.
Demonstrations of anti-machine shoemakers took

[1] The first machine in England was erected in the Kendal factory of
Somervell Bros.   The machine was introduced into Norwich by Mr.
Edwin Bostock, uncle of Mr. Frederick Bostock of Northampton.

Plate 35

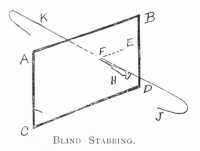

BLIND STABBING.

Sketch by Mr. Frank Plucknett.

See p. 173.

A, B, C, D, the leather.

E, F, the line of stabbing.

H, the awl.

J, the thread on the right hand.

K, the thread on the left hand.

When the awl is withdrawn the workman does not look for the hole on the left hand side, he works like a blind man—by feeling; for while the awl is still in the leather he feels for its position, and has the bristle ready to put in the hole as the awl is withdrawn. The hair is the hog's bristle which is fastened to the end of the thread in lieu of a needle. Both threads, the one from the right hand and the other from the left, pass through each hole.

THE COBBLER OF BAGHDAD. See p. 85.

Illustration to "The Arab Shoemakers of Baghdad," by Mr. Roland Gorbold, *Footwear Organiser*, Oct., 1919, p. 404.

Photo Mr. Roland Gorbold.

BEARD-IN-BIB (Stitchman with hand-leather and brainband).
See pp. 176 and 178.

Plate 36

John Bagford, Antiquary. 1657—1716.

See p. 136.

Johann Joachim Winckelmann,
Critic and Historian of Greek Art. 1717—1768.

See p. 148.

place all over the country. At a gathering, with banners and bands, on Northampton Market Place (August 25th, 1858), inflammatory speeches were made to crowds of sympathisers. There was to be no compromise—all the machines were to be destroyed; and the men of Kendal and other centres were equally furious. Nothing daunted, however, the manufacturers decided at all hazards to use the machine, being convinced that without it they could not possibly compete in the trade. " The will to do anything," says Shaw, " can and does, at a certain pitch of intensity set up by conviction of its necessity, create and organise new tissue to do it with." Evidently in this instance the new tissue came into being. The answer to their resolution was a strike (March 9th, 1859), during which hundreds of work-people left the town, and much of the trade drifted to Leicester, where the feeling against machinery was less acute. There were also strikes at Stafford and elsewhere. The Northampton strike collapsed in July; within a few months closing machines were in general use all over the country; and gradually the animus against the innovation subsided. The strike at Stafford lasted for years. Indeed it never was formally abandoned. It petered out.

In many towns the Truck System was then in general use—an evil combated by the incisive pen of Disraeli (in *Sybil*). At Daventry all the firms had adopted it, with the exception of Stead and

Q

Simpson.   Mr. Simpson, who married Mr. Stead's sister, had a polite and urbane manner, but Mr. Stead was a great, rough, uncouth Yorkshireman, who loved to tell of his early struggles.   " I was apprenticed to a country shoemaker," he used to say, " for seven years, and I had a penny a week for cleaning the shoes of a lodger.   In after years this lodger on meeting me said, ' Mr. Stead, you're a big man now.   I remember when you cleaned my boots ! '   ' Yes,' said I, ' and didn't I earn the money !   Fourteen pairs a week for a penny !'"

Following the introduction of the closing machine, there was soon established a new branch of the industry—the **Closing Trade**, the pioneer being Mr. Richard Roe, who had previously been in the employ of (Sir) M. P. Manfield.   The general trade was good, and three wars in quick succession—the Austrian-Italian (1859), the Civil in America (1862), and the Franco-German (1870) —gave it a great impetus.

At the time these changes were taking place only hand-sewn work was done at **Olney.**   The employer, Thomas Harris, of No. 2 High Street, did a good general business, and among his many hands were J. Ruffhead, Joe and Harry Neudegg, Alfred Peters and " Gaffer " and Tom Knight (father and son).   Shoemaking, however, did not become the staple industry of Olney till after the Great Fire of 1854, when the northern half of the town was entirely destroyed.   On June 30th, 1864,

Thomas Harris's house was burnt down. (It was Cherry Fair day, and he and all his work-people were on the Market Place.) Among the many rare things destroyed was a Devil among the Tailors[1] board [Pl. 41], with which the work-people used to amuse themselves during the dinner-hour. At Kislingbury the sport was battledoor and shuttle-cock, the battledoor being a piece of stout leather.

The **Blake Sewer**, introduced in 1859, began to make headway in 1861. It sews right through the inner and outer sole, and at the same time catches the edges of the upper leather and the lining between them, but the toe part was still, for a time, done by hand. When the machine was perfected, Machine Sewers to the Trade sprang up, obliging the employer to find workmen for his lasters; and most riveters (who require iron lasts and a firm stand) went into the factories.

The first sewing machine worked in Olney was sent by Robinson of Kettering to Thomas Harris, and an instructress from Northampton accom-panied it. One of Harris's workers, a very beautiful girl, attracted the attention of an Olney gentleman who resolved to marry her, notwithstanding the objections of his family. One day he came upon one of his sisters when she was giving herself a

---

[1] The "Tailors" were toy skittles. At the end of the board was a peg (the Devil) shaped like a mushroom. The whipcord string, which had a button at the end to prevent it from slipping through the hand, was wound round the peg. The peg was held firm by placing the thumb of the left hand on the top and the forefinger in front. The string was then drawn sharply but evenly with the right hand, when the peg would spin up among the skittles.

few finishing touches at the glass. " Ah," he said,
" you may put on ribbons, you may prink and you
may paint, but you'll never come up to my Sal ! "
" Y-o-u-r-e Sal ! " she replied, scornfully—the first
word being long drawn out. It is only fair, however, to the sister to mention that she too had
attractions; and it must be added that the marriage eventually came off, to the entire satisfaction
of the Olney people, who dearly love a romance.

118. The village of **Turvey,** Beds, was at this
time still[1] a shoemaking centre. Mr. George
Wooding, who resides there, tells me that he and
his fellow workmen made Army boots, and that he
often walked to Wellingborough (distant 14 miles)
with his bag of work. I saw him, March, 1921, at
his little low bench, with its kit and candle holder
at the side for heating his iron ; and he spoke
with enthusiasm of the old days and of his watch-
dog—a jackdaw which assumed control of his
household, called him familiarly " George," and
chased away intrusive children by hopping after
them and pecking their legs.

Mr. S. R. Owen of Olney " gave out " for the
Northampton firm, Turner, Hyde and Co., bag or
Hamper Work, and matters were managed
similarly in all the towns and villages round. The
carrier, John Boswell (predecessor of the late
George Field), used to take the work to Northampton three times a week, and return with the pay

[1] See p. 108.

and more leather. Boswell had started with a very ramshackle turn-out, but later he grew bold, and about 1860 ventured on a large new van which was built by John Negus, painted sulphur colour, and placed for three days on the Market Place for all the world to admire. Indeed, nothing at the time was talked about but Boswell's new van.

119. A little later came a tremendous revolution in the industry—the introduction of the **Hand Riveted Boot**, an event scarcely second in importance to that of the advent of the Machine Shoe. The Riveted Boot as we now know it was first introduced into this country (for Brunel's riveting was of a very tentative and experimental kind) by Derham Brothers in the late fifties. A metal mostly composed of zinc was first used, and copper and subsequently steel and brass tacks (which are the best of all) followed. In 1860 Crick of Leicester began to attach soles with French rivets. The earliest to make riveted shoes in Northampton were Mason and Co., a London firm, who had a branch business in Newland. John Field,[1] from whom I had this information, worked as a youth of 18 for Mason's and did riveting there. Other firms followed, and among them Turner, Hyde and Co., who in 1861 had a tremendous order for riveted goods. Much of their business was done with the Southern States

---

[1] In 1854, as a boy of 14, Field had worked for Joseph Barker of Olney, who represented Muddiman's of Northampton.

by means of blockade running. If one cargo in
three reached its destination the profits were handsome. As a result of the rush of work, one of
their agents, Abram Whitmee, brought a Blucher
boot in the rough to Olney and persuaded S. R.
Owen to take up riveting. The first pair of
riveted boots made in the town was finished in
the shoemaker's workshop in his garden at the
back of 94 High Street. Owen made one boot
and John Field (who had left Northampton to
become Owen's foreman) the fellow to it. Iron
lasts, procured in quantity, then took the place of
the old wooden lasts; and on Field devolved the
duty of teaching, but within a little while there
were other instructors. The **Colt,**[1] as the learner
was called, was initiated with religious solemnity;
that is to say, he lifted his right leg and the sole
of his boot was struck with a strip of leather. The
fee—the price of a gallon of beer—having been
paid and his health drunk, the ceremony of "shoeing the colt" was considered to have been satis-
factorily performed. I have often watched the
riveters at work, with their mouths full of rivets,
but I used to be afraid to speak to them lest in
replying to a question they might swallow, and so
waste, I knew not what weight of marketable
metal. Subsequently John Field left Mr. Owen in
order to serve under his brother-in-law, Mr.

[1] This term was used in the time of Queen Elizabeth : " He shall forfeit
and pay a pottle of wine, or be counted for a colt."—*Deloney*, Ed. by
F. O. Mann, p. 89.

Sheffield (Ward and Sheffield), of Earls Barton.

120. The **Riveting Machine**[1] in its perfected form was by this time in general use. The **Screw Machine** appeared in 1876. Rivets may work loose in the leather and fall out, or work in and wound the foot, but the screw cannot work either in or out. It is automatically cut off to the exact length required, the wire, whether of iron or brass, being supplied in rolls with the screw thread cut. To the rivet succeeded the sprig, and to the sprig the peg.[2]

Hand-pegging[3]—that is, the attaching of the bottoms of boots to the uppers by means of wooden pegs—was introduced into England from America about 1851 by Mr. Josiah Walker (ob. 1904), head of the firm of Walker and Abbott, Earls Barton, who also became famous as the largest makers of sea-boots in the world. Olney in particular obtained a name for efficiency in this kind of work, and there was a saying in the trade, "All Olney men can peg," but it could have been said truthfully also, "All Olney boys," for regiments of them might have been seen working together, each on his little stool so as to be high enough for the bench. The Mills Turn-shoe

---

[1] See p. 223.

[2] Rivets have heads, sprigs have not. Pegs will not hold in common leather.

[3] Pegging is now done by machinery. The pegging machine was introduced into Northampton by Mr. Thomas Tebbutt, father of Mr. G. M. Tebbutt, J.P. (see p. 174). Improvements were made by various persons, and finally Sturtevant invented the Peg-Wood Strip.

Machine was introduced into this country in 1868, and the Goodyear Welter and the Goodyear Chain-stitcher in 1872.

121. The Franco-German **War of 1870** gave, as already remarked, a great impetus to the English trade (" We were thragged up with work," said John Field to me, using a local expression), and a little later, owing to the collapse of the Commune, the English again benefited, for most of the shoemakers of Paris, who had been Communists, were either dead or in exile. The first factories built in Olney were those of S. R. Owen and G. A. Drage. In 1890, just after the death of Mr. Owen, was founded the enterprising firm of Hinde and Mann, who later housed themselves imposingly at the junction of the Midland and Wellingborough roads. Other Olney firms are those of S. Cowley, Ltd. (makers of the S. O. S. brand of boots and shoes), who have adopted the American or one floor system, and Thomas Johnson. At the south end of the town is the tannery of W. E. Pebody and Co. What Olney, as a shoe district, is to North Bucks, Chesham is to the south of the county, where, however, most of the firms turn out men's heavy-nailed footwear.

122. Of shoemaker life in the sixties a vivid account has been given by Mr. William Arnold, of Northampton. His father, a shoemaker of Everdon, could by working hard make six pairs of shoes in a week, but as his employers frequently had insufficient trade to keep their men fully at work, his earnings rarely exceeded 16s. per week. On this pittance had to be kept fourteen children as hungry as fourteen wolves. At the age of seven William was set to the second process of riveting, the first process, that of fitting the upper to the last and fixing the sole in its proper place ready for the nailing, being done by men. The second process consisted of knocking in the rivets with a " driver " (a flat iron rasp). Sometimes sprigs were used, hence the term " sprigging boys." And then he tells how, step by step, he rose to be a manufacturer in a large way.

Among the romances of the shoe world is that of the **Rossendale Slipper** trade, an instructive paper on which, by Councillor W. Hardman[1] was reported in *The Shoe and Leather News*, April 14th, 1921. As far back as 1840 there was a building called Slipper Hall, where slippers were made from rabbit-skins, but the trade as now known grew out of the felt industry. At first workpeople made for their own use slippers from the tab ends of the felt. In 1874 J. W. Rothwell, of Waterfoot, began to turn the small traffic into a wholesale trade ; in 1876 Samuel McLerie commenced operations ; and from the businesses founded by these pioneers have sprung Sir H. W. Trickett, Ltd., and other firms. Everything is now done by the maker to tempt the public. He or she is presented with

[1] Of Hardman Brothers, Slipper Manufacturers, Waterfoot, Lancs.

charming colour combinations, including pink and
black, violet and black, and saxe and darker blue.
Women's slippers in particular are conceived in
every thinkable degree of daintiness of design and
colour scheme, and to please the children both
slipper and carton are printed with pictures of
fairy-book favourites.[1]

In 1871 Harry Vine of Northampton improved
the Bunk Wheel, a little appliance which enabled
manufacturers to produce an artificial stitch, and
thus to compete more successfully with the hand-
sewn boot.[2]

123. Among the shoe manufacturers in the
sixties none was more original than **William
Jones**—Billy Jones, as he was familiarly called,
whose factory stood at the Market Square end of
Newland, Northampton. Of middle stature, aristo-
cratic looking, luxuriantly bearded, and with a vivid
scarlet birth-mark on his face, he was one of the
most noticeable local figures. A Wesleyan of the
aggressive type, he took an active interest in
church work. He loved a merry tale, his conversation was racy, and he had himself taken part in
many odd incidents—he was an odd incident
himself, an encyclopædia of wit—and he would
run on for hours, piling one comic story on the
top of another. He was original in all that he
did. When the country workers brought in their

[1] See *Footwear Organiser*, August, 1921, p. 102.
[2] See Devlin's *The Shoemaker* (Part 1, p. 47), published in 1839.

shoulder loads of boots they usually waited for
Mr. Jones and his brother "Sammy," who presided
at the desk. On entering, " Billy " would go,
" H'm, h'm, h'm ! " and then with a sweep of his
arm send the whole of the nearest collection of
boots on to the floor. " H'm, h'm, h'm !" and over
would go another collection ; " H'm, h'm, h'm ! "
and a third was treated in the same way, and he
would then make his payments.

Some of his workers thought him hard, but he
had many difficult men to deal with—those, for
instance, who resorted to the dishonest system of
procuring "cabbage," that is, of obtaining more
leather than they needed or were entitled to for
the making up of the goods. " Strap " or " Dead
Horse " was another pernicious system. A man
would go in on a Monday morning, get the
materials for three dozen pairs of boots, "strap "
on them, that is, have a certain sum in advance,
be out on drink all the week, and go in on Saturday
and get more "strap." Some would carry on like
this till the third week. They would also steal and
sell for beer the jean that was used as lining for
the uppers. It was this sort of treatment that
made Billy a martinet; and when, prosperity having
come to him, he took a many-windowed house at
the corner of Palmerstone Road and Billing Road,
he became stricter than ever. The boots being
deposited on the counter, he would scrutinize them
very closely, and if not satisfied would call out to

his brother, "Dock him, Sammy!" On one occasion one of the workers who had been docked said angrily, turning to a chum, "I don't mind paying for one of his d—— windows, but it's jolly hard luck to have to pay for the d——d lot." Occasionally on a Sunday some of the operatives would take a walk as far as Palmerstone Road in order to have a look at what they called their windows.

A few years passed by, and at the election for Mayor (November 9th, 1872) in the Town Hall, and in the presence of the public, Billy was chosen. He was naturally the butt of every wag in the building, while those who were not conspicuous for wit could at least call out, "Dock him!" which they did very vociferously; but he took it all in good part, and indeed he was really no worse treated than his predecessors. The year of his mayoralty was marked by an important event—the Northampton Exhibition of Leather Work—the first of the kind held in the county. His finishing up as a shoe manufacturer was quite characteristic of him. Having called in a friend, Joseph Burton, he said, "Joe, I'll sell you every 'top' in my shop [these tops filled a great room] for £5." Burton, who had a wonderful bargain, sold £15 worth of them in one afternoon, and their removal seemed to make no difference to the great accumulation.

Sammy Jones, who outlived his brother, was one of the founders of the Co-operative Society of

Northampton. Like William he had a luxuriant beard which had become white, and one day he, "looking like father Abraham," took his concertina (on which he was a skilled player) to a gathering presided over by Mr. S. S. Campion, who jocularly introduced him to the amused audience as "young Mr. Jones," adding, " I knew his father, old Mr. Jones."

Many sensational events have occurred in the shoe trade, one of the most sensational being that connected with the mysterious "J. B.," and to this day nobody knows who " J. B." was. However, millions of pairs of boots were shipped to him until 1874, when all of a sudden the orders ceased.

124. The story of the firm of H. E. Randall, Ltd., is inextricably interwoven with the personality of its founder, **(Sir) Henry E. Randall,**[1] J.P. [Pl. 45], who, after entering the factory of his uncle, Wm. Jones, started business on his own account in Lady Lane, Northampton. The firm, which in 1896 became a limited liability company, caters for both sexes, the many departments turning out every popular style and design. In 1894 and 1897, when Mr. Randall was Mayor of the Borough, Abington Park was, owing largely to his efforts, acquired for the public, and he has played a prominent part in many other movements for the

[1] An account of Sir Henry Randall's career appeared in *The Northampton Independent*, Dec. 13th, 1919.

good of the town. He was knighted in 1905, and in 1909 he became High Sheriff of the county.

In 1919 the oldest of the Northampton firms, that of **Frederick Bostock, Ltd.** (which was established by Thomas Bostock[1] in 1836), amalgamated with that of Edwin Bostock and Co., Ltd., of Stafford and Stone, forming the **Lotus Company, Ltd.** It was a happy idea to link present-day shoemaking with old Egypt—the land of the lotus and of beautiful foot-gear—to say nothing of the Delta, the name given to one of their leading brands. In the time of Mr. Frederick Bostock's father the shoemakers used to bring in their boots in boxes on wheels drawn by large dogs, —six in hand—and it was quite a sight to see Tommy Dunn and Tommy Knocker, two of the most famous charioteers, race their dog-carts down hill by the Fever Hospital on the London Road, and outstrip the stage coaches.

The Manfields are a west of England family, descended from the Conqueror's Geoffrey de Mandeville. Moses Philip Manfield, born in 1752, at Hemyock, in Devonshire, drifted to Bristol, where was probably born his son, also named Moses Philip, who became a cordwainer in that city, and who in turn had a son, Moses Philip the third, born July 26th, 1819, who became **Sir Philip Manfield** [Plate 42]. When Philip was

---

[1] The present Mr. F. Bostock's grandfather. The firm made a speciality of handsewn work.

only two years old his father, who had fallen a victim to paralysis, gave up the shoemaking and took to selling second-hand books. Philip, who learnt shoemaking at Bristol, soon showed that he had remarkable gifts. After saving a hundred and fifty pounds he made for Northampton, where, in 1844, he started in business as a shoe manufacturer, and in 1892 he purchased a four acre wood—Monks Park Spinnie—where he erected, on the American system, the present magnificent factory. He took an active part in politics, being a staunch supporter of Bradlaugh, whom he succeeded in 1891 as a member for the borough, and in the following year he received the honour of knighthood. A Unitarian by conviction, he in 1897 presented to the Unitarian congregation of the town a church and schools, at the cost of £7,000. He died on July 31st, 1899, just after his 80th birthday, honoured and respected by all who knew him; and he was succeeded by his two sons—Harry, who in 1906 was elected M.P. for Mid-Northants, and James [Pl. 42], to whom this volume is dedicated. The business is now known as Manfield and Sons, Additions to the number of its many retail shops were made in August, 1921, by the opening of new and palatial premises at the corner of Oxford Street and Newman Street, London, and Argyle Street, Glasgow.

The firm, **W. Barratt and Co.,** of " Foot-shape " fame, Northampton, was founded in 1903, and their handsome factory was erected in 1913. With them originated the Boots-by-Post idea, and they were the first to send (in 1911) boots by aeroplane. For beauty of construction and facilities for light and ventilation, their factory is unsurpassed.

Among the partners of W. Horton, of Stafford (see p. 154) was William Elley, who became associated with the firm of Thomas Benson Elley and Co., whose business was, in 1901, taken over by Messrs. Mason and Marson. In 1920 this firm, which during the War had supplied enormous numbers of boots to the British, French and Russian armies, as well as quantities of Italian mountain footgear, joined hands with Messrs. Padmore and Barnes, Ltd., Northampton; and their factory at Stafford is now known as the **Moccasin Works.**

Other well-known firms in Northampton are A. E. Marlow (St. James's Works), W. B. Stevens and Co. (St. Andrew's Street), C. and E. Lewis (Greenwood Road), Crockett and Jones (Magee Street), J. Sears and Co. (True Form Co.), and G. T. Hawkins (Overstone Road). The business of Henry Marshall (Northampton) was founded in 1848, that of John Marlow and Sons, Ltd. (Phoenix Works) in 1866, and that of Henry Wooding and Sons in 1867. Numbers of men associated with the shoe trade have been elected to the Mayoralty of various towns, among those

Plate 37

Stendhal, Henri Beyle (1783—1842), dancing in boots. From a sketch by Alfred de Musset, 1833, reproduced in "Henry Beyle-Stendhal," by Pierre Brun, 1900. See chapter 10.

Tartar Boot. See chapter 9.

The Half Moon Inn, Grendon, Northants. See p. 189.

Plate 38

THE COBBLERS OF PARIS. Aug. 1, 1641. See p. 189.

From Hone's *Every Day Book*.

who took office in Nov., 1921, being Councillor
J. W. Heath (W. Heath & Co.), of Leicester, who
succeeded Councillor G. E. Hilton (S. Hilton and
Sons) ; Councillor W. W. Chamberlain, of Higham
Ferrers ; Councillor H. N. Holmes (Edwards and
Holmes, Ltd.), who became Lord Mayor of
Norwich [Pl. 51] ; and Councillor William Smith
(Messrs. Smith Brothers), who was re-elected
Mayor of Ilkeston. Cartons—cardboard boxes for
shoes—are made at the works of Messrs. Horton
and Arlidge, Northampton.

Of late years Mansfield, Derby and Nottingham
have become shoe centres. The President of the
Manufacturers' Association representing this district is Mr. W. A. Royce of the Mansfield Shoe Co.
The President of the Irish Boot Manufacturers'
Association is Mr. Thomas Smalley (James Win-
stanley, Dublin) ; of the Scotch, Mr. C. W. Allan
of Edinburgh. Maybole, Glasgow, Kilmarnock,
Aberdeen and Dundee are also well-known centres.

The history of the **Saxone** Shoe Company, of
Kilmarnock, commences in 1820 with the foundation of the firm of Clark and Sons. In 1902, at the
time of the American Shoe Invasion, the firm of
F. and G. Abbott was founded, and their endeavour
being lightness, flexibility and perfect fitting in
machine welt shoes at a commercial price, they
were able to hold their own against the invaders.
In 1908 the two firms were merged under the name
of the Saxone Shoe Co., and thenceforward their

R

story has been one of continual progress. Most considerable towns in the British Isles have Saxone stores, and the factory has been again and again extended. The company is also the sole agency in this country for the famous American " Sorosis " shoes.

To deal with the great leather firms is beyond the scope of this work, but a word or two may be spared concerning one, as an example—**Dri-ped, Ltd.** The parent firm was that of William Walker and Sons, Ltd., Rose Hill Tannery, Bolton, established in 1823, but in 1919, owing to the popularity of the output, it was decided to form a separate company—" Dri-ped, Ltd." Dri-ped, which advertises itself as " The super leather for soles," is made from the finest hides obtainable, and is manufactured by an exclusive process, the purple diamond with which its goods are stamped being its guarantee. Mr. James Collier, head of the Globe Leather Works, Dunster Street, Northampton, is developing his Spinnie Hill Estate, which will form a pleasant and healthy garden suburb for Northampton.

125. In all the principal bootmaking centres there are **Technical Schools** where lads are instructed in the craft. To the College at Bethnal Green I have already referred (p. 71). On Jan. 18th, 1922, I went over the institution (formerly the old Grammar School[1]) at Northamp-

---

[1] The Grammar School was transferred to the Billing Road.

ton, and was greatly impressed both by what I saw and by the enthusiasm of the Principal, Mr. John Blakeman, M.A., and his staff, and the pride they take in their work. Normally there are 200 boys who are released from the factories for one morning a week, 60 day students (including full and part timers), and 300 in the evening classes. In 1911 huts were erected for machinery, and in 1919 a small factory at the back was purchased. The School has now a complete plant for the manufacture of all kinds of upper leather and of boots and shoes. Mr. D. Woodroffe, Mr. Roland Farey, and Mr. William James Barnes (who hails from Olney) each explained his special department. The Northants Boot and Shoe Students' Association was revived on August 27th, 1921, when by invitation of Mr. Owen Parker, a social gathering was held at the Parochial Room, Higham Ferrers; and the Wellingborough Technical Institute (Principal, Mr. C. J. Thorpe) was publicly opened on Sept. 23rd, 1921. The Technical School at Stafford is superintended by Mr. Frank Plucknett, Lecturer in Boot and Shoe Manufacture for the County, who has placed the industry under an obligation by his well known work, *An Introduction to the Theory and Practice of Boot and Shoe Manufacture* (1916).

The *Leeds* Technical School (Leeds Institute, Cookridge Street) was founded in 1903. The Principal is Mr. R. E. Barnett, B.Sc., and there is an efficient staff with Mr. J. S. Harding as the Head. The School in Gower Street, which is devoted to the Department of Boot and Shoe Manufacture, is said to be the largest and best lighted building used for the purpose in the country; and this and the modern equipment enable Leeds to offer invaluable facilities for the study of the Trade in all its branches. Boot and shoe classes were first held in *Norwich* in 1892, the present Municipal Technical Institute was built in 1901, and adjoining premises have since been utilised for extensions of the work. The Principal is Mr. Hugh Ramage, M.A.; the Lecturer, Mr. A. F. Neve.

At *Bristol* Boot and Shoe Trade Evening Classes are held at the Merchant Venturers' Technical College (Principal, Prof. J. Wertheimer, B.A., D.Sc.), the Chief Instructor being Mr. S. J. Glass.

The Principal of the *Leicester* Technical School —which calls itself, finely, " The Gate of Opportunity "—is Mr. John H. Hawthorn, M.A.; and Mr. J. L. Browett is at the head of the Boot and Shoe Department.

126. Allusion has several times been made to the shoemakers' interest in politics, their sympathies being almost invariably with the Radical side, and the names of George Odger (a shoemaker by-the-by) and other reformers were very dear to them. In the middle of the 19th century the Liberal candidates for Northampton were **Gilpin and**

Lord Henley, and these were the days of open voting, for the Ballot Act did not come into force until 1872. The very babies in their cradles screamed out, and the parrots on their perches squarked, "Vote for Gilpin and Henley." Boys of tender years were mature politicians. If another boy was suspected of an inclination for the unpopular colour he was "called out." " When I was eight," says Mr. Alfred Ager, " my grandmother said to me one day, ' Alfy, you go on to the Market Hill, in front of the booby hutch [hustings], and when they are asked to vote for Gilpin and Henley,[1] you put up two hands.'" And he did—with a feeling of unworthiness, however, because he had only two.

On polling day there was in every town unblushing bribery. Often a candidate would stand more barrels of beer than he got votes. Many an " incorruptible elector " would take money from both parties. Northampton, which at such times differed little from other towns, drew upon itself in 1868, as an election centre, the eyes of the whole world, that being the year when **Charles Bradlaugh,** the secularist orator and reformer, came forward as a candidate. It was the last election before the passing of the Ballot Act. A " Booby Hutch " seventy feet long was erected in the Market Place, and the usual scenes occured. The excitement was intense. The rival parties

[1] C. Gilpin and Lord Henley—Liberals.

displayed their colours obtrusively, Bradlaugh's[1] being green, mauve and white, and the Conservatives' orange and blue. Immense rosettes were worn and streamers carried, and when, as sometimes happened, the rival bands met, " Oh, then they went at it ! " Gilpin and Henley, who were returned, obtained respectively 2,623 and 2,111 votes, Bradlaugh's figures being 1,068. In January, 1874, Gilpin was returned again, but a Conservative (Phipps) took the place of Henley, Bradlaugh being last with 1,653 votes. The popularity of Bradlaugh among the Northampton shoemakers was tremendous. An eye-witness, speaking of one occasion, February, 1874, said, " Bradlaugh left Bridge Street Station and got into his phaeton. The people took off the horses and drew it through a mighty throng—a human river—up the hill to the Market Place, while from every throat rose the words of James Wilson's[2] song, ' Toil, men, toil; toil in Freedom's cause.' It stirred your blood ! It carried you away ! Bradlaugh addressed the crowd from a window on the Market Place. He was the grandest, most eloquent speaker I ever heard. Never was there such enthusiasm." In the

[1] It was in connection with this election that was made " the Bradlaugh mug," decorated with mauve and green, on which was inscribed the words, "Bradlaugh for Northampton." A photograph of a specimen that belonged to Mr. E. J. Wright appeared in *The Northampton Independent* April 26th, 1913.

[2] Wilson died in 1878 at the early age of 30. He is buried in the cemetery on the Billing Road. Bradlaugh usually stayed when in Northampton with a dwarfish friend named Stimson, a man of means.

autumn of the same year, 1874, there was another election, polling day being October 6th. The comic always trenches on the serious, and this election was no exception. In Compton Street lived a fishmonger, Jim Allard, whose bitterness against the Radicals had become proverbial. " It was not so much what he said as the wounding way in which he said it." Allard had in his paddock a goat. Some of the shoemakers caught it, arrayed it in Bradlaugh's colours and let it loose ; and all day long it capered about the town urging everybody to vote for its master's antipathy. Not even Allard's goat, however, could save the green, mauve and white, and Bradlaugh failed for the third time. After the declaration of the poll a riot took place, the military were called out, and guns were placed in Newland, St. Giles's Street, and at other points. However, the crowd was at last persuaded to disperse, and beyond the breaking of a few heads, which were of no great beauty, and a number of windows, little harm was done. The scene formed the subject of a drawing by Mr. C. J. Staniland, which was reproduced in *The Northampton Independent*, Dec. 16th, 1911, and doubtless it was a truthful drawing, though one misses Allard's goat. Subsequently the " old Liberals " joined the Bradlaugh party, and at the election of 1880 Bradlaugh and his colleague, Henry Labouchere, were returned. Bradlaugh, who had to be elected three times[1] before being allowed to take his seat in Parliament, died in 1891.   A statue of him was set up in Abington Square, with James Wilson's verses on the pedestal.

About 1870 spring-side shoes—called by the profane, Jemimas—had a vogue in this country,[2] and their popularity extended even to China, where they were prettily called "Cheaty Coks," to distinguish them from "boots ploper."

127.   In the autumn of 1887 the operatives of Messrs. Cove and West of Northampton demanded higher wages, and the workers for other firms followed suit.   The Manufacturers' Association[3] endeavoured to settle the dispute, but without success, and in October occurred what is remembered as the **First Great Lock Out.**[4]   Twenty thousand persons were thrown out of employment, the distress was frightful, and the factories were not re-opened until January 2nd, 1888.

In 1889 the new Goodyear Welter[5] was brought into England by Mr. J. H. Hanan, and first used by a Kilmarnock firm.   The Munyan Lock Stitch Machine also appeared the same year; other devices were introduced later, and at the present

---

[1] To commemorate these three victories, a razor with a suitable inscription was made.   A specimen is in the possessiou of Mrs. Jackson, of Olney.

[2] The *Brodequin à entrée élastique* was in common use in France as early as 1850.   *Lacroix*, p. 105.

[3] Manufacturers' Association founded 1879.

[4] This first Great Dispute was not National.

[5] It does in 18 seconds what in the old days took a man an hour.   The old stitchman conld never turn out more than one pair of boots in a day.

day almost every operation in the trade is done by machinery.

128. The **Lift Industry** was in full swing about 1890. Previously each lift, or portion of leather that made up the heel, was in one piece. It then occurred to someone to utilise the small waste pieces of leather by cutting them in such a way that they should when pieced together form a lift. Thus there are " threes' lifts " and " fours' lifts," the name denoting the number of pieces of leather used. Among those who took up this business was Mr. Sheffield of Earls Barton, who sent a waggon load of leather, mallets, &c., to Olney, and in a short time hundreds of girls were busy with the work.

In 1894 occurred another extraordinary revolution in the trade, the employers having conceded to the demand of the Shoe Union that *all work*, except closing, should be done indoors. Then, too, whereas previously the factory workers had come into the factories and gone out again when they liked, thenceforward there were settled hours for work, and a man who was late found himself excluded. " On a certain day," to use the words of Mr. Alfred Ager, " the men all went out **Piece Men** and on the next they came in **Day Men.**" One after another the little workshops in back gardens fell into disuse, and additional and larger factories rose in every shoemaking town.

129. In 1895 a new wages statement was

demanded by the operatives and opposed by the Manufacturers' Federation; and negotiation having failed, there commenced in March the **Second Great Lock Out**.[1]   Some 60,000 unionists and non-unionists were thrown out of employment— the towns chiefly affected being London, North-ampton, Birmingham, Bristol, Kettering, Leeds, Leicester, Rushden and Higham Ferrers; but happily in seven weeks a settlement was effected, owing largely to the good offices of the Board of Trade.

Attention was then turned more than ever to machinery, and as the plant required larger space new and important factories sprang up, some manufacturers adopting the **American** or **One Floor System,** and departments were arranged in accordance with the progress of the material from first to finished product.   About the same time the **Multiple Shop** system, originated by Freeman, Hardy, Willis and Co. (the managing director of which firm is now Sir Jonathan North) and Stead and Simpson, began to extend.   The firms of Manfield and Sons, H. E. Randall, Ltd., J. Sears and Co. (founded 1891), the British Boot Company, and the Bronson Shoe Company have each of them many retail shops (J. Sears and Co. have 84), a number of them being palatial buildings.

In 1895 commenced what is known as the

[1] This Second Great Dispute was National.

American Invasion, which occasioned, for the moment, a serious repulse to the English home trade. The style and appearance of the American goods took the popular fancy, the fittings covered a wider range than those of the English goods, and the prices were favourable. It was soon discovered, however, that the wearing qualities were inferior to those of the English shoes, but even that discovery did not work much change. The manufacturers then decided to fight their rivals with their own weapons. They adopted the best in American methods, and within a few years the imports from America showed a decline, and the English not only had their own again, but began to carry the war into their rivals' own country by shipping high-class goods to the States.

In 1887 there were in Northampton 130 shoe manufacturers, exclusive of sewers and closers to the trade; in 1892 there were 169. The tendency, however, of recent years has been for the factories to become larger and for the number to decrease. There are now about 80 factories in the town.[1]

130. We may next give in a few words an idea of the way in which a shoe is at the present day built up. In hardly any two factories would the procedure be precisely the same, but the general system and plan differ little. Of course, to understand thoroughly the various processes,

[1] Men's Boots are roughly—Derby, Bal., and Open Tab Bal. ; Men's Shoes—Oxford, Derby and Brogue ; Women's Boots—Derby, Bal., and Open Tab Bal. ; and Women's Shoes—Oxford and Gibson.

personal inspection is necessary.   The visitor to a factory is usually first taken to the **Last-making Room,** where a wonderful machine converts pieces of rough-hewn wood into lasts precisely like a model.   The Skin Room[1] with its variety of skins —all of most beautiful surface—and its machine for measuring them, having been studied, he is taken into the **Rough Stuff Department** where soles, insoles and stiffeners are cut.   Stiffeners are pieces of uncurried leather, which can be mellowed by wetting and moulded while mellow.   When dry they retain their moulded form.   They are placed between the upper and the lining at the heel part of the shoe.   Persons who examine the boots and shoes of bygone days and compare them with those which are now produced, cannot fail to notice the superior shape of the modern boot at the back.   Stiffeners did not come into general use until about 1850.   Previous to that date they were

[1] In a lecture delivered at Northampton Public Library Hall, Jan. 21st, 1921, Mr. James Randall, of Messrs. Randall and Porter, tanners, Ulverstone, said : " Light coloured leathers should be avoided.   The chemicals required to produce a light colour take away a very great deal of the wear.   Our supplies of oak bark having become practically exhausted, tanners have to go abroad for tanning materials.   There is a big move on now by tanners to use materials from within the Empire, such as gambier (an extract from the leaves of *uncaria gambir*, a Straits of Malacca plant). mimosa (bark of the Australian variety), and myrobalans (the dried fruit of an Indian tree).   Besides English hides, market hides as they are called, many come to us from distant countries to be tanned.   These are either ' dry ' hides (which have either been dried in the sun or temporarily preserved with arsenic) or ' wet salted ' (also called ' green ') hides." Leather may be alum dressed, vegetable tanned or chrome tanned. Upper leathers may be produced by anyone of these processes, but sole leather only by the last two ; thus Dri-ped is a chrome tanned leather used for soles.   Kips, one of the terms in frequent use in the trade, are the leather of yearlings or small cattle.   They form a grade between calf and cow hide.

placed only in such boots as could be removed from the foot by the help of a boot-jack, e.g., Wellington Boots or Riding Boots ; consequently, the lighter kinds of footwear of those earlier days, although often beautifully made, did not retain their shape.

131. THE UPPER CUTTING OR Clicking Department.

In the Upper Cutting Department one's attention is first drawn to the Clicking Machine, which does by means of metal dies what the clicker formerly did by hand. In most factories, however, hand clicking is still the rule, while in others hand clicking and machine clicking go on side by side.

The cutting board—whether for hand or machine work—has the end grain for its surface. This is an American idea, and it is an undoubted advantage, because the knife can sink into the board easily and yet keep in good condition very much longer than it would if the surface were formed from the length of the tree, as in an ordinary plank.

A machine, *The Royal Perforator*, punches a design on the toe-cap—different designs being obtained by changing the die ; and another machine, *The Stamping Machine*, stamps on the top lining (or on a slip to be stitched on to it) the name of the Firm, the order number, and size of the shoe.

Skiving Machine.—The parts of the uppers which have to be doubled over or folded must then be skived at the edge in such a way that the part which is folded will not be thicker than the unfolded part. The edges of other sections, which on account of their thickness might cause discomfort in wear, or mar the appearance of the shoe, must also be suitably skived, the work being done on a small machine capable of very fine adjustments.

Stitching Machines.—Previous to the introduction of the Sewing Machine, the sewing together of the uppers was done by hand, and our Museums abound with specimens which attest to the wondrous skill of the workers. After examining some of them, it is easy to understand Devlin's remark that it takes fourteen years to learn the trade. At first only one machine was invented for putting together the many sections of the upper, but to-day there are machines for each separate operation, so that in up-to-date closing rooms as many as twenty different machines may be in use.

With the *Eyeletting Machine*—a gauge having been set—the eyelet-holes are made and eyelets inserted.

This finishes the shoe upper.[1]

---

[1] There are also machines for fixing hooks at the top of laced boots— blind hooks as they are called because they are covered with lining ; and machines for button sewing. The latter drop a button on to the marked place on the leather and then stitch it.

132. The Making Departments.

There are *Four* principal methods by which the uppers of boots may be fastened to the soles.

(1.) **The Turn-shoe or Sew-round.** A suitable last is selected, and the stiffeners are properly prepared by skiving their edges—with a view to preventing discomfort, and in order to avoid spoiling the appearance of the shoe. The leather to be used for the soles is shaped to the last and tacked to its bottom with the back of the leather uppermost. The upper is then *turned inside out* and strained over the last, so that its edge laps over on the sole, in which position it is temporarily held with suitable tacks. The upper is next secured to the sole with sewing, using either one or two threads and making a horizontal seam. It is important that the stitches form a true outline, because these determine the shape of the shoe. When they have been sewn round, any surplus upper which stands above the sewing is cut away, and the shoe will then be ready for turning the right side out. This is far from being a simple operation, but through experience the workman acquires such dexterity that it is soon accomplished. The sock lining is next put in, and the last for the *opposite foot* (not the one on which it was made) is inserted, in order to restore the shape impaired by the turning. This finishes the shoe—unless a heel has to be attached.

(2.) **The Veldtschoen** method is so called

because the Dutch people make their boots for the Veldt by it. In England it is used principally for children's shoes, ward shoes and slippers. The sole is first fastened to the bottom of the last in order to hold it in position while the shoe is being made. On the surface of the sole (which is left wider than the last) a channel is cut and opened so that the stitch can be sunk into the leather, and thus be protected from wear. The upper is then strained over the last and bedded down, so that its edge, which is turned outwards, lies flat on that part of the sole which extends wider than the last. In this position it is then secured with a row of stitches that are vertical to the surface of the sole. The channel having been closed, the heel is attached.

(3.) **The Handsewn** or **Welted Process.** This is far more difficult to make, although its durability and comfort justify the care and labour necessary in its production. A piece of leather called an insole is first placed on the bottom of the last in such a way that its smooth side or grain comes next to the foot. This is shaped to the last, and then the upper is strained to the last and its edge lapped on to the insole, in which position it is temporarily kept by nails driven partly in. A strip of leather about half an inch wide—the welt—is prepared, as is also a waxed[1]

[1] The wax is to preserve the thread, and also to prevent it from slipping back after the stitch is pulled up.

Plate 39

WILLIAM HUNTINGTON, S.S. 1745—1813.
See p. 161.
From the *Life of William Huntington*, by Thomas Wright.

ROBERT BLOOMFIELD. 1766—1823. See p. 159.
Author of "The Farmer's Boy," &c.
From the *European Magazine*, Published, Dec. 1, 1801.

Plate 40

FRONTISPIECE OF CHAP BOOK.

From copy in the Public Library, Northampton. See p. 216.

Photo Coldham & Son, Northampton.

thread, at each end of which is attached a hog's bristle. A horizontal or flat seam is made with a curved awl, which passes through a part of the insole, the upper and the edge of the welt. Both ends of the thread are passed through the same hole, one entering from the right hand side and the other from the left. The thread must be pulled sufficiently tight so that the seam formed by the upper, the welt and the insole may be waterproof. The shoe being sewn round and the nails withdrawn, all surplus leather is trimmed away. The bottom is then filled up level with the seam. This is often done with ground cork, to which has been added some water-proofing composition. The sole and welt are next shaped to the outline of the last, a channel is cut in the surface of the sole, as in the *veldtschoen*, and the sole is sewn to the projecting edge of the welt with stitches vertical to the sole surface, also as in the *veldtschoen*. The heel is next attached, and the shoe finished.

Formerly the hand-sewn welted boot was made entirely by hand, but to-day there are machines which copy the processes fairly well. The shoe can be lasted by machine, which can be adjusted so that the lasting tacks are driven in only part way (because they are removed as the welt is sewn on), the welt can be sewn on by a machine, and the sole rounded and stitched by other machines. In all, eleven different machines—in some factories

s

more—would be employed when making boots on the hand-sewn principle.

(4.) **The Blake Process.** By far the greatest number of boots are made by what is termed the *Blake Process*—Blake being the name of the inventor of the first machine used for sewing on the sole by this method. A last is selected having an iron plate on its bottom ; an insole is then attached to the last by nails driven through holes in the plate. Then the upper is strained over the last and its edge lapped over on the insole, to which it is secured with small nails called " tingles," which are usually about five-sixteenths of an inch long, their points being burred over on the iron plate. After the bottom of the shoe has been made level by filling up the part not covered by the edge of the upper, the sole, which must be already shaped and channelled, is temporarily secured in position with nails. Then the last is removed. The permanent attaching of the sole is done on a sewing machine which uses a waxed thread, the boot being held on the tip of a long arm termed a horn, the extreme end of which is about the size of a farthing. The boot is quickly sewn round, after which the channel is closed to protect the stitch, and the shoe is ready for heel attaching and finishing.

133. The Finishing Department. In wholesale manufacture, the heels are always made first and attached afterwards. The small pieces, or sections, of which the heels are made are placed in moulds the exact shape of the required heel, and after being nailed in order to keep these various pieces or sections in position, they are placed in other moulds and subjected to considerable pressure in a machine designed specially for this purpose. The final shaping of the heels and edges is also effected with special machines. Knives of suitable shape are rotated at a great speed, and the heel or the edge, as the case may be, is brought into contact with these knives, and trimmed to the desired shape. The heel is then made perfectly smooth by contact with a revolving wheel covered with a suitable abrasive, such as emery cloth, after which it is stained and burnished. The edges are likewise stained and burnished with a hot iron which is shaped to fix on the edge. The surface of the sole is also finished.

To the Boot Repairing Machinery of Messrs. Keats and Bexon, Ltd., Stafford, and other firms, allusion only can here be made. In most towns to-day shoe repairing is done with a machine. There is one kind of boot—" the Cripple Boot," for persons with deformed feet—which is necessarily still made entirely by hand.

134. The human mind is perpetually making bold and yet bolder excursions. Of recent years **Sole Leather Substitutes**—zome (an amalgamation of fine rubber and vegetable fibre), neolin and others—have found a very large market, and as they wear well they will no doubt continue to push their way. One of the greatest revolutions of modern times has been the introduction of **Rubber** soles and heels, which are turned out in enormous quantities by Phillips (Old Street, London), Redfern (Hyde, near Manchester), Chess and Stead (Brinscombe, Glos.), the Metropolitan Rubber Company, and Wood-Milne. In America steel-soled shoes are made, the steel being one piece from toe to heel, but they have a springy insole of hair; and Mr. J. W. Hastings, of Northampton, has recently patented a metal heel.

135. It would be quite impossible, in a work of this kind, to deal with the output of the many factories in the British Isles, but the specialities of a few firms may be mentioned. Speaking generally, men's shoes are made at Northampton, women's at Leicester, men's and women's at Stafford and Stone; farmers,' labourers' and miners' at Bristol and Kingswood; dress and turnshoes at Norwich. In respect to the heavy shoes made by A. Lovell and Co., Kingswood, the shank of every nail passes through a metal sheet inserted next the sole, which gives the required grip and makes it impossible for nails to fall out in ordinary wear. The Norvic Shoe Company, of Norwich, has produced some of the finest ladies' shoes of the century. In old times the employers supplied the more important materials for the home workers, but the smaller things, such as inks, stains, polishes,

Plate 41

PILLAR HEEL JOCKEY BOOT.
T. 441—1920.

SHELL HEEL JOCKEY BOOT.
T. 419.

A 19th CENTURY BOOT.
T. 416—1920.

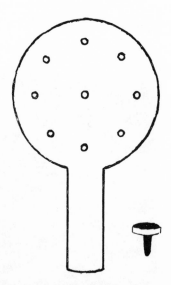

DEVIL-AMONG-THE-TAILORS-BOARD

From sketch by Mr. Alfred Peters, of Padiham.

Length of board 5 feet. It was enclosed by sides
about 3½ inches high. See p. 227.

All the above boots are from specimens in the Victoria and Albert Museum, S. Kensington.

Photo Mr. Geo. Avenell.

Plate 42

Mr. JAMES MANFIELD, J.P.

See p. 239.

Sir PHILIP MANFIELD.

See p. 238.

emery paper, bristles, waxes, sponges, heel balls, &c., they had themselves to find or supply. Hence these articles are generally known as **Findings**,[1] and they are supplied by Shoe Findings, Ltd., of Stafford (who also manufacture cartons), and other firms. Under the head of **Mercery** come laces, hooks, loopings, bindings, socks, threads, needles, cotton and linen drill, canvases, eyelets, &c. Almost everything the shoemaker requires can be obtained at what are called Grindery Shops. Every kind of shoe mercery is manufactured by Faire Brothers and Co., Leicester, who also specialise in stiffeners. Mohair bootlaces are produced at Leek in Staffordshire, and Johnstone in Scotland. Hobnails are made at Leicester and Manchester, but wire hobs, which are cleaner in finish than the British malleable article, though they do not possess its wearing qualities, are imported from Belgium. Louis Sandy, of Stafford, and other firms, specialise in shoe buckles.

The 19th century was the golden age of **Blacking**. Day and Martin have never erred on the side of modesty in proclaiming the merits of their wares, but they were hopelessly outdistanced by their rival, the omnipresent Turner. This active and self-satisfied gentleman spent the whole of his life in trumpeting his own praises, and when he

[1] Interesting article on Mercery, Findings and Grindery by Mr. Edward B. Knowles, President of the National Federation of Leather and Grindery Merchants' Association.—*Footwear Organiser*, March, 1920.

wearied of loading the press and the hoardings with his prose, he touchingly broke out into anacreontic verse upon the same delightful theme.

The old blackings held sway till (in 1883) the introduction of chrome tanning, which led to the use of glacé kid, willow and box calf as materials for the manufacture of boots, and called into existence the forerunners of modern wax boot polishes, creams and cleaners,[1] which are made from china wax, the product of the tiny insect, *cocus pela;* Brazilian wax, derived from the leaves of the palm *copernicia cerifera;* and ozokerite, a mineral found in Galicia, Poland and Moldavia.

An idea comes from America respecting the ugly name, "pumps," which has attached itself to one of the most beautiful kinds of footwear. A writer in *The Boot and Shoe Recorder*, Boston, March 27th, 1920, suggests in its place the really pleasing "cameos." It would be far better, however, to use something we already have in the Shoe vocabulary; for example, the word Pinsons or Pynsons, old English for a thin shoe (see p. 102), putting the word "pumps" in brackets beside it until the public get used to the term.

At Lynn, Massachusetts, a company has been formed called the Foot-o-Scope Corporation, to exploit a new invention in which an X-ray apparatus is used, by means of which a purchaser of

[1] *Footwear Organiser*, Sept., 1921, p. 162. An article based upon material supplied by E. Brown & Son, Ltd., makers of the Meltonian Polishes and Creams.

shoes may know whether or not the shoe fits, as the machine enables him to see the bones of the foot through the leather of the shoe. This machine in its perfected form is now manufactured by X-Rays, Ltd., 11 Torrington Place, Gower Street, London, and advertised as **The X-Ray Pedo-scope.**

136. In 1894 was established the International **Shoe and Leather Fair** (held in the Royal Agricultural Hall, London), which has become one of the great events of the industrial world. At the Fair held in October, 1921, over 400 firms were represented. On October 7th, 1921, was held at the Fair the First National Convention to discuss Trade Outlook and Trade Problems, among the speakers being Dr. A. D. Denning (of the Lotus Company), and Messrs. G. E. White, Owen Parker,[1] J.P., C.B.E. [Pl. 44] and Edward Lewis.

An important event of 1920 was the securing, by the Committee of the Northampton Public Library, of the Shoe collection made by the late **Mr. Stewart Beattie,** which can now, thanks to the valuable labours of Mr. Reginald W. Brown, the librarian, be examined by the public. *A Shoe and Leather Trade Bibliography* which Mr. Brown is compiling will be of great service to students of

---

[1] Head of the firm of Chas. Parker, boot and shoe manufacturers, Higham Ferrers, and in 1921 President of the Incorporated Federated Associations of Boot and Shoe Manufacturers of Great Britain and Ireland. He did a wonderful work as trade leader during the War. See *Footwear Organiser*, Feb., 1922, p. 68.

the trade.[1]   It is always cheering to learn that the working classes are thrifty, and of the 73rd Annual Report of the Northampton Town and County Benefit Building Society (Feb., 1922), its officers have reason to be proud.   Its assets amount to £1,071,497, proving that the number of working men in Northampton who own their own houses is very large.

137.   In these pages I have dealt chiefly with the Shoe Industry of Great Britain, and have referred only occasionally to that of America.   To give some idea of the business done there it may be observed that one firm, the **Endicott-Johnson** Shoe Corporation, Binghamton, New York, employs 13,000 hands, and does "thirty millions of tannery business a year."   Mr. George F. Johnson, of that firm, when asked the secret of its success, said, " It is as simple as the Golden Rule.   It is putting yourself in the worker's place, and doing by him as you would have him do by you."   In other words, the heads of the firm have tried to carry their souls with fairness through a difficult world, and to earn the kind thoughts and approval of their fellow men.   The great American shoemaking city of Lynn (see p. 121), has been styled, " The Shoe-shop of the United States." Looking into the future, the trade is probably tending towards specialisation, and some manu-

[1] See *Footwear Organiser*, 1919 (June, Oct., Dec.), 1920 (Jan., April, June, July, Oct.), 1921 (Aug., Dec.).

facturers ardently desire it. Mr. Frederick Cook, of Long Buckby, in a recent speech, pleaded that the manufacturer should be "a producer in the broadest sense of the word and not a shoe assembler." He should ensure "a continuity of the supply of his raw materials by broadening the basis of his undertaking, and bring within the sphere of his activities the production of the leather he requires to use ; " and under the head of specialisation he says, "It would be well if a manufacturer would lay himself out to make one boot, and one boot only, at a given price." How far Mr. Cook's views are shared by the trade in general I do not know.

138. The Japanese have straw shoes which slip on and off easily. Siamese shoes are sometimes in the shape of a canoe with an open toe. The sole is of wood, the upper of wood and embroidered cloth clinquant with gold and silver. The Armenians wear red shoes and boots ; the Oriental Jews blue or black. The Turks revel in slippers of soft leather, yellow or black, and shoes and boots of red morocco. The Morocco women (at Fez there is a great manufactory of slippers) are allowed to wear footgear of any colour except yellow. To an English mind, however, the oddest kind of footwear is the **Hoodoo Boot**,[1] which finds favour in parts of Asia, Hawaii and Cuba. Made of fanciful shapes, these boots are under-

[1] See *Canadian Shoe and Leather Journal*, June, 1906.

stood to bring good luck to the wearer.   Over one
of them in a shop would be a ticket with the price
—a high one—and the information, " whosoever
shall wear this boot will never be ill."   Occasionally the part between the golosh and the leg
resembles a cage.   This is to allow the devil to
come out, if by chance you should put on your
shoe without taking the precaution to look inside
first.   Above a pair of Cuban sandals was the
announcement, " He who walketh in these sandals
is the son of good fortune."   You can also buy
boots " to create activity in dull feet."   This is
done by means of spirals of fine wire inserted in
the sole, which tickle you as you walk.   If only
somebody would invent a boot that would tickle—
create activity in—dull minds (for the boot, good
or bad, incontestably *does* affect the mind)—
medicinal soles for sick souls, say—we could all of
us be right at both ends, and the world would
really begin to improve.

Russians love mighty boots.   The men of rank
under the old régime wore the Kassam high-low
pattern of dark crimson leather, and happy was he
who could swagger in the luxurious wear of
Tamboof, reaching to mid-thigh, scarlet in colour,
and made of deliciously-scented Russia leather.
Tartar boots [Pl. 37] are a delight to the eye.   In
Brazil the majority of the people wear shoes made
in the factories of Rio or Sao Paulo, or clogs—
just a thick wooden sole with an upper of leather

covering the front half of the foot.   The villagers walk to the town on Sundays barefooted, carrying in their hands conventional shoes, which they put on when approaching it, and remove when leaving it.   With them, indeed, the shoe is purely an ornament, and the Brazilian village dandy who walks in torture and grimacingly in a pair of shoes looks down with utter disdain on his less fortunate brother, who is walking in comfort with bare feet.   Circassian bootmakers soak their goods, when finished, in resinous gum and water, and the purchaser is advised to wear them wet for a few hours, in order that they may take the exact shape of the feet and fit with the pliability and comfort of a glove.   We also hear of shoes that have been evolved from the skins of such exotic creatures as the python, the Java lizard, the crocodile, and the shark.[1]

I have seen a number of fine private **Collections of Oriental Shoes**.   Mr. Roland Gorbold, for example, brought back from Mesopotamia and Persia some most interesting specimens.   Another excellent Northampton collection is that of Mr. H. G. Barker (G. Barker and Co.), who returned from India in 1921.   It includes specimens with the decorated back (a peculiarity of Indian makes) and the heel pushed in.   He also showed me a pair with the uppers prettily ornamented with green needlework ; red shoes from Rangoon made

[1] See *Footwear Organiser*, Feb., 1922.

of native leather tanned with mangrove bark ; and coolie boots (which are convex, instead of flat, to the foot) made by jobbing makers who go from street to street and do their work on a doorstep, just as the English cobbler did in the time of Elizabeth. The Burmese women like a raw hide sole covered with blue velvet, or an upper decorated with the most enchanting colours, amid which shine the wing cases of a green beetle. The boots of the Indian rajahs, and even of the petty chieftains [Pl. 47] are very gorgeous with turned-up toes. The snow shoes of Cashmere have felt soles, and the uppers are lined with lambs' wool. The peasantry of India pay twopence a pair for shoes which consist of a wooden sole with a peg of brass for the toes to grip. Many of Mr. Barker's specimens were purchased at Delhi, Cawnpore, and in Bentinck Street, Calcutta, a thoroughfare that is almost entirely monopolised by shoemakers. The Wilson collection of Oriental shoes (collected by Miss A. E. Wilson) was at one time in the possession of Mr. C. M. W. Turner, of 22 Dawson Place, London. Mr. Padmore's (Padmore and Barnes, Moccasin Works) fine collection of North American Indian shoes was the delight of visitors to the Shoe and Leather Fair of 1921. The imprint of the moccasined foot in the dust indicates the trace of a friend or a foe. Two little tabs wide apart at the heels betray the Sioux, one tab marks the Winnebago, three tabs mark the

Plate 43

THE COBBLERS' ROUND.

Maze at Boughton Green.   Diameter, 37 ft.   See p. 195.

SIR JAMES CROCKETT, J.P.

Lent by
The Northampton Independent.

SIR JONATHAN NORTH.

(Managing Director of Messrs. Freeman,
Hardy & Willis).   See also *Footwear
Organiser*, Feb., 1922, p. 69.

Plate 44

Mr. OWEN PARKER, J.P., C.B.E. See p. 243.

The Late Mr. A. E. MARLOW, J.P.
President of the Federation, 1922. He died on July 11th, 1922.

See p. 240.

Chippewa. The skins are dressed by the squaws.

139. Owing to the efforts of Mr. Edward Carpenter,[1] the democratic author and poet, and other enthusiasts, there has of late years been a continually increasing demand for **Sandals.** Messrs. Holden Brothers, of Harewood Place, Oxford Street, London, and other firms, now specialise in this kind of work, and the sandal is very much in evidence at our sea-side resorts.

The biggest boot ever made is said to have been the one completed in March, 1906, by Mr. Frederick Cook, of Long Buckby, for a customer who wanted it for advertising purposes. Its length from heel to toe was 44 inches, 41 square feet of willow calf were used in the upper, and 51lbs. of sole leather for the bottoming. Every detail of construction was carried out with extreme care.

140. In no department of the Shoe World has greater advance been made in recent years than in the Footwear Press. The Trade has reason to be proud of its journals. **The Shoe and Leather Record** (weekly), 42 Finsbury Pavement, E.C., founded in 1886 by Mr. John T. Day, the gifted founder and manager of the International Shoe and Leather Fair, author and critic, deals in a masterly way with machinery and tanning materials, as well as with the boot and shoe trades,

---

[1] Edward Carpenter, b. 1844. The story of his life at Millthorpe, near Sheffield, is told in his breezy work, *My Days and Dreams* (1916).

and one recalls its excellently written series of articles (which commenced Jan. 26th, 1894) on " Celebrated Shoemakers."

On Jan. 2nd, 1869, appeared the first number of that very human and delightfully lively periodical, **St. Crispin**, edited by John Bedford Leno. Besides dealing with technical matters relative to the trade, it published a brightly written series of articles entitled, " Biographies of Noted Shoemakers," by John Blackman (see p. 168), the Rembrandtesque " Fifty Years' Experience of an Irish Shoemaker," by John O'Neill (see pp. 168 and 169), and the " History of Boots and Shoes from the Earliest Times." To *St. Crispin* succeeded *The Boot and Shoemaker* (also under the editorship of Leno), March 16th, 1878; *The Boot and Shoe Trades Journal*, Jan. 3rd, 1880 ; and **The Shoe Trades Journal**, Sept. 24th, 1915 (weekly, 74-77 Temple Chambers, E.C.4), which is printed in good, clear, large type, and is cleverly edited, its attractive pages being studded with shoe news from all over the world. A new, blithe and go-ahead spirit has of late come over the Boot and Shoe Newspaper Press, notwithstanding our difficult times, and *The Shoe Trades Journal*, which seeks to be a real help to its readers (and it succeeds), is in the van of it. From time to time it publishes thoroughly rousing articles, and I sometimes think that such articles should be signed, so that the writer may have the credit for them.

Everything from " H. A. P." (whoever he is) is good, and his contribution on April 23rd, 1920, "A Philosopher who Sells Shoes," was a masterpiece. He says, to give a little bit of his wisdom, that the world waits for psychological direction, and generally speaking, this is quite true ; but readers of *The Shoe Trades Journal* need not wait for psychological direction. They get it.

The Shoe and Leather News (South Place, Finsbury, E.C.2) also gives news from all quarters, and its contributors have a knack of making everything they write not only useful but interesting. The paper is all alive. Its reports of lectures and meetings are admirable, and nothing likely to be of value to the leather trade is omitted. The admission (March 10th, 1921), " We love a picturesque phrase," is welcome indeed from a professedly trade journal. Everybody turns to the instructive and racy section presided over by the young lady in furs, with a foot (and a shapely one, too) on the Trying-on Stool, which to my own knowledge she has occupied for four years, but although she may be tired of sitting there, I hope that her patience will not for a long time be exhausted, for it is certain that the reader will never be tired of the lively paragraphs over which she presides. To put the best last, the leading article is always valuable and usually stimulating. It seeks to raise the trade above itself. It insists (I recall particularly the article of August 18th, 1921, " The Elevation of Business ") on the importance of culture, and believes that the trade " is about to step forward on to a higher plane, where life will be fuller." That is the sort of writing to give spring and courage to the reader, and an impetus to trade. The paper that can widen our outlook, and at the same time give elasticity to our step, is our friend.

The Footwear Organiser (Monthly), published by The National Trade Press, Ltd., Regent House and Windsor House, Kingsway, W.C.2., is beautifully printed and most attractively illustrated, many of the plates being in colour. They are a feast for the eye. Turning over its pages is like walking through a picture gallery. It is the Royal Academy of the Shoe World. The special articles on the various Shoe Centres that from time to time appear have a decidedly literary flavour.[1] Its presentation of the British footwear industry to overseas buyers is worthy of the best productions of the industry. A praiseworthy feature of *The Footwear Organiser* is its recognition of the fact that true journalism is educational. It regularly includes articles which have a high educational value. The Acting Editor, Mr. T. A. Roberts, is an enthusiast and he is replete with ideas. He understands the value of novelty and the stimulus which it gives ; and if he were

---

[1] Among them have been articles on foreign shoes supplied by Captain Roland Gorbold, who also supplied the excellent photographs for the illustrations. *The British Shoeman* is a supplement to this periodical.

Plate 45

Mr. H. J. BOSTOCK (Lotus Co.).

President of the Federation, 1922, in succession to the late Mr. A. E. Marlow. See p. 238.

Sir HENRY RANDALL, J.P.

See p. 237.

Plate 46

FACTORY OF W. BARRATT & CO., NORTHAMPTON. See p. 239.

MR. WILLIAM BARRATT (W. Barratt & Co.).
See p. 239.

unable to offer it his soul would suffer. There are no bounds to his enterprise. All these journals lay themselves out to give those who seek their help bold, original and striking advertisement; and advertising has, in the shoe world at any rate, become a fine art.

Other valuable publications are *The Official Handbook of the National Federation of the Boot Trades Associations, Limited.* The cover, in colours, of the 1920 issue shows a medallion containing the figures of SS. Crispin and Crispianus, with a quotation from Devlin :

> " The Crispin trade, what better trade can be ?
> Ancient and famous, independent, free."

The statement by Councillor A. Tallant, of the ideals of the Federation, is excellently put. There is a brotherly ring about it that makes us want to go straight away and grasp his hand. The local press of the various shoe towns also contains a large amount of trade intelligence. *The Northampton Mercury*, dating from May 2nd, 1720, is particularly happy in its name, taken, of course, from the god with winged feet. Among its editors have been Mr. De Wilde and Mr. S. S. Campion, whose volume, *The Delightful History of Ye Gentle Craft*, appeared in 1876. The present able and cultured editor is Mr. W. W. Hadley. *The Northampton Echo*, a daily, issues from the same house. *The Northampton Herald*, a paper with a

T

fine record, under the editorship of Messrs. Butterfield, has a corresponding daily, *The Northampton Chronicle*. The pictorial side of local shoe-life is furnished by *The Northampton Independent* (edited by Mr. W. H. Holloway), a publication that has, and justifiably, advanced in popularity by leaps and bounds.

The Halford Publishing Co., Ltd. (Leicester) issues *The Shoeman's Guide* (an annual) and *The Shoeman's Foreign Terms and Book of Commonplaces*, with illustrated pages on Types of British Footwear, both of them volumes of first importance to the Trade. Their information is compendiously conveyed, and the maps in the former of the principal shoe towns are most useful. These and the **Shoe Manufacturers' Monthly** (a review rather than a furnisher of news) are edited by Mr. Martin Wright, whose style is lucid, who has a genius for order, and who possesses in an almost uncanny degree the gift for supplying to his readers precisely the information they want. In May, 1920, the " Monthly " arrived at its 25th annual number, and Mr. Wright was warmly congratulated by the trade. *The Journal* and *The Year Book* of " The Incorporated Federated Associations of Boot and Shoe Manufacturers of Great Britain and Ireland " are valuable publications.

The following newspapers are published in the other shoemaking towns :—

Leicester.	The Daily Mercury.
	The Leicester Advertiser.
	The Weekly Chronicle, illustrated.
	The Leicester Mail.
Norwich.	The Eastern Daily Press.
	The Eastern Evening News.
	The Norfolk News and Weekly Press.
	The Norwich Mercury.
	The Norfolk Chronicle.
Bristol.	The Bristol Times and Mirror.
	The Western Daily Press.
Leeds.	The Leeds Daily News.
	The Yorkshire Post.
	The Yorkshire Weekly Post.
	The Leeds Times.
Stafford.	The Staffordshire Advertiser.
	The Staffordshire Chronicle.
Wellingborough.	The Wellingborough News.
	The Wellington Post.
Kettering.	The Kettering Guardian.
	The Kettering Leader.

Among the Continental and American Shoe Journals are :

Paris.	Moniteur de la Cordonnerie (weekly).
	La Chaussure Française (monthly).
Berlin.	Schuh und Leder (weekly).
Boston.	The Boot and Shoe Recorder.
	American Shoemaking.
Toronto.	Footwear in Canada.
	Shoe and Leather Journal.

Of recent works on the technical side of shoe-making, *The Modern Boot and Shoe Maker*, four vols., issued by the Gresham Publishing Company, is the most ambitious. *Kelly's Directory of the Leather Trades* reached in 1922 its Fourteenth Edition. In 1921 appeared *The Organisation of the Boot and Shoe Industry in Massachusetts before 1875*, by Blanche Evans Hazard, a work partly founded on interviews with old shoemakers.

141. Among the most charming **Advertisements** in the shoe world are those of the *Sherwood Shoe Co., Mansfield*, whose specialities are " Devonshire shoes for ladies" and the Zephyr ladies' shoe. One of their advertisements shows a Devonshire young lady—a relative, surely, of Keats's delicious " Devon Maid "—seated on an antique chest. A very amusing advertisement is that of *Paton's Laces* (Johnstone, Scotland), in which an old shoemaker, while examining a terribly worn pair of shoes, exclaims, " Leave 'em with me an' I'll see wot I can do for yer—the laces ain't so bad." The *Moccasin* Company offers us an Indian all in his war paint and feathers. *Horace Wright* of Summit Works, Rushden, indulges in an aeroplane in flight, with a boot resting on it, and the motto, " Wright on top." The Beehive is the familiar trade mark of *John Cooper and Sons*, of Leicester. *Smith and Foster*, of Kettering, give us a boot stuck on the spire of the Parish Church. *A. Lewitt*, of Leicester, rejoices in a lady figure that might have been drawn by Mucha, and the word " Andolit." Delightful is the appeal of *A . E. Crane*, Wigston, near Leicester, " May I help to bring colour to your business ? " He specialises in boots and shoes for children. The man who will bring colour into any business or any life is a benefactor of his species. I raise my hat to him. The advertisement of the Diana shoes (*William Mason*, of Leicester) gives us the figure of that chaste huntress and goddess. *Samuel Beal*, of Leicester, turns out the Cynthia brand, and there is Cynthia herself looking down and admiring them. *H . Cahen and Son* (London), who specialise in shoe buckles, display four daintily-winged fairies who are removing their wares from a cabinet. The *Norvic Co.*, Norwich, has a most effective view of the Cathedral of that city, with a telling background of Verona brown. The wares of *Louis Sandy*, Stafford, are ornamented with effective buckles. *Green and Sons* (Northampton), give us a fine picture of the Argosy, with bellying sail and many oars. The Jack Horner brand, with Jack trying on a pair of their shoes, is the pleasant idea of *White, Breward and Sons*, of Barwell. Another Barwell firm (*George Ward*), that makes boys' boots, allows us to be confronted with a highwayman in the act of drawing a pistol from his holster. Golden Dawn and Silver Dawn are two fine advertisements (female figures) of *Hill and Cunningham*, Leicester. *Wilkes Bros. and Co.*, of the same city, fascinate us with the *Gypsy Queen*. *Orson Wright and Son*, of South Wigston, Leicester, are bold people to sell their shoes as the " Delilah " brand, but shoes that entice are, after all, the most likely shoes to sell. We should have preferred, however, a real Oriental Delilah instead of the very English-looking beauty who takes her place. Another striking advertisement is that of *Frederick Cook*, of Long Buckby—a young lady with dainty footgear seated in a garden chair in front of a vista of hollyhocks. The brown ochre lion of *Coe, Church and McPherson*, Bristol, step-ing on the letters L I O N is very effective ; but not less striking was the vast semicircle of green which, in *The Footwear Organiser* of Dec., 1921, advertised the manufactures of *Sir Henry W. Trickett*, of Waterfoot shoe and slipper fame. (See p. 233.) Attractive, too, is the advertisement of the Little Duke—he was quite the feature of the Shoe Fair of 1921—(*B. Toone and Co.*, Desborough), with a picture of a little 18th century aristocrat in cocked hat, ruffles and knee breeches. *Liberty Shoes, Ltd.*, show their enormous premises at Leicester surmounted by a figure of Liberty. *A. Sudborough and Son*, of Higham Ferrers, use the arms of that ancient borough ; *Edward Penton and Son* (London), a box of shoe laces ; and *Dowie and Marshall* (West Strand, London), the Facsimile of a Testimonial from Thomas Carlyle. The *Kiwi Polish Co.* give us a picture of that attractive little bird, the New Zealand kiwi, examining with lively curiosity a tin of the polish.

To Mr. Gorbold and other **Lecturers** on the Shoe I have several times alluded. Dr. A. D. Denning, of the Lotus Co., never fails to illuminate any subject with which he deals. Mr. F. Y. Golding has the gift of making his lectures, which are witty, deeply interesting even to persons outside the trade. Mr. J. Billington has dealt with his experiences among the shoe workers of India, and Mr. George Haldinstein with " Shoemaking as exemplified in the modern factory."

CHAPTER X.

142.   A number of **Anecdotes of Shoemakers**
have already been given, and I now add a few
others.   In old times, I am sorry to say, the
cobblers used to join in the sport of bear baiting—
the day chosen being usually a Sunday.   In a
town in the north some of them took the unusual
course of going to church, but while they were
there part of the roof fell in, and several were
badly bruised.   This to their old friends seemed a
judgment.   "You see," said one of them, "what
it is to be at evensong when you ought to have
been at the bear baiting."

The next story is also ancient, and has often
been told with variations.   A shoemaker, a barber
and a bald-headed tailor once travelled together.
Losing their way, they were forced to sleep in the
open air, and to avert danger they agreed to keep
watch by turns.   The lot fell first on the barber,
and secondly on the shoemaker.   The barber for
amusement, while on duty, crept up to the sleeping shoemaker, shaved his head, and then woke
him to tell him that it was his turn to watch.

Picking up his awl to scratch his head, the shoe-maker protested, " You've made a mistake, barber, you've waked the bald-headed tailor."

Of the shoe as a death-bringer many stories are told, one of the most curious being the legend of Sir Ralph de Shurland, Lord of Sheppey, who kicked and killed a Franciscan monk.   An old hag in a red cloak having prophesied that the horse, **Grey Dolphin,** on which Sir Ralph rode, would be the cause of his death, he, in order to make the prediction impossible, severed the horse's head from its body.   Some time later, seeing the bleached skull lying on the beach, he kicked it towards the water, but as it fell a loud " Ha ! ha ! " issued from the jaws, and at the same time Sir Ralph felt a pain in his right foot.   One of the horse's teeth had pierced his boot and entered his great toe.   Gangrene ensued, and within a few hours the knight lay dead.   His remains were interred in Minster Abbey, and on his tomb is the figure of a horse's head.   The legend with embroideries is included in *The Ingoldsby Legends.*

It was a misadventure with a shoe that caused the death of one of the Archbishops of Magde-burgh, " who broke his necke dancing with a damsell."[1]   Just how it happened history does not say.   Perhaps it was the fault of the shoemaker, but I am not sure that Archbishops ought to dance with " damsells."

[1] *Wit's Commonwealth*, p. 273.

The *Moniteur de la Cordonnerie* had a story[1] of a Persian Ambassador under the first Empire, **Mirza,** who loved boots of red morocco embroidered in gold colour.   After wearing a pair he was seized with a horrible pain in the right foot and died.   Two other persons who subsequently drew on the boot were similarly seized.   Eventually a shoemaker, M. Abbot, examined the boot, and found embedded in the leather a small white object which he extracted, and which proved to be the tiny tooth of a uraeus, a venomous snake.

It was a kick from a sabot administered by a drunken Brittany sailor that crushed the ankle and contributed to the end of that marvellous genius the French artist, Paul Gauguin (1848—1903).

Lord Chatham was a sufferer from the gout, and one day a thief got into his house and stole a pair of the great man's " large gouty shoes."   A servant, not finding them, began to curse the thief. " Never mind," said Lord Chatham, " all the harm I wish him is that the shoes may fit him."

About the year 1820 Joseph Staub, a French shoemaker, made a pair of shoes for the Vicomtesse de Save, who was so pleased with them that she exclaimed, " Monsieur Staub, you are the king of shoemakers."   He replied, " I would very much rather be the shoemaker of kings."   She took the hint, and thanks to her recommendation he became court shoemaker.

[1] Given in *St. Crispin*, Vol. 3, p. 267.

The love of the shoemaker for sport has already been noticed. As an angler he has no rival. You may see him in the hazy distance any day in the season, solitary as the blue heron, rod in hand, his eye intent on a bobbing bit of coloured cork. With a horse hair and a hook he can do what he likes. The line goes in and the fish comes out. As for bait, the fish so respects a shoemaker that he will take anything from him. **Eli Billingham** of Kislingbury, certainly was never at a loss under this head. A typical old stitchman—with forget-me-not blue eyes and coal-black hair—even when his body was at the bench his soul was among the butomus by the glittering river. He fished in a black coat and a tall hat, otherwise the fish would not have known that he was a stitchman—and if he ran short of worms, he would tear a bit out of his coat, and the fish would rise to it just the same. When dibbling for chub, indeed, this was the only bait he would ever use. One day in November, when he was after dace, he hooked a fish of incredible size (it always is), and was about to land it when a huge jack darted from under a bank, snapped at the dace and was also hooked. The line was a fine one, but Eli was resourceful, and without a moment's hesitation he threw the rod into the river after the retreating pike. " I thought you a bit of a fool," remarked a friend who stood by, " but I didn't think you would lose your rod as well as the dace." But when the pike

began to tire, it was Eli's turn. Into the water he
went after his rod, and a few minutes later both
pike and dace were flopping helplessly on the grass.
The Northampton shoemakers know every hot
corner not only of the Nen but also of the Ouse.
They have been seen returning through Olney with
a cart load of bream. Sixty pounds weight have
been taken from one hole in a morning. Mr.
Senior, of *The Field*, used to speak disrespectfully
of this fish, calling it a pair of bellows, which it
certainly in shape resembles, but it is good eating
all the same if cooked properly, which is more
than can be said of most pairs of bellows.

Not all the stitchmen, however, were lovers of
fishing, or sympathetic towards their piscatorial
apprentices. One of this sort, says the writer of
" Retail Topics " in *The Shoe and Leather News*,
hung a piece of sacking up across his little window
so that his apprentice should not waste time by
looking out. " Master," said the boy to him one
day, very wistfully, " they tell me the roach are
biting like billy-ho in the canal." " That's all
right," said the old man, " you be a good boy and
get on with your work, and they wont bite you."

Eli Billingham had seven sons, one of whom,
William, kept a bookshop at the corner of
Marefair and Quart Pot Lane (now Doddridge
Street), and he made shoes in a workshop at the
end of the garden. Some of the Northampton
people objected to the altering of the names

of streets; and one of the Councillors—Mr. S. S. Campion—stood out manfully when it was suggested that the name of another thoroughfare should be altered from Cow Lane to Swan Street. He contended that of the two creatures the cow is the more useful, and he even, in the heat of the moment, went so far as to assert that a cow yields more milk than a swan. The Cow Lane people, who naturally could not accept so wild a statement, obstinately refused to give way, consequently the name was changed. Eli Billingham's grandson, Walter Ernest, has now a bookshop in Bridge Street, and this and the shops of Mr. Joseph Billingham (also grandson of Eli), Mr. W. J. Slade (Slade's Stores), Abington Street, Richard Harris and Son (Bridge Street) and Mr. F. Mutton (formerly in Derngate and now in Lower Mounts), have for long been favourite haunts of the book-loving shoemakers.

Eli Billingham used to lead the **Singing** in the chapel at Kislingbury. People do not sing in places of worship nowadays; they make a murmuring noise like zephyrs passing over a wood. In those days it was different. With the aid of violin, horse's foot, serpent, and other instruments of astonishing shape and eccentricity of movement, they produced results that made the rafters ring, the windows rattle, and (on great occasions) blew out the candles that stuck up out of the sockets in the pew tops. Eli's grandson, recalling those great days, says, " There was heartfelt singing in that chapel for certain. I've never anywhere else heard anything like it." "Singing," said a shoemaker once to me, " is our delight, we pride ourselves on it." The choir of Messrs. Manfield's is famous throughout the county. Some of the shoe manufacturers who were choir-leaders were apt to be overbearing at the chapels. If the parson or any other influential person interfered too much, they would stay away for a Sunday " in a twake,"[1] as the Buckinghamshire people say, drawing the choir with them. When this happened on one occasion at Olney, the congregation would not at all have known what to do if a kind, bald-headed old gentleman had not come to their rescue, and launched them into a long metre tune for a short metre hymn ; though even then, somehow, they did not get quite so far as they had expected. Next morning two of the members called humbly on the choir leader and were graciously received. On the following Sunday the choir were present in full strength, and were profusely thanked ; but, by a curious omission, it did not occur to anybody to tender even a word of thanks to the bald-headed old gentleman who, on the previous Sunday, had so kindly come forward as a substitute.

Some of the shoemakers, like their ancestors the " astrologians," were students of **the Stars,**

---

[1] In a fit of ill humour.

and George Brown, of Northampton, was one of these enthusiasts. The three golden nails in Orion's belt stirred him more than any three golden sovereigns. The sickle of Leo, the square of Pegasus, the chair of Cassiopeia—he knew them and loved them all. During his nightly wanderings, he made the acquaintance of a policeman of kindred tastes, and many excited talks they had on their favourite study; furthermore, each promised to acquaint the other, if necessary, "when anything unusual was going on overhead." One night in 1868, when Brown and his wife were snugly asleep, there came a tremendous knocking at the door. Mrs. Brown jumped out of bed declaring that the house was on fire; and it really seemed to be so owing to the lights seen at the window. Brown lowered the upper sash and looked out, when he was accosted by a well-known voice, "George, George, get up; the stars are shooting like one o'clock." In less than no time he was in the street, and the two friends walked about the town till peep of day, admiring the wonders overhead, and thanking God for His goodness. It was indeed a marvellous display. At Kislingbury somebody roused all the shoemakers, who dressed and gathered together in the village street. They were all singers and, as with one consent, they of a sudden and with deep full voices, burst out with Haydn's glorious strain, "The heavens are telling;" and while the firmament rained gold their grand notes rose in the cool, quiet air. It was a moment that none ever forgot.

Shoemakers have usually been great smokers. Those who lived at Upton were in the habit of returning home from Northampton in the **Carrier's Cart**, and they persisted, in spite of the remonstrances of the carrier, not only in smoking, but in throwing down matches which sometimes ignited the straw at their feet. At last, tired of warning them, the carrier stepped down from his seat and walked at the horse's head. One of the men shouted to him, "What do you want to walk for ? Do you think the old hos'll break down ? " " Oh no," replied the carrier gaily, " but there's fourteen pound of gunpowder under one of the seats, and when it goes off I shall be safer at the horse's head than at his tail." At this the shoemakers, scared out of their lives, promptly hopped, one after the other, out of the cart, and did all the rest of the journey on foot, while the carrier remounted his seat, and he and the old horse, who was also in the secret, and who benefited by having a lighter load, had a quiet laugh together.

In the days of thatched houses **Fires** were not uncommon in the villages, and as the only way of dealing with them was for a string of men to pass buckets from one to another, the conflagration usually burned itself out. The destruction of property, however, was less thought of than the state of the cellars at the ale-house. At a fire at one of

Plate 47

BRITISH AIRMAN'S BOOT

with leg turned down showing lamb's wool lining. It is a full Wellington with a seam up each side of the leg.

FRENCH ARMY ANKLE BOOT,

made in England. War, 1914—1918. A whole-cut, unlined, welted Blucher.

In the War of 1870 the German Army marched one mile per hour faster than the French Army because they were better shod, hence the determination of the French to have specially good boots of English make for the recent War.

BRITISH MACHINE-MADE INFANTRY BOOT.

Introduced at the beginning of the War to take the place of the handsewn boot.   War 1914—1918.

This—the Regulation Boot—may be described as an open tab-bal; the legs were cut the same shape as a derby, and were fitted under the golosh so as to form the place for the stiffener. There were three different specifications for the material. The uppers of Nos. 1 and 2 were cut from dull black chrome, the vamp was cut from basil, and the tongue from goat or other suitable material. The No. 3 upper was cut from vegetable tanned leather. There was a chrome sole on the No. 1 boot, and a vegetable tanned sole on Nos. 2 and 3. The boot was rivetted and stitched.

SHOE OF PETTY INDIAN CHIEFTAIN.

From the Collection of Mr. H. G. Barker (G. Barker & Co., Ltd., Countess Road, St. James's, Northampton).

Photo Coldham & Son, Northampton.

Plates 1, 2 and 3 appeared in *The Leather Trades' Review,* Nov. 10th, 1915, as illustrations to a valuable article, " The Making of an Army Boot," contributed by Mr. Roland Gorbold, who supplied the photographs. One French order amounted to 3,000,000 pairs. British boots were delivered roughly at the rate of 60,000 a day. Three distinct types were made for the British Army (1) the Regulation Pattern (2) the Standard Pattern, and (3) the Old Hand-sewn Pattern. A special boot with a rope sole was made for the men in the tanks. Ours is the finest shod army in the world.

Plate 48

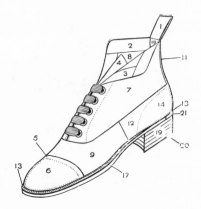

BALMORAL BOOT.

Footwear Organiser, October, 1920.

BALMORAL BOOT.

1, Loop, 2, Inside Top Band. 3, Inside Facing. 4. Tongue. 5, Toe Cap. 6, Leather Toe Puff. 7, Leg and Quarter. 8, Fabric Lining. 9, Vamp. 10, Inside Back Strap. 11, Outside Back Strap. 12, Golosh Quarter. 13, Welt. 14, Leather Counter. 15, Felt Bottom Counter. 16, Insole with Feathered Edge. 17, Outer Sole. 18, Split Lifts. 19, Heel Lifts. 20, Heel Top Piece. 21, Seat Piece. Nos. 15 and 16 are of course invisible from outside.

STRIKING DESIGN

From *Footwear Organiser*, March, 1920.

NORVIC "SHOE DE LUXE."

Fine Willow Calf 2-Bar and Buckle Shoe with white buck vamp and quarter.

Footwear Organiser, March, 1922.

these shoe-making villages, Great Billing, the
people of Ecton, two miles off, came to help, and
that which was dreaded happened. The beer did
not hold out. The Great Billingers were loud in
their indignation. "It was the Ecton people,"
they said, "who drank the beer. What did they
want to come and drink our beer for ? It wornt
their fire."[1]

In those days, when there was a fire in Northampton (and many of the houses were thatched),
it did not occur to the firemen to attempt to put
it out, but the hose and the brightly painted engine,
neither of which did anything in particular, made
a grand impression on the crowd. When, for
example (it must have been some seventy years
ago), "Uncle Tom's Cabin," an inn that faced
Regent Square, caught light, old Charlie Smith,
the fireman, was seen to lift the thatch again and
again in order to give the flames fresh hold. The
beauty of the paint on the engine, however, satisfied the subscribers that they had good value for
their money, and they were more than satisfied
when they learnt that Olney and other towns that
had no Fire Brigade were thoroughly envious of
them.

To the depths that **Intemperance** has been
able to carry some of the shoemakers the following story bears painful witness. Some years ago

[1] As this story is told of several pairs of villages, the reader may alter
the names to his taste.

U

a Northampton shoemaker, whom we may call "old F.," had, with two or three pals, been on the drink and had run out of funds. "They'd got to have more beer some road." Says F. to his pals, "Look here, I know my daughter has a few shillings saved, and I know too that we owe a lot of rent. I'll tell you what I'll do. I've got a pair at home to make. I'll go home and start work, and you, Tom (addressing one of his pals), come along as a bum and say you've come for back rent, and must have it or part of it." F. goes home and starts work. His daughter, a poor pale-faced girl, says, "I am glad you're going to start work again, father; I don't know what we shall do if you don't. It makes me happy." Half an hour after comes an aggressive knock at the door. The girl answers it. "Morning, Miss F. I've come for that there rent that's owing." "Well, I am sure I can't pay. We have no money, but father's just started work, and I'll pay next week." "That wont do for me. I must have it now, or part of it." "Well, I've only got five shillings altogether, to get coal and food with." "Then I'll have that." The poor girl parts with her last five shillings, and off goes the sham bailiff. F. waits a few minutes, then he gets up from his seat, and goes out to join his pals and help them spend the money. I have told the story just as it was told to me. It requires no comment.

In the days of Charles II., Bunyan and other godly divines used to administer to their flocks at a spot called **Three Shires Lane,** where the counties of Bucks, Beds and Northants meet. If the constables of one county appeared, it was an easy matter to step over the borders to another county, and so evade the law. The same spot was used for a very different purpose in the middle of the 19th century, though the reason it was chosen was the same—the facility it offered for avoiding arrest. To it congregated representatives, as they were pleased to call themselves, of Northampton, Wellingborough and Olney, not for the purpose of worship, but to take part in dog-fights, cock fights, prize fights, and other elevating recreations.

In the Franco-German War, Messrs. Stead and Simpson, of Daventry, had from the French Government a " leviathan " contract for little tab shoes and long boots with nails. As the time for delivering the goods drew near, the firm, fearing they could not fulfil their promise, asked for more time. The French Government would not give them a moment. The workmen, however, responded nobly to the request of the firm. On the Sunday night at 12 o'clock (the goods were to be despatched early on the following Wednesday) the men were at their posts—there were hundreds of them—and not a man quitted the factory till seven o'clock on the Wednesday morning—55 solid hours. It was a record that the old hands still speak of with pride ; the goods were delivered to time, and the period is generally spoken of as the **55 hours day**. All honour to those splendid men ! Some of the old stitchmen worked for the same house for many years. One of them, at the age of seventy, after 45 years' service, was dismissed with a small pension. " If I had known this was not a permanent job," he commented, " I'd never have took it."

Some of the **Olney shoe hands,** though nowhere are there better fellows at heart, are wanting in manners. They have an inconvenient habit of standing at street corners and other places in groups, and of not moving to let people pass. One of them one day made himself the victim of a witticism. A gentleman went to post a letter at the Olney Post Office, and in front of it stood a short man in such a way that his head was just in front of the slot. Instead of moving off he opened his mouth, and pointing to it indolently said, " Put it in here." " Oh, it's only a letter," said the gentleman ; " if it had been a parcel I would."

Under the old system, by which the shoemakers' work was done in their own homes, the wife, instead of being what she should be—a housewife —was often expected to help by stitching uppers, doing lift work, &c., with the result that the poor woman could attend properly neither to her appearance nor to her house duties. Dirt naturally accumulated, and she having no time to attend to herself grew as black as a nigger, and as ragged as

Plate 49

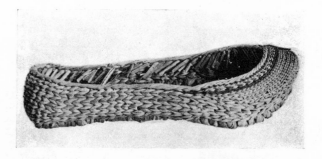

CHINESE GRASS SHOE.

Photo Mr. Roland Gorbold.

FRENCH SHOE.

Mauve satin, with patent leather facings, revers at tops, lacing in front, black laces, square toes. French prize work. Bought at the sale of Mr. J. Daniels, Regent Street.

The Museum, Northampton. *Photo Coldham & Co.*

MOCCASIN (North American Indian). See chapter 9.

Photo Mr. Roland Gorbold.

Plate 50

An Amusing French Advertisement,
A Post Impressionist Cobbler.

A Striking English Advertisement.
Messrs. Padmore & Barnes, Northampton. See p. 240

Brocade Court Shoe with oval paste buckle.

Model by Goochs, Ltd.

Footwear Organiser, December, 1920.

a moulting crow. In those days, among my tenants was a Mr. X., and, when I called, Mrs. X. always answered the door. One morning before calling on her I looked in at Mrs. Z.'s, and while we were chatting somebody passed the window. "Who is that?" I said; "I thought I knew everybody in this street." "Why," replied Mrs. Z., "it's Mrs. X." Then noticing that I was sceptical, she added, "But she's washed herself!"

At Olney the shoemakers have various tastes. Some are expert rose-growers, and waves of fragrance meet us as we pass their gardens; others cultivate pork. Next door to one of the rose-growers lived a man who kept pigs inconveniently near to the two houses, and the rose-grower complained that he could never walk in his garden without smelling the pigs. "If you have a grievance," said the pig-rearer, "so have I; I can never walk in my garden without smelling your roses."

When another person complained of a shoemaker's pigs, the good man said, "In the first place, my pigs don't smell; in the second, I clean out the sty every week; and in the third, I have no pigs."

Apparently that harmony which should always subsist between man and wife does not invariably obtain in Buckinghamshire. "How long has your wife been dead?" asked a friend of a shoemaker. "She isn't dead." "But," added the friend, "I read it in the papers, and I thought the papers

were always reliable." " Unfortunately," sighed
the shoemaker, " not always."

The small town of Kilmaurs has for long been
a shoemaking centre. In 1820 there were 42
shoemakers out of a total population of 919, and
to-day the boot and shoe factory of Messrs. Kellie
and Co. employs many hands. One of the old
stitchmen, who had put away his lingle (shoemaker's thread) and elshin (awl) to spend the
evening at Hallowday Fair, became so noisy that
it was necessary to lodge him in the **Tolbooth.**
Unfortunately the bailie had mislaid the key of
the padlock, and diligent search was unavailing.
At last a happy idea struck him ; he went to his
garden and pulled up a " gaucy kail runt " (a lusty
cabbage stalk), which he thrust into the vacant
staple, observing that as the prisoner was drunk he
wouldn't know the difference. Early next morning, however, one of the town cows which was
being driven to pasture, caught sight of the tempt-
ing runt, and giving it a vigorous pull, secured it
for herself. The door flew open of its own accord,
and the prisoner walked out into the sunlight,
politely saluting, as he did so, the obliging cow.

On another festive occasion an offender in the
same town was brought before the two reigning
bailies, one of whom wished to dismiss the case
while the other was unwilling. Ultimately the
sentence of the court was announced as a fine of
half-a-crown, upon which the prisoner said he'd

see them both in hell before he'd pay it. At this the lenient bailie, turning to his colleague, remarked in a very audible whisper, " There na, I tell't ye ; he'll no' pay't ; and what can we dae ? "

Another Scotch story is of a shoemaker who was brought before a magistrate for stealing a signboard. " He stole my signboard last week," said the plaintiff, " and what does your honour think he did with it ? " " That," said the magistrate, " would be hard for me to say." " Well," said the plaintiff, " he brought it into my ain shop with my ain name on't, and offered to sell me't, as he said he thought it would be o' mair use to me than to anybody else."

During a preaching tour through Ireland, a Scotch minister, the Rev. Dr. Guthrie, was in the habit of addressing his audience by the name of their city or town thus : " Dear Belfast souls," " Dear Dublin souls," and he was listened to with gravity. When, however, he addressed another congregation as " Dear Cork souls," a ripple of laughter went round the church, and he wondered what caused it.

John Silvey, an old stitchman of Hale, was in the habit of walking to Methodist services at Bromedge, five miles distant, and of soliloquising on the way. The expression, "Glory be to God !" was in particular often on his lips. One dark night when returning home, he called at the village inn and rebuked the company for their tippling.

This gave offence, and one of the number, a young man, determined to have his revenge ; so he stole to his bed, wrapped himself in a sheet, and ran a good distance to a certain large holly tree which he knew the old man must pass. Behind it, with the sheet over his head and shoulders, he waited for his victim. Presently footsteps and the well-known exclamation, " Glory be to God!" were heard. After shaking the holly tree violently, the young man came from behind it, and stood stock still with outstretched arms. But Silvey, who was not afraid of any human being, was not afraid of ghosts either. He drew himself up and said, " If tha' be a good spirit, tha' winna' hurt me ; and if tha' be a bad spirit, tha' canna' hurt me. Glory be to God!" and then he unconcernedly pursued his way home. The ghost, however, was so unnerved, that his knees knocked together and his teeth chattered. But he managed to find his way back and often told the tale, but in telling it he never failed to speak with reverence of Old Silvey.

Another devout old shoemaker and **Kidderminster local preacher** was much given to superlatives. One Sunday he took as his text, 3 John 11 : " Follow not that which is evil ; " and he urged his hearers to follow instead the way of the Lord. " It is the most wisest course," he said in his powerful, rich bass voice. Then after a pause, " It is the most safest course ; " and finally —with emphasis—" It is the most honourablest course!" That sermon has been remembered while thousands of others by learned divines have been entirely forgotten.

When Mr. W. Steward, of Bedford, was a boy, he often used to go to see an old cobbler at Kidderminster, **John Trow**, and sometimes read to him. One day Trow, who was seated at work with the lapstone on his knee, handed the boy a book about the Devil and his tricks, probably the volume entitled, *The Christian Armed against Satan's Devices*, saying, " Willie, read it to me." To the boy the book seemed dull and tedious, but it worked Trow almost into a fever, and raising his hammer he said, " Ah, the old villain, if I had his head on this lapstone he would never tempt poor sinners any more ! "

A gentleman who may or may not have come from Dublin tried once, and in vain, to draw on a pair of new boots. At last he gave up the attempt, saying, " I perceive clearly that I shall never get these boots on till I have worn them a day or two."

A Yorkshire cobbler, Isaac, or more familiarly, **" Aud Ark,"** added to his work as shoe-mender the duties of clerk and sexton. He was great at funerals, when he appeared in an aged " bright black-green, semi-frock coat and flat square black tie," and he was a welcome guest at the feast that followed. Unfortunately he used to be too regular a frequenter of *The Fox and Hounds*, where, purse empty, he often mortgaged prospective funerals. On such occasions he would walk unsteadily down the village and knock at some door in the room above which a light burned, and ask after Henry, or George, or whoever else it might be.

" Hoo is he teneet ? "

" Oh ! he's warse, Ark. You'll soon hev to be gettin ready for him."

" Aye ! I suppose so," and then he would add, " You might just let me have a shilling, will ya, an' I'll knock it off when the time comes," and then he would return to the tavern. He is now a very temperate man, but there is still unpleasant-ness between him and a family from whom he received an advance on account of a funeral which never came off, chiefly for the reason that the subject of it still appears good for many years.

In the village of Bradwell, in the Peak of Derby-shire, a Wesleyan minister, who had been newly appointed to the place, called on an old cobbler, but could make nothing of him. At last, with his hand on the latch, he said as a final effort, " But don't you ever pray ? "

" Good heavens, sir, nobody more fervently ! "

" And what is your prayer ? "

" My daily prayer is that I may be kept out of the hands of doctors, lawyers, and parsons."

During the War there was a difficulty in dealing with orders, and a customer, an Irishman, writing to a Stafford firm, said, " I suppose you'll deliver the goods on the Day of Judgment." The head of the firm, who had the reputation of being the wittiest man in the town, wired : " Very busy day for Irishmen ; will send them the day after."

The opinion which the tanners hold of themselves is not always shared by the shoemakers. The shoemakers, as we have seen, have four saints of their very own. Major E. W. Lennard of Bristol once asked a shoemaker if he ever heard of a saint among the tanners ? " Eh ! what ? " he replied. " A saint among the tanners ? No fear ! "

Of **Dwarf Shoemakers**, one of the best remembered is " Tuppenny Rice " of Yarmouth, whose shop stood near the site of " Peggotty's Hut," and who often had to repair a smacksman's sea boot taller than himself. It is said that his wife, a big, strapping woman, used, when she thought he had been at the tavern long enough, to follow him there and to carry him off, kicking, in her apron. In later days fortune smiled upon him, for a local showman inveigled him into a frock coat and a top hat, put a gold Albert on his chest, and toured the country with him.

A pretty story was told in *The Shoe and Leather News*, 1920, by Mr. C. Raven, of Collumpton, Devon. He says, " I have often been amused at the various reasons given for requesting prompt attention to repairs. On one occasion a pretty little flaxen haired girl came with a pair of babies' shoes which she wanted mended. I asked her by what time her mother wanted them. She replied, "'Fore [before] baby wakes.' Such a request," adds Mr. Raven, " coming through such a medium, could only be regarded as a command."

Another little girl was in trouble because the button of her shoe had come off. Her grandmother being too busy just then to sew it on, told her to take it to the shoemaker next door. " How much is it ? " asked the child. " Just one kiss," replied the shoemaker. " Granny will pay," said the little girl.

A young **Berlin shoemaker,** who in the year 1878 resided in London, was engaged to a German girl, but he had not the means either to marry or even to buy the materials to execute his orders. At last, on a holiday excursion, he confessed to her in the Whispering Gallery of St. Paul's his hazardous position. Shortly after there came an order for work, and the leather merchant with whom he had dealt offered him credit. Success followed, and when he paid his last bill the leather merchant told him that the credit had been allowed owing to the good word of Mr. Gladstone, who, it seems, had been in the Whispering Gallery at the opportune moment, and had overheard the tale of the young workman's poverty. When Gladstone died, in May, 1898, a plain oakleaf chaplet came from Berlin to be placed round the great statesman's casket. It was the German

Plate 51

COUNCILLOR HENRY N. HOLMES

(Edwards & Holmes, Ltd.).

Lord Mayor of Norwich, 1921—1922. See p. 241.

shoemaker's gift of remembrance—after twenty years.

Wilhelm Voigt, the **Cobbler of Koepenick,** about the year 1906 made all the world laugh. Attiring himself in the gorgeous uniform of a captain of the Royal Regiment of Guards, he ordered two detachments of Fusiliers in Berlin to march with him to the station. He said they had to carry out an arrest in the Kaiser's name. On arriving at Koepenick, he ordered three coaches and drove to the town hall, where he arrested the Mayor and ordered the treasurer to deliver over all money in hand, some 4,000 marks (£200). After giving a receipt and inserting in the books that the amount was short to the extent of nearly one mark, he sent the prisoners who, he said, were arrested because of defalcations, under escort to Berlin. It then transpired that Voigt, instead of being a captain, was a rogue who had spent half his life in jail. His exploit earned him four years' imprisonment, and gifts, said to have amounted to £2,000, from admirers. In 1910 he settled in London, where he sold signed postcards, and he died at Luxembourg in January, 1922.

Solutions to give longer life to the soles of boots are now on the market. The public, however, require to be educated on the subject. An American druggist advertised a patent concoction labelled, "No more colds! no more coughs! Price, 75 cents." A man who bought the mixture came back in three days to complain that he had drunk it all, but was no better. " Drunk it all! " gasped the druggist, " Why, man, that was an india-rubber solution to put on the soles of your boots ! "

To the weakness that people in all ages have had for shoes that make a noise, allusion has several times been made. A South Sea Islander and his wife having secured a pair of " shoes that talk," the question arose which should have the pleasure of walking into church in them. The difficulty was got over, however. The husband entered the church with the boots on and marched, to their music, all down the nave. On reaching the chancel he dropped them out of the window, and by-and-by his wife entered wearing the identical shoes. She had, it seems, been waiting for them, and so was able, likewise, to enter the church in the same style, and to draw upon herself, in her turn, the envy of the rest of the congregation.

In old times it was the custom of the people of Old Neston, Hants, to wear new boots on St. Swithin's Day (July 15th), but the squeaking that they made so troubled a benevolent gentleman of that parish that he founded a charity which was to supply the poor with bread four times a year, one of the conditions being that hay should be strewn in the church on St. Swithin's Day. The custom was observed as late as 1908, and is probably observed still.

There is a saying, " Shoemaker's children are always ill-shod," but this certainly does not apply in the great shoe districts. However, a dentist's son once jeered at a shoemaker's son, saying, " Look at your boots, and your father a shoemaker, too ! " To which came the retort, " Look at your baby, she hasn't a tooth in her head, and your father a dentist, too ! "

A poor old Christian woman who lived in the East of London was in the habit of shouting out, " Praise be to God ! " " **Hallelujah!**" &c., when anything in the sermon at her chapel particularly appealed to her. One of the members of the congregation remonstrated with her, and said that if she would promise to remain quiet during the service for six Sundays he would give her a pair of new shoes. The shoes were badly needed, so the old woman promised, though she said, " It will be hard work, sir." For three Sundays all went well, but on the fourth the sermon precisely met her need, and so cheered and encouraged her that she pulled off her shoes and, throwing them into the table pew,[1] shouted, " Shoes or no shoes, I must say, ' Glory be to God ! ' " That is all we are told. Let us hope, however, that, nevertheless, the shoes were not forfeited.

Perhaps it will be alleged that the humour that

[1] The large pew in old chapels just under the pulpit.

gathered round the shoemaker of former days has quite disappeared in these serious times. That this is an error the following examples will show.

To one of my shoemaker friends I complained of the rising of the rates and taxes, adding that the Government were constantly creating new officials and increasing the salaries of the old ones. Said he, " There is a bright side to all this. I am looking forward to the time when every inhabitant of the British Isles will be a salaried official with nothing in particular to do, and a staff of clerks to help him do it."

" But," I objected, "as all will be officials, there will be no clerks to be had."

" I had not foreseen this difficulty," said he, " but no doubt it can be got over."

About six months after the commencement of the War with Germany, a gentleman fell into conversation with an old shoemaker at Hanslope, Bucks.

" Well," said the visitor, " what do you think about **The Great Battle** yesterday ? "

As the old man proved to be deaf, the visitor repeated the question, bawling it in his ear, " THE GREAT BATTLE YESTERDAY."

" What battle ? "

" WHY, THE GREAT BATTLE BE-TWEEN THE FRENCH AND THE GER-MANS."

" I don't know nothing about no battle," said
the old man. " However, they had a nice day for
it ! "

143. The **Shoe in Fiction** is a pleasant
subject. I have already referred to the original of
Cinderella, the story of whom is one of the delights
of the nursery. What multitudes of little folk
have been held spell-bound by the histories of
" The Old Woman who Lived in a Shoe,"
" Goody Two Shoes," and " Puss in Boots " ! We
all envy the gentleman who wore Seven League
Boots. Robin Goodfellow, however, still drops
sixpences into the shoes of little girls who are good.
But I am not sure whether we ought to be grateful
for this. If it goes on much longer there will be
no naughty girls left, which would be a pity.

In *Grimm's Tales* we find " The Elves and the
Cobbler " and " The Dancing Shoes." Among the
earliest and most delightful shoemaker stories is
that in *The Arabian Nights* of " Ma'aruf the
Cobbler and his Wife Fatimah," which, as translated by Payne, is one of the most beautiful things
in English literature. After reading it one may
well say, quoting the words of the Third Kalendar
in the *Nights*, "Such gladness possessed me, that
I forgot all the cares of the world, and said, ' This
is indeed life ! ' "

In *Don Quixote* (as we have seen, p. 63) much
is made of leather. Rabelais, too, overflows with
shoe lore. There is the tale of the cobbler and

x

the pitcher of milk, the description of Gargantua's shoes of blue crimson velvet, which " took 11,000 hides of brown cows to sole them "; and we are told about Queen Whims, who did all impossible things, and whose officers cured people by touching them with a piece of a wooden shoe. They could even turn old women entirely into young ones— with painted lips and eyes all complete—" except their heels that were now much shorter than in their former youth "—a sly allusion to the changes of fashion. On the Island of Sandals they found an Order of jolly old Mumbling Friars, who went to bed in their boots, walked about all day barefooted, and laughed at Fortune and the Fortunate.

In Stendhal's *Lucien Leuwen* (written in 1834) are references to the French shoemaker's love of liberty; and one recalls the odd portrait of Stendhal himself, drawn by Alfred de Musset (1833), dancing in furred boots in the courtyard of an inn [Pl. 37], during some moments of excitement—the only moments, he insisted, when he really was worth anything.

Dickens portrays in *A Tale of Two Cities* a distinguished maker of shoes, Dr. Manette; and in *Sketches by Boz*, a shoe-binder, Miss Evans. *Shoemakers' Village*, by Henry Holbeach, is a series of humorous sketches rather than a story; but the shoe and the shoemaker are prominent also in the Northamptonshire story, *The Blue Firedrake*, and in Sarah Dowdney's *Pilgrims of the Night*.

Two shoemakers stand out in special relief in the novels of Maxim Gorki—who as a lad was errand boy to a cobbler—Orloff, in *The Orloff Couple*, and Perfishka, in *Three of Them*. Whenever you come upon Perfishka he is singing joyous songs to the accompaniment of an old harmonica, which seemed to be a part of his body. Pashka, Perfishka's apprentice, was, like so many other shoemakers, easily fascinated by a book. He says, " I kept reading poetry — Lermontoff, Nekrasoff and Poushkine. There is, Ilia, such poetry that, when you read it, it's like your sweetheart kissing you ; " and this was something from him, seeing that he said of the girl he loved, " You'll see what she's like ; she can set your whole soul on fire ! "

Tchekov has a story entitled, " The Shoemaker and the Devil ; " Anatole France, in *The Red Lily*, depicts a Florentine shoemaker who kept as a pet a sparrow with a false leg made of a bit of a match ; and Virgilio Brocchi, in *Sul caval della Morte*, *Amor cavalca*, tells of the passion of Giacomo, cobbler and student of Machiavelli, for the Countess Orsella.

144. To some of the **Poets** who have dealt charmingly with the shoe and the shoemaker allusion has already been made. The roving fancy of Blake gives us the lovely and melodic :

" Lift up thy blue eyes, Vala, and put on thy sapphire
　　shoes,
　O melancholy Magdalen, behold the morning breaks ; "

and he represents Los (Imagination) drawing on his
golden sandals and stepping from mountain to
mountain.　Burns sings of Tam o' Shanter ; Scott
(in *The Lay of the Last Minstrel*) of Watt Tinlinn,
shoemaker and border spirit, who " in vain never
twanged the yew " ; Edwin Markham has given
us *The Shoes of Happiness*, and Mrs. Coralinn
Daniels the pretty street scene entitled :

" HER SHOE.

" She tied her shoe, her little shoe of brown.
　She was a dainty maiden !　In the town
　Few such a round and taper ankle showed ;
　Few ankles bore so fair and fresh a load
　As she, who glanced aside and then stooped down.

" World's praise or blame what cared she ?　And to tie
　A heart within what maiden would not try ?
　So, with a little flutter of her gown,
　　　　She tied her shoe.

" A longing heart, a yearning heart had I ;
　Fond looks I gave, and then a sudden sigh ;
　My soul, myself leapt to that shoe of brown—
　Courage I took unheeding of her frown,
　Kneeling I kissed it,—but she did not fly !
　　　　She tied her shoe."

As these pages have borne witness, many shoemakers have been great readers.　About 14 years
ago died at Bedford a shoemaker, Thomas Robinson, who had committed to memory the whole of

Cowper's *Task,* and would repeat any passage if given the opening words. His well-thumbed copy is now in the possession of Mr. E. Anderson, of Bedford.

145. To some of the **Plays** relating to the shoe and the shoemaker I have already alluded.[1] Mention should also be made of *The Cobbler's Prophecy*, by Robert Wilson (1594) ; *Bartolomeo the Shoemaker*, by Paoli Ferrari, 1847 ; *Le Cordonnier de Crecy*, by August Lucket et Desbuards (1855) ; *A Pair of Spectacles*, by Sydney Grundy (1890) ; *Chu Chin Chow* (1916) ; and *Hunky Dory* (1921).

146. I must soon take leave of my readers. To go over the story of the shoe from its incipience to the present moment has been a great joy to me. May there still be progress and yet further progress in this wonderful industry! The life story of many a manufacturer, of many an operative, of many a retailer, has been a romance. The life of every just man is a miracle. As we have seen, every shoemaker is a king's son. Until quite recently it was common in Olney to hear a child addressed as **"My king."** I often heard my father use the expression when thanking a boy for opening a gate or for some other little kindly service. William Rufus, not by any means an ideal king, was nevertheless in the secret, for while crossing the channel in a storm he said scornfully to a trembling

[1] *The Shoemaker's Holiday* (Dekker), p. 115; *Henry V.* (Shakespeare), p. 113; *A Shoomaker a Gentleman* (Rowley), p. 121; *The Cobbler of Preston* (Charles Johnson), p. 141.

courtier, " Kings never drown "—never go under—
nor do they. Their courage and their spirit keep
them afloat. Let self-reliance be the watchword.
" Wherever we wish to go," says Sallust, " we
must carve a passage with our own swords [or
shall we say, " Prick one with our own awls " ?] . .
Woe be to him who relies not on the vigour of his
own arm." " Persevere, persevere," says Carlyle,
in his burst-through way, " that is the strength of
a man. I will promise you all manner of good if
you persevere. You shall have victory ; more
conquest, perhaps, than you yet believe ; you shall
have heroic battle, which is the noblest conquest
of all."

When we consider the story of the shoe from
the Tab-teb age to the present day, no narrative,
whether in *The Arabian Nights* or any other work,
can be stranger, more absorbingly interesting, or
more encouraging to those who love adventure,
innovation, and progress,—and aim at perfection.

The feeling is abroad that the time has come for
the conferring of **Degrees in Boot and Shoe
Manufacture**. As the subject is a difficult one,
I have invited expert opinion. Mr. J. H. Hawthorn, M.A., Leicester, after pointing out that the
Shoe Industry as a trade consists of (a) Operatives, (b) Foremen, (c) Managers and Proprietors,
writes :

" Now the (a) class is obviously out of the question
in the matter of degrees. The (b) class, in common with

(a) class, is usually restricted in ability to some part or other of the process of manufacture, so that its members would not come into consideration. As to the (c) class, it is not usual to find its members expert in particular processes. They attain their position from a general knowledge of the completed article, together with some special business aptitude. This business aptitude is not necessarily confined to one trade, and if degrees are given for something of this kind, I should have very little to criticise. To widen the scope of University recognition so as to include anything of class (a) and (b) would be extremely undesirable, if not indeed impossible. My approval of giving degrees for business aptitude is absolutely contingent upon students passing the necessary examination dealing with general education before taking up any business subject for a degree."

Mr. R. E. Barnett, B.Sc. (Leeds), observes :

" There is, as you suggest, a growing feeling in favour of the extension of University influence in many directions hitherto regarded as being outside the University field. In some places this is effected by a definite affiliation of the Technical School or College with the local University, the former ranking as the ' Faculty of Technology ' of the latter. In such cases, study at the Technical School qualifies the student to sit for examination for a special Technological Degree.

" It must be remembered that the distinguishing mark of a University Degree is its implication of a thorough general education in addition to technical knowledge. In the case just referred to, for instance, the students of the Technical School must also have passed the Matriculation Examination of the University with which it is affiliated, or at least have some equivalent proof of adequate general education.

" Would the Shoe Trade regard a University Degree as justifying the expenditure of so much time upon general education ? Would the possession of the Degree bring

such material reward to the Shoe Trade student in his
subsequent career as to compensate him for the time and
labour involved in acquiring it ? "

Mr. John Blakeman, M.A., B.Sc. (Northampton), says :

" At the present time it is possible to take at British
Universities degrees in all branches of Engineering, including Electrical, Mining, Gas Engineering; also degrees
can now be taken in Agriculture, Textiles and Leather
Manufacture.   Much of this is a development of recent
years.   I realise that boot and shoe manufacture by
machinery is a very new industry, and that science has not
yet been applied to it to any great extent.   Nevertheless,
the industry is only passing through a phase similar to
what has been passed through by each of the above mentioned industries.   It is practically certain that within
the next twenty years Degrees in Boot and Shoe Manufacture will be developed.   At any rate, all those engaged
in education in relation to the Boot and Shoe industry
should work with that idea in view."

Mr. Frank Plucknett (Stafford) says :

" There can be no doubt whatever that the possibility
of taking a University Degree would result in developments that would astonish the industry; for it would
attract a different type of man, and then equip him so
that he could introduce improvements.   For ages men
have studied the subject, but have guarded that knowledge so carefully that they took it with them to the grave,
and this is why progress has been so slow.   The earliest
text book is only 100 years old.   There is now, however,
a sufficient accumulation of knowledge which extends
over such a wide field that a University Degree, as
suggested, would be of real service as an index of a wide
knowledge in a complex subject, and it would soon be
recognised as the essential qualification for all those
appointed to the higher positions in the industry.

" The first step would probably be the founding of a ' Chair ' at a University, and the scope of study for the degree could soon be defined, but it should certainly include the study of :—

" 1. The foot.

" 2. The relation of the boot to the last and the foot.

" 3. The making of boots by hand processes, where these have not been surpassed by machinery.

" 4. The available machinery to replace hand processes.

" 5. All the materials used in boot and shoe manu-facture.

" 6. The science of management.

" 7. Systems of costing and accountancy applicable to the industry.

" 8. Finance and commerce, including the various markets and what they require.

" It has only been in the last few years that it has been possible to take a degree in tanning (Leeds), or in the Motor Industry (Bristol), or in Commerce (Manchester and London), and the benefit to the Shoe Industry would not be less than the benefit in these subjects."

Mr. Reginald W. Brown, of the Public Library, Northampton, reminds me that in the year 1238[1] Northampton was very near becoming a University Town. Let us trust that the hopes which were then raised will soon be realised. It would be delightful also to be able to refer to the Universities of Leicester and Norwich, and to speak of them as proudly as we are accustomed to speak of the Universities of two other great shoe centres—Bristol and Leeds.

[1] See Wetton's *Guide to Northampton*, pp. 37, 38.

147.　In **Conclusion,** as regards Northampton from the art lover's point of view, one of the most cheering signs of the times is the public spirit being shown by the Corporation and private persons. The mediæval town was highly picturesque, but later there was a terrible falling off, and " Northampton the Beautiful " forfeited its right to the name. At the end of the last century, however, a new era dawned, and there was a gradual revelation of soul. As Messrs. Manfield and Sons, Messrs. W. Barratt and Co., and others have shown, Shoe Factories can be exteriorly as attractive as other buildings. Streets have been widened, parks and recreation grounds laid out. The valuable Public Library and the splendid Museum are constantly adding to their attractions. It is true that both the railway approaches to the town are still, to use a mild expression, uninviting ; but to the hesitating traveller I would say, adapting the words of Heraclitus, " Enter, boldly, for here too there are gods." Beauty is to be sought in the hearts of men as well as in architecture. With beauty in the heart, beauty in the façade will soon follow, and there is as much poetry and romance in Northampton to-day—for those who have eyes to see it—as there was in ancient Sicyon when Apelles painted, and Susarion, or whatever other artificer with cunning fingers and melodious name, made foot-gear for Rhodope and Sappho.

Norwich, Leicester and other shoe towns have also moved in the right direction.

In the course of these pages I have again and again alluded to the fact that so many persons in the Shoe Trade are intent on progress. I should like, in closing, to say a few words on the employment of leisure. The ambitious men in the trade, whether manufacturers or operatives, will, of course, give a certain amount of their spare time to the study of what immediately relates to their business. Let me, however, put in a plea for the study of art and literature. I know I am not speaking to deaf ears, for the shoemaker has in all ages been a lover of the beautiful, both in word and object. Time spent in the study of art and literature will not be wasted. It will produce an uplifting that nothing else can effect. Everywhere, already, I see evidence of aspiration in this direction—the artistic appearance of the advertisements, the justifiable pride of the window dresser, the passion for form and colour, the æsthetic appearance of the goods, especially those intended for ladies, the literary touches in the great Trade Journals. In the Victorian era shoemaking was very largely a mere sordid, money-making industry, bringing little joy to those engaged in it. There is far more money made nowadays in the trade, but it is recognised that along with the money-making should go colour, novelty, beauty, enlightenment.

Art and literature have the power to serve the trade royally.

A wise and exhilarating leader on this subject appeared in *The Shoe and Leather News* for 24th November, 1921. After quoting with approval Lord Haldane, whose ambition was to get the University atmosphere into every industrial town, it said: " We feel certain that as the intelligence of the democracy increases, there will be an increase in the happiness and prosperity of the people." More than that, he who puts himself into line with this movement will not only acquire power and happiness, he will be moved to ecstasy, he will become electric—radiating fire, enthusiasm, vitality. He will be a man worth knowing—not merely now, but (death being merely transition) *in secula seculorum*, for ever and ever—to the end of time. " Take fast hold of instruction, for she is thy life," said Solomon; and he, too, though not particularly illustrious as a shoemaker, was the

SON OF A KING.

THE END.

APPENDICES.

APPENDIX I.

ANCIENT COBBLER'S STAND.

Discovered at Isham. (See Plate 32.)

This was used for heating the burnishing tool by means of a candle flame. The candle holder could be adjusted as the candle burnt down. In connection with the stand was also an appliance for melting the wax used in hand-stitching.

This stand was superseded by the Beatrice Oil Stove, which was brought out on purpose to meet the requirements of the cobbler.

APPENDIX II.

There has recently come into the possession of Dr. William Cock, of Appledore, Kent, a relic of William Huntington. It is an oval iron plaque, which has evidently been fastened to something, as there are four holes for screws. On the front is painted, on a whitish ground, a crown, the letters " W. H.," and below them "S. S." It may have been removed from a pulpit or from a piece of household furniture. Perhaps some reader can throw light on the matter. See page 161, and also my *Life of William Huntington* (C. J. Farncombe & Sons, Ltd.).

INDEX.

Y